Daily Meditations for
Parenting Our Kids

THOMAS WRIGHT

. . . .

Recovery Publications, Inc.
San Diego

Daily Meditations for Parenting Our Kids

Published by Recovery Publications, Inc.
1201 Knoxville Street
San Diego, CA 92110
(619) 275-1350

Library of Congress Cataloging-in-Publication Data
Wright, Thomas, 1942–
Daily meditations for parenting our kids / Thomas Wright. — 1st ed.
p.   cm.
Includes index.
ISBN 0-941405-18-4 (pbk.)
1. Parenting—Religious aspects—Christianity—Meditations.
2. Parents—Prayer-books and devotions—English.   3. Devotional
calendars.   I. Title.
BV4529.W75   1993
242'.645—dc20   92-37756
                                                    CIP

Printed in the United States of America
First edition
10 9 8 7 6 5 4 3 2 1

*This book is dedicated
to my wife Judy, with whom I
share my dreams, my three children,
and my counseling practice.
Her love, encouragement,
and gentle enthusiasm continually
nurture me.*

I thank my wife, Judy, who encouraged my writing, offered valuable suggestions, and accommodated my being in the home but not of the home while I worked on this book.

I thank our three children, Sarah, Kara, and Adam, for their patience in training me in the fine art of being their father.

I thank Scott Edelstein, friend and mentor who guided me through the labyrinth of publishing this book. Without his expert knowledge, this book would still be nothing more than an interesting idea.

I thank Jan Johnson, whose skillful editing and numerous suggestions kept my writing focused and clear. Her gentle humor and sensitivity to my internal process made our collaboration a real joy.

I thank my daughter, Sarah, for her totally biased enthusiasm for the project, and for her able assistance in helping me assign 366 different meditations to the 366 days of the year.

I thank Margaret Kallsen, Judy's mom, for reading the manuscript with her proofreader's eye and appreciative spirit.

I thank Valerie Deilgat, Ron Halvorson, and the crew at Recovery Publications for making my first book publishing experience such a rewarding and delightful one. Every writer should be so fortunate.

INTRODUCTION

THIS BOOK is a natural outgrowth of my lifelong interest in helping people improve the quality of their lives. I have pursued this interest as a hospital chaplain, minister, teacher, family counselor, and parent. I chose the format of daily meditations because of the tremendous power of systematic focused attention. Of all the methods and techniques for achieving personal growth, none is more effective than a discipline of daily attention.

I hope this volume will be your companion for comfort, insight, and encouragement as you seek to improve the quality of all your relationships, and especially those with yourself and your children. Recovery is both a painful journey and a terrific encounter with ourselves, our spiritual nature, and the Holy Other. In recovery, this mysterious other who seeks to lift us from our unnecessary suffering and show us the path of serenity is called Higher Power, or God, as we understand him. Although I am comfortable calling my Higher Power God, and do in this book, I encourage you to use whatever name or symbol fits for you on your journey.

For me, faith is following the path as far as I have light to see, and taking another step. Faith is acting as if the universe is being run by a friend of mine. I don't have to stay awake at night worrying about how everything will turn out. I don't have to manage all the outcomes of life. God, my Higher Power, the Holy Other, is in charge of the universe. I can sleep peacefully and awake each new day to do the best I can to seek and do his will in my corner of the universe. Even when I fail, as I often do, I am surrounded by God's love.

As a counselor, I've had the privilege of hearing the life stories of thousands of men and women in recovery. I admire their honesty, courage, and determination to improve their lives and deepen their spirituality. I see them reach out to others with both compassion and humility as they seek to share the serenity they have experienced.

When I seek to touch the lives of others with hope and healing, I am regularly reminded that I live by grace and not by gumption. If I have been able to offer you a word of hope and healing, it is not by my superior intelligence, outstanding effort, or unusual talent but by amazing grace. The words of John Newton's great hymn sum up my life as well as the lives of those I've come to know in my work.

> *Amazing grace! how sweet the sound*
> *That saved a wretch like me!*
> *I once was lost, but now am found,*
> *Was blind, but now I see.*

THOMAS WRIGHT
Minneapolis

Live Through Children

· ·

*W*e feel sorry for children whose parents force them into sports or other activities because the parents want the glory. Such parents are insensitive to their children's feelings and push them to participate in activities they have no interest in. These children often feel embarrassed and humiliated, and are not allowed to follow their own curiosity and develop their own interests. They are expected to fulfill their parents' lives through their activities.

Sometimes it's easier to look down on these parents than it is to see the ways in which we, too, live through our children. We want them to be well behaved in public so we look good. When we are together with other families—in church, at a restaurant or an amusement park—we worry about what other adults think of our children, and ultimately of us. Wanting our children to make a good impression so we can be proud of them is another way of living through them.

We're learning to be conscientious, responsible parents without living through our children. We are teaching them how to act in public. While we are legally and morally responsible for their behavior, they are not responsible for our self-worth. We accept our responsibility to train them in appropriate social conduct. We are learning to depend on ourselves and our Higher Power, not our children's behavior, for our sense of self-worth.

I enjoy my children more when I live my own life.

Accepting Others

. . . .

As children, we never felt like we fit in. We felt different, set apart, and lonely. We didn't know how to connect well with others, including those in our own family. We were afraid that others wouldn't accept us. If we had friends, we weren't close to them. We never talked about our inner thoughts, feelings, or fears to anyone. We were afraid to face ourselves.

The Twelve-Step program helped us look at ourselves and others in a new way. Once we began to face ourselves honestly, we no longer felt so alienated from others. When we began accepting ourselves, we noticed we were less prone to criticize others. Our growing self-acceptance has improved our relationships with others. We notice other people's gifts instead of their liabilities, and this reciprocal acceptance is one of the biggest benefits in our recovering lives.

We accept our children more now. We are softer and gentler with them and see them through new compassionate eyes, not our old critical eyes. As we accept ourselves, we are also less envious of our children because we have begun to take care of our own needs. When we take care of our own needs, it's much easier to take care of our children without resenting them. We feel less fearful about our children's future. We have placed our trust in God, and not in our worrying.

As I accept myself, I learn to accept others and to feel close to them.

Trusting Myself

· ·

*W*e want our children to have self-confidence, so they won't be overly dependent on the opinions of others. We want them to be able to validate themselves and their judgments and to be able to hold their own when others question their motives and opinions. Many of us lacked this self-confidence in our childhood and pre-recovery days. When others questioned us, we immediately felt stupid, self-conscious, and eager to adopt their point of view, even when their point of view was critical of us. We easily abandoned ourselves in arguments.

We've come a long way in overcoming our codependence and in standing up for ourselves since we began our recovery. As we grow in self-confidence, we become less defensive when others disagree with us. We speak our truth confidently, even when others challenge us. We've learned to carefully consider the views of others without automatically abandoning our own positions.

In helping our children learn to trust their own judgments, we never belittle their views or tease them when we see things differently than they do. Instead, we encourage them to share their thoughts and explain their positions. These conversations can help them to clarify their thinking and increase their self-confidence. We're also willing to let them know when they've changed our minds.

I encourage my children to trust themselves and stand up for their points of view.

Now That It's My Turn

. . . .

As children, we longed to grow up and become adults. Adults had the power to make the rules, and they controlled our lives. We dreamed of the day when we could make rules and control other people. We played house with our friends and took turns being the boss, teacher, mother, or father, telling others what to do in stern voices. It was great fun then.

Now that we're parents in recovery, we try not to be bossy, controlling, and domineering. We don't want our children to feel powerless, victims of our whim. Yet, we have to admit that at times we are sorely tempted to demand obedience and exercise control—now that it's our turn to be the grown-ups in charge. We feel especially vulnerable to this temptation when we're tired, when we're feeling like somebody else's victim, or when our kids have been fussing and demanding things of us all day.

We may think it's unfair that we don't get to have our turn being controlling, bossy parents. Of course, we could act this way if we wanted to. In fact, we probably did before we began our own recovery. In recovery we're learning new, healthier ways to relate to people, and we no longer enjoy putting people down.

I let go of my desire to be a dominating, bossy parent and replace it with learning respectful ways to relate to my children.

Anger

. . . .

*I*t seems like at least one of our children is angry all the time lately. Every attempt we make to soften the hard edges of their anger results in more hostility. They seem determined to stay angry and refuse to be comforted.

We've been working on patience and listening. We've even avoided the temptation to give advice. When we listen patiently and invite them to share their feelings, they eventually relax a bit, and some of their frozen animosity melts. We still may not understand why they are angry, but we're gradually learning to be better listeners.

This is a hard lesson for us. When our children are angry, we feel distressed as well. We tend to worry, even when their feelings aren't directed at us or anyone in the family. Anger wasn't acceptable when we were children; we grew up believing that parents should prevent their children from feeling anger or at least prevent their open expression of it. And, as children, we were supposed to cooperate by not feeling angry. We're learning that people in healthy families own their own feelings. They even encourage children to express all feelings, including anger. That means listening patiently and telling our children that it's okay to feel anger. It also means letting them know what we're feeling.

Today I will draw out my children's buried feelings, even if it means listening to their hostility and anger.

The Truth Works

. . . .

*H*onesty was not always the best policy for many of us as children. We got punished so often for things we didn't do that we lost faith in the value of telling the truth. Honesty wasn't practiced, encouraged, or rewarded. The shrewd person was the one who got away with the most and still looked good. We've spent most of our lives being careful not to say the wrong things. We never thought of this as lying until we got into a Twelve-Step program.

In our recovery we have learned a new way of relating to what others called honesty. This has been very difficult for us to cultivate. We believed we were responsible for everyone else's feelings, so we were very careful about what we said. We didn't want to hurt anyone's feelings, especially our children, so we tiptoed around them, watching their eyes and changing our stories as we spoke.

The more we learn about emotional honesty, the harder it is for us to go on living with emotional avoidance or dishonesty. We are learning to tell the truth in our relationships. We feel so much better when we don't have to worry about which white lie we've told to whom. When we tell our children our true thoughts and feelings, we're amazed that they aren't hurt by our new honesty. And we've stopped telling little white lies to protect them from disappointment. We're learning that the truth works.

I am practicing honesty in my relationships.

Apologizing

. . . .

*N*one of us likes to make mistakes and have to apologize. We've always believed we should be perfect—happy, in control, and on top of things. Mistakes are for other people. Mistakes make us feel guilty. We will do almost anything to avoid feeling guilty and needing to apologize. Perfection—or at least the appearance of perfection—seemed like the only way to avoid guilt and recrimination.

Everybody makes mistakes, though. We sometimes treat our children as if they are irritants, annoyances, or unpleasant interruptions we have to put up with. When we're busy, we often say in any number of ways, "Go away and leave me alone." When we're irritable, we may yell at them just for being in the room. After we have treated them harshly, or merely harbored unkind thoughts about them, we feel guilty and inadequate as parents.

In recovery, we try to be more self-accepting and forgiving of our behavior. Then we can acknowledge our mistakes, apologize, and be forgiven. Before we can fully accept forgiveness from our children, we must first make amends to ourselves and cleanse ourselves of crippling guilt. Being above reproach is no longer our number one priority. We'd rather have close relationships with our children than feel isolated by our perfectionism.

Making amends to myself for not being perfect enables me to apologize to my children.

Embarrassment

. . . .

*S*ometimes we're embarrassed by our children. They don't act the way we think they should or dress the way we'd like. They bicker in public and express themselves loudly. They insist on wearing weird T-shirts or other inappropriate outfits to school—and even to church. They don't talk the way we think they should. We worry about what other people will think of them—and of us. We're afraid people will think we're bad parents.

Feeling uncomfortable with our children doesn't mean we're bad parents. We're working hard to let our children be themselves, to be individuals. We know they need to "try on" different looks, different words, different behaviors. They need to have their own clothes and language in order to bond with their peers. And it isn't always easy to let go and let them.

We can share our values with our children without passing judgment on them. We can stand back as they try their hands at life, giving them reassuring smiles that let them know we like them just the way they are. Accepting them just as they are supports their development. We can impose limits without placing stumbling blocks in their paths as they discover themselves. When we feel embarrassed, we can own our feelings and not blame our children for them.

As I learn to be myself, I am able to let my children be themselves.

Provocation

. . . .

*W*hen we feel provoked by our children, we immediately think we must be doing something wrong. Or we think they are. How could our children, who are sweet and happy most of the time, turn irritable and crabby for no apparent reason? When our children are crabby, they pester and tease each other and end up in tearful fights. That drives us crazy, and we end up being part of the problems, rather than offering solutions. Things rarely improve when we intervene and stop their fights.

Getting angry at them when they provoke one another only makes things worse. Although we try not to lose patience with them, that isn't always easy. We get so irritated with their behavior that we want to scream, scold them, shake them, or send them to their rooms. When we reach this point, it's time for us to stop and listen.

If we listen to what they're really trying to express, we may be able to understand what's behind their annoying behavior. In recovery, we're learning to ask our children about their feelings. When we know what's upsetting them, we can try to suggest some possible solutions without fully directing their behavior. We can teach them how to talk about feeling afraid, sad, or angry as an alternative to picking fights or throwing toys.

I patiently and carefully observe my children's annoying behavior and strive to recognize the unmet needs they are trying to express.

Discipline

· ·

*N*o one enjoys scolding children. Those of us who were severely scolded may have done everything, short of taping our mouths shut, to avoid yelling at our children. We've quickly learned, however, that undisciplined kids become monsters. Children need discipline for proper development. In our recovery, we're learning how important it is to give children consistent rules, clear guidelines, and firm limits. We expect them to know right from wrong, and we correct them when they break the rules, go beyond our limits, or disobey our guidelines.

Knowing the importance of good discipline doesn't necessarily make our jobs any easier. How can we correct their behavior without damaging their self-esteem, enthusiasm, or creativity? Many of us grew up without proper discipline. For some of us that meant rigid rules with abusive punishment. For others it meant loose, inconsistent rules that were randomly enforced with unpredictable punishment.

We want to nurture our children's self-esteem—something our parents didn't consider important. We try to focus our discipline on their misbehavior, not on their characters: "That was a dumb thing to do," not, "You're dumb because you did it." Our goals are to be consistent and firm, not wishy-washy. Then our children will respect us without being afraid of us.

I am consistent and firm in my discipline without being physically or emotionally abusive.

Over-Responsible

· ·

*M*ost of us learned to be in control during childhood when doing so was essential to our survival. Living with so much chaos in our families, we did everything we could to maintain some control in our lives. When we became parents, we continued this attitude and behavior because we didn't know any other way to be. In fact, it felt perfectly natural and appropriate to be in control because, after all, we were parents.

In our controlling, however, we took on too much responsibility for our kids' behavior. That meant they took too little. The more we did for them, the less they did for themselves; our overinvolvement led to their underinvolvement. We pampered and rescued when we should have stepped back and allowed them to discover their own solutions, thereby enhancing their self-confidence.

Twelve-Step programs taught us the perils of trying to control others. It took us a long time, however, to recognize that the first step—admitting we are powerless—could be applied to parenting. First, we learned that by controlling adults we were causing ourselves serious relationship difficulties, anxiety, and personal distress. Later, we gradually realized that our controlling interfered with our children's development. Now we are learning humility as it applies to raising children. As we're learning to step back, they are taking on more self-responsibility. And we are experiencing more serenity.

I can step back when I am tempted to step in and control my children.

Positive Focus

. . . .

We used to think negatively about everything, including our children—especially when they misbehaved. We
were so pessimistic about life that we believed "whatever can
go wrong, will." Our recovery programs have helped us to
look at things from different perspectives. We are learning to
maintain positive attitudes toward our children and avoid expecting negative outcomes.

When our children act in ways that concern us, we no longer
focus on the problem behavior. Instead, we think about positive action and plan ways to help them move toward new behaviors rather than constantly scolding them for the old. We
begin each new day with positive outlooks and plans for making changes easy for them. We talk to them confidently about
new behaviors. By staying focused on a positive outcome, we
easily resolve most problems without power struggles and
without inflicting shame.

As we develop positive attitudes toward our children, they
change too. We can tell that they are feeling more confident
and worthwhile, without carrying the shame we carried. It is a
joy to see our children grow without having to experience the
humiliation and shame that we felt as children.

*My positive approach helps me and my children overcome
problems that used to overwhelm me.*

Mirroring

· ·

*W*e want to communicate to our children that we are genuinely interested in their lives. We realize, however, that we are often preoccupied and unavailable when they come to us with concerns. Sometimes we're even irritable and cranky when they interrupt us. We want to change this. We never want our children to feel afraid, or even reluctant, to share their concerns with us.

We stopped sharing our inner lives with our parents at an early age because they were always too busy to listen. When they did listen, they often offered us little support and were rarely enthusiastic about what we told them. They seemed to judge us as bad or inadequate if we had concerns. When we see parents who are enthusiastic in support of their children, we see how lucky those children are.

We're learning to give our children enthusiastic support when they're excited and empathetic concern when they're upset. This is easiest with our youngest because they bring more enthusiasm with them. All we have to do is mirror it back to them by responding in kind. Our older children seem to have lost some enthusiasm along the way. They are more reserved, and we have to listen more carefully to show them our support. They often test us before sharing their concerns or letting their enthusiasm show.

Mirroring the enthusiasm my children express to me enables me to better connect with them.

Hypervigilance

· ·

*H*ow can we ease off from constantly worrying about our children? Many of us feel exhausted by our anxious hovering over their lives. We feel totally responsible for protecting them from every imaginable adversity. We worry about accidents, muggers, sickness, kidnappers, molesters, thunderstorms, electrical outlets, radiation, germs, violence on television, playground bullies, household cleaners, dogs, pesticides, drugs, and nuclear war—just to name a few possibilities!

We want our children to be happy, well adjusted, and optimistic, without worrying about their physical safety or emotional security. Yet we know that keeping them safe and secure in a precarious and dangerous world is impossible, in spite of our constant vigilance. We cannot guarantee that nothing bad will happen to them. Not only are we preoccupied with worries about them, but we sometimes persecute ourselves with the fear that our worries will turn them into hypochondriacs and neurotic worriers.

Thankfully, we are learning to trust our Higher Power. We are gradually letting go of the illusion that we are alone in the universe—the only ones assigned to our children's safety and welfare. We first learned to trust our Higher Power in our own lives and are now learning to entrust the safety and welfare of our children to our Higher Power. We no longer feel alone and overwhelmed by the responsibilities of protecting our children.

I am learning to trust my Higher Power to both protect my children and calm my worried mind.

Listening to the Silence

. . . .

*W*e stopped sharing our feelings so long ago that many of us can't remember ever doing so. Most of us had little or no emotional support growing up; we were on our own as far as emotions and feelings were concerned. We never talked to our parents when we were upset, scared, or insecure. We learned to suppress our uncomfortable feelings until we hid them from ourselves as well.

We have only recently begun learning to identify feelings and sharing them with others. We want our children to feel comfortable and safe about talking to us about their fears and insecurities. As we learn the vocabulary for putting our emotions and feelings into words, we want to share it with our children so they will be able to express, rather than repress, their feelings.

We are learning to create safe places for our children by listening to the silence as well as the words. We reassure them that we will not scold, tease, ridicule, or even question their feelings. We create this safety by being available when they seem unusually quiet. By turning off the television or putting down our reading, we make sure we don't discourage them from talking to us. After a comfortable silence, they'll often start a casual conversation that tests our attention. When we listen carefully, they will open up to us.

I listen to the silence as well as the words to help my children express their feelings.

Time Management

. . . .

*M*any of us rush through life, always in a hurry to get somewhere else—to work, to meetings, to the store, or home. The faster we hurry through a nonstop day, the longer it takes us to slow down and unwind. In our haste we too often ignore the needs of our children. We can be so preoccupied with our own lives that we don't realize how much our children need our time and attention until they act out or get in trouble.

When we practice slowing down and relaxing, we find we can pay attention to what's going on around us. It's important to be more sensitive and to listen to our children, no matter how rushed our day has been. We can pace our lives more reasonably in order to be available when they need us, as well as to set a better example for them.

As children, many of us had parents who were too busy to notice us until we were in serious trouble. In recovery, we are learning the importance of getting attention for doing the right thing. We want to catch our children being good and give them the attention and recognition they need before they act out. In order to do this, we have to slow down and focus our attention on them rather than rushing through each day, preoccupied with our lives.

I can be still long enough to listen to my children and really hear what they are saying.

Inferiority

· ·

J A N U A R Y   1 7

*F*eeling inferior has nothing to do with facts or reason. When our children are discouraged, telling them how wonderful they are doesn't help at all. They don't see what we see in them or recognize their own abilities. They feel inferior to others when, in fact, they are gifted in their own ways. We hate to see them become discouraged or give up on themselves simply because they are different from their peers. When we try to sway them out of their discouragement, they defend themselves and their despair.

We see our children's uniqueness, their gifts, and their abilities. Why can't they see them? We find it difficult to understand why our beautiful, gifted children feel worthless and inadequate at times. They have so much going for them, if only they would realize it. Discouragement is a cruel bondage that can make it impossible for us to hear the truth about ourselves.

Learning not to argue with a discouraged child is important. Telling children that they have nothing to feel discouraged about because they're smart, creative, capable, and so on only makes them feel worse. We are learning instead to listen, draw out their thoughts and feelings, and assure them that we understand. When we allow them to fully express their discouragement, their moods brighten. It's amazing how quickly our children recover when we offer them emotional support rather than advice or criticism.

Today I won't argue with my discouraged child but instead will listen and offer emotional support.

Gentle with Me

. . . .

A wonderful part of our recovery is learning to be gentle with ourselves. We used to be very critical and hard on ourselves. We like this new attitude we have adopted, and we seem nicer than we used to be. We treat ourselves more like we treat our friends. And, happy result, we don't get so depressed and angry.

We used to go into an awful funk every time we made a mistake or upset someone. Then we would agonize about all the neurotic habits we were passing on to our children. Now we see that the kinder and gentler we are with ourselves, the kinder and gentler our children are. They are happier, less irritable, and nicer to us, themselves, and one another. Our new attitude is catching. We enjoy seeing them pick up our healthy traits.

The happier we are each day of our lives, the calmer they are. We no longer start our days together with fights, tears, and tantrums. When we do have conflicts, we are able to handle them without sinking into depression over our imperfections. We like this new way of living, and we like our new way of relating to our children.

I thank my Higher Power for being gentle with me and teaching me to be gentle with myself.

Simple Joys

· ·

*A*s teenagers, our chaotic lives dulled our senses until we needed a pretty big jolt of adrenaline to feel alive. The more risks we took, the less these risks moved us. We needed progressively more and more excitement to get high. We couldn't feel any rush unless our lives were at stake. We craved danger and excitement like an alcoholic craves alcohol. We were addicted to speed and intensity. For some of us this meant fast cars, fast boats, and fast motorcycles. For others it was the drama and energy of sex.

We were clearly on a path to self-destruction. Our feelings were so deadened that we had no sense of danger. It has taken us a long time, but we're recovering our ability to feel life around us without creating chaos and crisis. Our feelings have gradually reawakened. First, we regained our ability to feel our own physical sensations. Then we began to feel our emotions, and finally we were able to feel empathy for others.

This reawakening of feelings changes our relationships with our children. We lost our connections with them, or never developed them in the first place, because we were so out of touch with feelings. Now we are learning what it means to get high on life, to feel a warm rush from simple things, such as a quiet, intimate conversation with one of our children.

I am learning to get high on life and find joy in simple things.

Yelling

. . . .

When our children yell at us in anger, many of us are tempted to yell back at them for talking to us in a disrespectful tone. Some of us want to shout, "Don't you ever talk to me like that!" Our parents punished us severely for expressing anger toward them. When we were told, "You can't talk to me like that!" we felt as if we had done something terrible or committed a horrible crime. Yet, we wanted our parents to hear what we were saying, and we probably yelled because we didn't feel they were listening.

In our recovery, we're learning new ways to deal with our own anger as well as our children's anger. It's not easy to accept their right to feel angry with us. Once we accept, in theory, that children have a right to be angry with parents, we are left with the challenge of teaching them how to express their anger toward us in a way that doesn't undermine our authority.

We don't want to punish our children for trying to communicate with us. They won't always do it "right," especially when they are upset. But then, neither do we. However, if we listen with care and respect to each other, no one will be forced to yell.

I accept my children's right to feel angry with me, knowing that their anger doesn't make me less of a parent.

Grieving

· ·

*W*e want our children to feel safe and emotionally secure enough to show their tears. We want them to grieve their losses freely. Many of us, especially men, were scolded and shamed for showing tears as children. We were told, "Big boys don't cry." While we experienced countless losses and disappointments, we received no support for dealing with them. We became emotionally stiff and brittle from our years of repressed grief. Whenever our grief was too huge to repress, we turned it to rage or depression—usually with the help of chemicals.

As we began uncovering repressed emotions in recovery, we opened up years of unmourned sorrow. Many of us cried more in the first months of recovery than in most of our previous life. Although this grieving process has been uncomfortable and emotionally draining, it has resulted in new emotional vitality. Our long-buried sense of humor, genuine spontaneity and our capacity to feel the whole range of human emotions are returning.

We encourage our children to grieve their losses, even when it's upsetting to deal with their tears. We listen to our young children's grief when they lose a game or get their feelings hurt. We support our teenagers in grief when they break up with a boyfriend or girlfriend. We all grieve together when one of our pets dies. We are now more comfortable letting our children see us express our grief.

When I grieve my own losses, I can support my children as they grieve theirs.

Overprotection

. . . .

*F*amily life was so threatening and scary for many of us as children that we couldn't face it without eventually turning to alcohol or drugs. We want to shield our children from this kind of distress. We want them to have secure, carefree childhoods. And yet, we find ourselves warning them about everything that could possibly harm them—crossing the street, talking to strangers, playing with matches and sharp knives, taking drugs, being taken by a stranger, getting AIDS. The list is nearly endless.

While we don't want to turn them into neurotics and hypochondriacs, neither do we want them to ruin their lives through carelessness and imprudence. Too often our children seem naive and unprepared, taking no precautions whatsoever to protect themselves from possible danger. Yet we don't want them to become anxious worriers from hearing too much gloom and doom or to tune us out altogether and fail to heed any of our precautions.

We realize that if we're constantly warning, they cannot possibly remember all of our warnings. Nor can they be expected to deal with all of life's hazards at once. We are learning to put our faith and trust in our Higher Power to watch over the lives of our children. We are learning to let go of our anxious worries and to temper our warnings.

I can teach my children how to handle the dangers they are most likely to face and then entrust them to God's care.

Judging

. . . .

*B*efore our own children began showing signs of maladjustment, we were smug in our belief that parents controlled how their children turned out. We were quick to judge those parents whose children were in trouble with the law or the school authorities or were on drugs. When our children began rebelling by experimenting with drugs and alcohol, we could no longer dictate their behavior. We realized that we were out of control.

Perhaps before we started attending support groups for parents of children in drug treatment, we knew we would not fit in. We thought that parents in this group would be very different from us. We expected to find single parents who had no interest in their children's lives. Needless to say, we were wrong. As we have come to know these parents, our attitudes have changed. We are discovering that family life is more complex and unpredictable than we had believed.

We are no longer quick to judge the parents of children who are in trouble, including ourselves. Too many factors influence our children's lives besides our words and attitudes. When our friends' children cause them grief, we can support them without judging them in our hearts. We now know there is no room for any of us to be smug about raising healthy teenagers.

I no longer stand in judgment of other parents or myself.

Children's Loyalty

. . . .

When we were sick of ourselves and sick of life, some of us manipulated our children into telling us they loved us and that they would never leave us, even when they grew up. Although this was wrong, we were too sick and discouraged to stop doing it. Our self-esteem was so low that we would do anything to make ourselves feel better, even at the expense of our children.

One of the richest joys of parenting is hearing a child say, "I love you." This expression of trust, loyalty, affection, and unconditional love lifts our spirits and brightens even our darkest hour. We can bask in the warmth of these words for hours. In these moments we vow never again to be irritable with them. When we're discouraged, however, we sometimes manipulate our children to tell us they love us.

In the program, we are learning to take responsibility for ourselves, and to take better care of our emotional needs so that we're not tempted to exploit others. Old habits die hard, however, and we often struggle to practice new and better ways to get our emotional needs met. It's easy to revert to our old habits of feeling sorry for ourselves and using these feelings to manipulate others. Our old behavior is especially tempting when we are discouraged or depressed.

I will turn to God, not my children, to lift my spirits when I'm discouraged or depressed.

Spirituality

· ·

JANUARY 25

*W*hen we began our recovery, most of us were not interested in God talk. God talk reminded us of all the things we weren't and all the things we've done that we shouldn't have done. Although many of us began our journeys to sobriety and sanity by ignoring the spiritual aspects of the program, we gradually learned that we were only cheating ourselves. We saw that those who developed their spirituality had a calmness and peace we longed for but never quite reached.

We came to see that the spiritual aspect of the program was nothing like what we had believed about a wrathful God. Spirituality is not about blame or punishment. It is a gentle resource that helps us live and love again. Spirituality is like a silent power source we can access if we are willing to be open to our Higher Power. This power source is available to anyone who will sincerely accept it.

This spiritual power helps us relate to ourselves, our partners, and our children in a more loving and nonjudgmental way. The acceptance we experience from God has released us from the self-blame and self-condemnation that once controlled our lives. We no longer blame or condemn others as we once did. And we no longer feel blamed or judged by those who disagree with us. We are learning, for example, that our serenity does not depend on our children's acceptance of us.

Genuine spirituality is my power source for becoming a more loving parent.

Being Alone

· ·

As children some of us remember being left alone when our parents went drinking. Sometimes we waited in the car for hours; sometimes we waited at home. These were frightening experiences that left us with lasting fears of being alone. We're more comfortable when we have people around us, even if we're not talking to them. Some of us experience real panic when we have to spend time by ourselves.

We became codependent as a result of our unhealthy need to have someone around us all the time. We sacrificed our independence and failed to develop a satisfying sense of self-reliance. We resented those we depended upon, often wrongly blaming them for our feelings of entrapment. We envied those who always appeared self-confident. We did not know how to free ourselves without feeling vulnerable.

Now that we are accepting ourselves more honestly, we are facing our childhood fears that have kept us from becoming full-powered adults. Although there were times we couldn't stand being left alone, we now enjoy it. We have come to regard time alone with ourselves as time spent with our best friend. Solitary activities like reading and going on long walks nourish our souls. This has given us a deeper appreciation of serenity, which is spreading to our relationships with our children. We teach them to cherish time spent alone and not be afraid of it.

I enjoy the solitude of spending quality time with myself.

Controlling My Children's
Inner Experiences

. . . .

*M*any of us have painful memories from childhood, and we want to ensure that our children have good memories. Consequently, we feel guilty when our children get upset, angry, or cry. We want to take away their pain, satisfy their needs, reassure their hearts that they are loved, and tell them everything is okay. We want them to be happy, content, and free from feelings of anger, loneliness, and fear. Although we know we can't control their inner experiences, we have a hard time letting go of our desires to do so.

According to experts, it is both healthy and essential for children to experience a certain amount of frustration. While we may believe this intellectually, it is hard to accept emotionally. Some of us get knots in our stomachs from the very sound of their angry voices—even before we know what they are angry about. Sometimes we over console. Sometimes we get so distraught that we punish them for making us feel anxious, angry, or guilty.

We're learning to resist the temptation to scold or punish them when they're angry and to let them have their feelings, experiences, and frustrations. We're learning to focus our efforts on listening and accepting rather than on controlling and stifling.

I surrender my need to control my children's feelings, and I respect their right to feel and express what they experience, even when I have to struggle with my own discomfort.

Staying Connected

. . . .

We learned very early to run away from our fears, troubles, and problems. When we were upset, we retreated to safe places. Withdrawal has always been our way of coping with life's difficulties. When we had conflicts with our friends, we isolated ourselves. If they did not seek us out, we rarely approached them. Instead, we became detached in order to minimize the hurt and loneliness we felt.

When we began our recovery, we were very lonely. Because we had withdrawn from them, most of our friends had given up on us. When we withdrew from our children, they begged us to talk or devised other ways to get our attention. We actually thought ignoring them was good for them, that it made them think about what they had done and behave better. Our partners disagreed, saying we were cruel and spiteful.

Now, we're learning to stay connected when we're upset. We're learning to identify our feelings and express them in appropriate ways. We try to express what we are experiencing without blaming. Because our impulses to withdraw were so strong, we couldn't stay focused on our feelings. With practice, we are able to stay connected and express our feelings. Our children are more responsive to us now. They don't cry or cling. Instead, we talk things over.

I stay connected when I'm upset.

Being Real with Kids

· ·

*O*ur kids look up to us, and their admiration makes us feel important, needed, and loved. When we feel compelled to live up to all their expectations, however, we feel as though their admiration places us on a precarious pedestal. Of course always living up to their expectations is an impossible task. Because we don't want to let them down, we try to hide our feelings of inadequacy, guilt, and shame. We don't want them to see our faults, weaknesses, and shortcomings or to feel ashamed of us.

We've worked to be more honest with our feelings. We've learned that we don't have to hide our emotions, pretend to have it all together, or be perfect. Participating in a Twelve-Step group is a blessing that frees us to be ourselves. We feel whole after attending our groups because we've been able to freely express our feelings, whatever they might be. Everyone there accepts us just the way we are.

We are learning to be emotionally honest and real with our kids. We are gradually becoming as relaxed and natural at home as we are at group. We are overcoming our fears that our children will be upset, embarrassed, or disappointed when they see our real feelings. We have decided to be ourselves with our kids. And our kids are helping us step down from the pedestal.

Being emotionally honest and real with my kids helps me be real with myself.

Idealizing

. . . .

*D*o you ever wonder if your family is normal? Many of us have come to accept that our childhood family was abnormal, but we're not sure what a normal family is. Some of us imagine that normal families never argue or experience conflicts. Others of us imagine that normal families resolve all their differences in calm, rational tones—or that people who live in normal families never act moody.

When we don't know what a normal family is like, we easily imagine we're doing something wrong. We imagine there is some secret that normal families have that prevents children from arguing with their parents and each other. Or we imagine that normal means everybody is happy. Or we imagine that normal parents know how to solve all their children's problems.

Many of us are willing to do almost anything to ensure that our children grow up in a normal family. Being willing does not automatically translate into either the knowledge or the skills needed to accomplish our dreams. In recovery, we're learning that all families have problems—that it is normal for families to disagree and argue. We're discovering the comforting knowledge that nobody is perfect and that our children will grow and develop in spite of our mistakes as well as because of our new attitudes and skills.

I am accepting myself as a good enough parent—not perfect but good enough for today.

Obedience

. . . .

*W*ho doesn't wish for obedient children? It would be so much easier if they would do exactly as we tell them, without any fussing, challenging, or talking back. How nice it would be if they were never defiant.

Blind obedience would certainly make our jobs easier. But would it be desirable for children to grow up under these conditions? How would they learn to speak their truths, express their points of view, or stand up for their rights? Their personalities would not develop properly, and they would be unequipped to live in the real world if they never learn how to assert themselves with authority figures.

Part of parenting is to teach our children the proper balance between respect for authority and self-respect. This is a big challenge for those of us who didn't learn this balance as children. The program has taught us the difference between self-respect and hostile defiance. We have learned that it is okay to question authority. We no longer automatically give up our personal rights to someone in power. We look to God and our program for direction and guidance in teaching our children these lessons.

I am teaching my children to stand up for their own feelings through encouragement and example.

Company

. . . .

Some friends came to visit today. We wanted to enjoy talking with them, but our children kept interrupting. We found ourselves getting angry with our kids for not leaving us alone. Then we remembered being sent away as children when company came to visit our parents. How we resented not being able to stay in the room with the adults. Now we're the adults, and we're the ones who want to send our children away—we resisted the temptation.

When we encounter this scenario, we can acknowledge their desires to be included by telling them they can stay in the room while we visit with our friends. We might also reassure them that we will talk with them and play with them, just not now. Now is time for adults' conversation.

Even if we are only moderately successful, over time our children will come to see that we have time for both them and our friends. The adult conversation may be interrupted many times by children's questions, but at least we don't have to yell at them or banish them from the room. Sometimes we involve them in a separate, special game or activity in the same room during an adult visit. We want our children to learn respect for others. But we know we have to show them respect first.

Remembering that children need to feel included makes it easier to treat them with respect.

My Recovery and My Children

. . . .

*A*lthough we believe our children are grateful for our recovery, they appear indifferent to the principles and values that have changed our lives. God and the Twelve-Step program saved our lives and changed them forever. We thank God for this daily. We were living in misery and despair, never looking beyond our next paycheck and our next high. We were medicating daily to dull the pain of our miserable existence. Our lives were going nowhere and our children were suffering from neglect, emotional abuse, ambiguous rules, and harsh, inconsistent punishment.

Although we wanted our recovery to govern their lives immediately, we are learning to be patient. Our old nature sought to control everything in our children's lives—including their thoughts and beliefs. We thought the evidence of good parenting was compliant, obedient children who agreed with our values. We are learning that we can trust God to work in their lives, even when they won't listen to us.

We used to think that God was dependent on us to reach our children. As we mature in our spiritual understanding, we are becoming less anxious about our children. We believe that the quality of our recovery will have a positive impact on their lives, whether they give us credit for it or not.

I put my trust in God to reach my children, with or without my help.

Feeling Stupid

. . . .

"*I*'m stupid!" How often we've heard this from discouraged children. Of course they're not stupid at all. In fact,
we know they're smart. Consequently, our first impulse is to
correct their mistaken impression about themselves. Next, we
show them they're wrong by reminding them of all their accomplishments. We're learning, however, that our first impulse
often misses the point entirely. We've come to realize that
when children make exaggerated, negative remarks about themselves or their capabilities, they're discouraged. And we're
also learning to neither accept nor challenge our children's
words when they're deeply discouraged but to let them talk.

We're learning by working our program not to squash our
own discouragement. By encouraging conversation, we will
discover what is behind our children's discouragement. Once
they begin to talk about their feelings, specific information
comes out about particular school assignments, test anxiety,
competitive pressures, or other inferiority feelings. We are
then able to provide help and encouragement in specific ways.

When we challenge that opening remark—"I'm stupid"—
we never get to the source of the discouragement. When we
set out to prove their intelligence, we often provoke arguments
that further alienate them and accomplish nothing. Where we
used to react impulsively, we're learning to listen first and seek
to understand what's beneath the dramatic words.

I will remember to listen patiently and encourage more
communication when my children express despair or
discouragement.

Confidence

. . . .

*H*ow gratifying it would be if we could simply transfer our new-found confidence and success at work to confidence and success as parents. Since we began our recovery, many of us have grown and are much more successful in our careers. Although we have accomplished many wonderful things in these past few years, we may still feel inadequate as parents. Challenges at work don't trigger our emotions the way our children do.

We feel like believable adults most of the time these days, except with our own children. When we are called upon to explain our actions at work, most of us are poised and confident. But when our children are upset, demanding, and loud, we feel inadequate, angry, and defensive. We don't even feel like adults when our children yell at us. We feel like we felt as children—angry and powerless.

As we practice staying in our confident adult mode with our kids, we don't feel so inadequate, defensive, or angry. When our children challenge our authority, we're learning to stay calm by breathing deeply, thinking clearly, and refusing to match their emotional intensity. Although we sometimes get flashbacks from childhood, we're learning not to dwell on these memories, but instead to dwell on our recent successes.

When my children challenge me, I dwell on my new-found confidence as an adult and not on the anger and powerlessness I felt as a child.

Life Without Crises

*C*haos and crises always seemed normal to us. In the early days of our recovery, we found ourselves wary of the new peace and calm in our lives. We kept waiting for the other shoe to drop. We were suspicious of life without the drama created by undependable people and bewildering events. While we wanted serenity in our lives, we didn't trust it.

One of the challenges of our recovery is learning to accept and appreciate a life without the drama and excitement of one crisis after another. At times, we unwittingly stirred up a crisis just so we could return to the familiar. If we hadn't had a blow-up in the family for a while, there seemed to be an electrical charge in the air. In this charged atmosphere, something as trivial as a broken cookie could easily turn into a disaster. After the dust settled and the hurt feelings were soothed, we would return to peace and calm.

We're slowly learning to trust the peace and calm in our lives without becoming suspicious. Through prayer, meditation, and working the principles of the program, we are learning to find serenity for ourselves and to promote a calmer, more serene atmosphere in our homes. We're learning to remain calm when our children come to us with their crises.

I am thankful for the gift of serenity and accept this gift graciously.

Cover-Up

. . . .

*W*e may have shared very little information about our traumatic childhoods with our children. For a long time, we were too ashamed to tell anyone, especially our own children. We didn't want them to know about the abuse we experienced because we were afraid of what they would think. We didn't want them to think that we were bad—as we'd thought ourselves for many years. We didn't want them to feel sorry for us because we feared they would lose respect for us as parents.

As we have progressed in our recovery, we have gradually become more open about our childhoods. We have come to accept that the abuse we suffered as children was not our fault. Although we now understand this intellectually, old feelings of shame and guilt come back to us at times. It often takes us a while to shake these feelings, even when we use all the tools of our recovery program.

As our children grow older, they ask more questions about their grandparents, especially after we visit them. We have decided to tell the truth about our parents, without being vengeful or dramatic. We want our children to trust their feelings and to maintain their self-esteem even while having confusing or hurtful interactions with our parents. We refuse to make excuses for their grandparents. Our loyalty is to our children.

I will tell my children the truth about my parents and about my childhood.

Mentor

. . . .

*W*e want to teach our children many things, but we don't want their lessons to turn out the way ours did when we were children. When our parents tried to teach us things, they often got angry with us for not catching on quickly, or they got bored with us, or they simply took over and finished the task themselves. We never did things well enough to please them. They got so frustrated while teaching us that they gave up. We want to teach our children without creating hard feelings, defiance, or rebellion.

In our recovery, we begin to let go of our need to control everything. We see how we can influence our children without controlling their thoughts, feelings, or behavior. When we create a relaxed, cooperative atmosphere free of dominance, authority, and power struggles, we become effective teachers. We do this by relaxing ourselves and letting things happen naturally.

We teach our children by sharing our stories and experiences. We don't use force or anger or focus on our authority. We can, for instance, teach them how to color Easter eggs by telling stories of how we used to, even if our experiences weren't perfect. By sharing our experiences, we put ourselves on their level and avoid authority issues entirely. If they make mistakes, we tell them about mistakes we made when we were their age. This keeps everything relaxed and friendly.

I am teaching my children by sharing with them in a friendly, relaxed manner.

Projecting Worry and Fear

. . . .

Worry has controlled many of our lives. We can't imagine feeling secure enough to stop worrying. We've worried as long as we can remember, and whenever we let our guard down, terrible things happened to us. We believed it was our worrying that stood between us and horrible disasters. When we saw carefree parents who seemed relaxed with their children, we wondered how they managed to avoid the disasters that would surely strike our children if we stopped worrying.

When we tried to relax and stop worrying, our minds began to picture frightening possibilities. Although we tried to keep these pictures out of our thoughts, we were rarely successful. We would warn our children and fret over them. They often acted puzzled by our worry and anxiety; they didn't see any danger, so they looked at us as if we were crazy.

We're learning to turn our worries over to our Higher Power. This helps keep us from projecting them onto our children. With the help of our Higher Power, we keep our frightening thoughts to ourselves. We carefully examine our fears to determine if they are based on reality or on our past lives. We're learning to do reality checks before warning our children. It is nice to see them happy and carefree. We don't want them to grow up to be worried because we projected our worries on them.

Not projecting my anxious fears and worries onto my children helps to dissipate my worrying.

Affection

· ·

*M*ost of our parents did not openly show affection for one another, especially in front of their children. They acted as if doing so was distasteful and immoral. Consequently, we became very self-conscious about touching other people, especially when we began dating. Eventually, as we grew more comfortable, it seemed more natural to express affection during our courtship. However, we remained stiff and unaffectionate when our parents were present. We were afraid that we would offend our parents if we touched our dates.

After marriage, many of us gradually stopped showing affection. Resentments set in as our relationships deteriorated because of increasing chemical abuse. In recovery, we are once again showing affection to our partners, even in front of our children. We want them to feel comfortable with tenderness. Our Twelve-Step groups have helped us become more comfortable with affection. We hug one another and our children and other friends without uneasiness or embarrassment. Many of us experienced giving and receiving affection in a nonsexualized manner for the first time in group. Sharing affection is now a part of many of our nurturing friendships.

Our children have always enjoyed affection. And, in recovery, we have been generous in our affection with them. It feels freeing to share our feelings for each other in the presence of our children.

Sharing tenderness with my partner in front of our children feels good and models healthy behavior for my children.

Spoiling My Kids

. . . .

*O*nce we started recognizing our children's emotional needs and taking them seriously, an inner voice accused us of spoiling our children. Many of us had parents who were harsh and unsympathetic, who ignored our emotional needs. They said no automatically to every request just to show us who was boss or to prove to us that life is hard and nobody gets everything they want. Although we don't believe we're spoiling our children, we can't help wondering about it.

Is showing our children kindness, consideration, and generosity wrong? We are learning in our program that it is not selfish or unreasonable to get our needs met, despite what some of us learned as children. Repeated denial is both unnecessary and unhealthy. We want our children to feel comfortable and secure in their neediness. We don't want them to hide their requests from us or to resort to sneaky means to get what they want. We want our children to be able to get their needs met by asking us. We will be responsible for setting limits on what we provide so they aren't overindulged.

On the other hand, we expect our children to contribute to the family by doing chores, running errands, and cooperating with others. We do not give them everything they ask for. We do, however, consider all their requests before we respond.

I can be generous and considerate toward my children without feeling that I should give them everything they ask for.

Disappointment

. . . .

We want to protect our children from disappointment, and we know we can't—any more than we can protect them from germs. If protecting our children from all disappointment is impossible, perhaps we could settle for never disappointing them ourselves. Even if we dedicated ourselves to avoiding all obvious causes of disappointment, they would still experience it. Life is filled with it. Our children will inevitably be disappointed by friends, relatives, siblings, teachers, grandparents, step-parents—just about anyone they associate with. Remember, however, that disappointment, like beauty, is in the eye of the beholder. Just because they're disappointed with us does not mean we treated them badly.

If we actually attempt to protect our children from all disappointment, we soon create havoc in their lives, as well as in our own. In an effort to immunize them we might, for example, try to give them everything they wanted. This overindulgence would turn them into demanding, unappreciative monsters. Or, if we try to protect them from loss, we'll leave them ill-prepared to deal with inevitable loss later.

Our children have certain basic needs and rights, but these do not include always getting everything their hearts desire. Experiencing disappointment and frustration is necessary for children to develop initiative, courage, and an awareness of the conflicting rights of others.

Part of respecting my children's rights and protecting them from harm is not promising them freedom from disappointment.

Fun with My Family

. . . .

*F*un was never much fun when we were growing up. In many families, having fun meant teasing, making fun of someone, getting drunk or stoned. We became distrustful of fun because it usually got out of hand and ended in tragedy. To this day, it is difficult for many of us to relax and have a good time. Even though we're now in recovery, we often become tense and guarded at parties and in situations where there is an atmosphere of merriment. It's been difficult to discard our fears that things will get out of hand, that someone will get hurt or lose control. Consequently, laughter, joy, and genuine happiness are all too rare for us.

Recovery has opened our eyes to a new world in which people have fun together without getting crazy and hurting one another. This has helped us discover that we, too, can laugh with and enjoy our children without shutting down emotionally. Genuine laughter without sarcasm, cynicism, or ridicule is energizing and relaxing at the same time.

We're learning to relax when our children have fun and to have fun with them, without letting our old fears shut off our feelings. We're learning that things do not always end in tragedy when we let go and have fun. We can relax and trust that nothing crazy will happen when we have fun together.

Today I will relax and have fun with my children.

Failure

. . . .

*M*ost of us associated failure with shame and humiliation because we were scolded and ridiculed whenever we failed. We did everything we could to eliminate failure from our lives; we even avoided activities we might not succeed at immediately. When we failed at things we attempted, we wanted to hide. We never learned how to rebound from our failures.

In recovery, we are overcoming the shame and guilt we associated with failure. We've begun to look objectively at our efforts and learn from our mistakes. We pick ourselves up and shake ourselves off when we make mistakes instead of spending hours or days in our shame, even when we fail seriously. We're learning to maintain enthusiasm and a sense of excitement about what we are learning from our mistakes.

Helping our children bounce back from their mistakes and failures without losing their momentum helps us as well. We never ridicule them, and we make certain we call attention to the things they do well, not to their mistakes. We remind them of the primacy of effort and enthusiasm. Skills will come in due time if they learn to truly enjoy the game.

My children and I are learning to bounce back quickly from our mistakes and failures.

Fighting

. . . .

*O*ur children are constantly arguing and bickering with one another. Although we fought with our brothers and sisters, our children may seem to fight more than we did. Is there something wrong with them? Is it the effect of television or social violence? Or is there something wrong with the way we are raising them—or our memories? We try to get them to work out their differences without fighting, but our words fall on deaf ears.

At times, it seems as though our children fight simply to annoy us. It's reassuring to note that experts think children fight with one another, at least in part, because they each want to feel special. They each want to be favored, preferred, superior, pampered, pitied—anything that gives them a sense of personal significance. This competitive striving for our attention and recognition takes the form of bickering and aggressiveness as they vie for most-favored-child status.

When we spend time with each child individually to reassure him or her of our love, our children become less aggressive and competitive. Our loving reassurances work miracles on their self-esteem. Loving reassurance is not like a piece of information that can be passed on once. Although we'd like them to feel loved and special without our reminders, they need ongoing reassurance. We never outgrow our need to be loved personally, individually, and specifically.

I reassure each of my children frequently, individually, and specifically of my love.

Broken Hearts

. . . .

We still remember our first broken hearts. We felt completely devastated—no one prepared us for this experience. When our teenagers fall in love, they will most certainly experience their first breakup as well. Even if they eventually marry their high school sweethearts, as some of us did, they will go through breakups along the way. Just as falling in love for the first time is a powerful emotional experience, so is breaking up.

We can remember being teased when our hearts were broken the first time. We felt absolutely miserable, and no one took us seriously. Consequently, we repressed our emotions and never talked about them. In recovery, we learn about the power of unfinished business. Many of us have unfinished business from our first romantic involvement. Because we never dealt with the strong feelings associated with our broken hearts, we remained emotionally aloof in subsequent relationships, trying to protect our wounded hearts.

Now we know that unmourned losses can interfere with our emotional well-being for years. We do everything possible to encourage our teenagers to mourn their broken hearts. We make it safe for them to share their feelings with us, being careful not to minimize their experiences. We treat their feelings with as much respect as we do when one of our friends experiences divorce or the death of a spouse. We listen with genuine empathy and understanding.

I treat my teenagers' feelings of loss as seriously as I do those of my adult friends.

Grace, Not Gumption

. . . .

*M*ost of us grew up too soon. We became little adults and learned to count on ourselves for the things that really mattered. Our parents were unreliable. We were proud of our self-reliance. We felt more grown-up than our friends because we could cook, do laundry, run the lawn mower, and buy groceries before they could. We didn't realize we were learning to distrust adults and God.

The very strategies that helped us through childhood soon led to loneliness and despair. It was inevitable that our self-reliance would eventually include trying to control our emotions. Once we began controlling our emotions with chemicals, work, gambling, sex, or even religion, we were doomed to become addicted to our method of choice. Our philosophy of total self-reliance led directly to addiction.

Giving up self-control was like abandoning ourselves. Once we acknowledged the futility of our own efforts to turn our lives around, we began to recover. For us, the only way to experience peace and serenity is to turn control of our lives over to our Higher Power. Although putting our trust in a power greater than ourselves seemed silly at first, it has made all the difference. We are learning to live in God's grace, rather than by our efforts. Our new serenity enables us to relate to our children in a more relaxed and confident manner as well.

Letting go of control is the key to peace of mind.

Overreacting

. . . .

*M*any of us were ridiculed for overreacting to poten-
tially dangerous situations as children. We were terrified by
the yelling and violence we witnessed in our families. When
we told our parents we were afraid, they discounted our fears,
saying things like, "Oh don't be ridiculous! There's nothing to
be afraid of. Go back to sleep. Just forget it." We became so
fearful of being ridiculed for overreacting that we lost the ability to distinguish an emergency from a nonemergency.

In recovery, we are learning to listen to our inner voices and
trust them when we are in danger. Because we lived in life-
threatening situations as children, we have trouble recognizing threats, danger, and potential violence. Even when we do
sense the presence of danger, we may not respond. Some of us
feel too inhibited to sound an alarm, while others are virtually
paralyzed by our fears of humiliation, lest our judgment turn
out to be wrong.

We are teaching our children to trust their judgments in
emergencies. We are teaching them it is better to overreact
than underreact. If our children call the fire department because they smell smoke, we will congratulate them on their
good judgment and presence of mind, even if there is no fire.

Encouraging my children to trust their judgments
in emergencies helps me trust mine.

Spiritual Progress

. . . .

*E*ven though we went to church as children, many of us did not receive much spiritual nurture there. Instead, we learned about moral demands, perfectionism, and God's wrath. Church, for us, was not a source of comfort and peace but a source of shame and guilt. The message we heard in church sounded like the same one we heard at home—that we were bad, stupid, and unlovable. Attending church reinforced our sense of unworthiness.

In recovery, we regarded Step Eleven with suspicion. Why would we invite God to remind us of how we had messed up our lives? We were far from perfect, and we had always believed that God demanded perfection. The spiritual aspect of the Twelve-Step program was difficult for us to accept. As we continued in the program, we heard people talk openly and honestly about their relationships with a loving God. We knew we wanted the serenity and hope they had in their lives.

Now we know that spiritual growth means progress, not perfection. This we can handle. With practice we learned to pray again, in a whole new way. God is now our friend and not the demanding, harsh judge of our childhood. We have come to think of prayer as conversation with a special friend. We now have a desire to communicate regularly with God. We now have a wonderful resource to turn to for our parenting, as well as for the rest of our lives.

I rejoice in my spiritual progress.

Losing

. . . .

*E*ach of us has felt the distress of losing games, races, contests, and competitions. When we enter a competition with enthusiasm and a strong desire to win, losing feels awful. This is true for adults as well as for children. My youngest child was crying. He had just lost a game of Chutes and Ladders and came to me for comfort. "It's only a game," I said, "don't get so upset." But my words led to more tears, rather than comfort.

Children simply don't like to lose. They expect to win and don't know how to hide their feelings when they don't. They show their disappointments openly and honestly. They haven't yet learned to act cool and indifferent toward winning and losing, as many of us have. When they lose, their disappointment is real, and their tears immediate.

When our children lose, we want to comfort them, ease their pain, and help them act maturely. We want them to be good losers, not crybabies. However, in our efforts to give comfort and teach maturity, we may minimize their feelings. We may unintentionally pass by their experiences and suggest they learn to be emotionally dishonest, like many of us are.

Remembering that my children have emotions and feel their pain deeply can help me comfort them rather than minimize their feelings.

Blame

. . . .

"It's not my fault!"
"I didn't do it!"
"He did it!"
"She did it!"

*W*e've heard lines like these countless times, yet we still wonder where our children get them from and why they are so interested in fixing blame. We hope we haven't taught them to accuse one another this way. Maybe we have, unintentionally. Blaming and being blamed played a big part in our childhoods. We can still hear our fathers' voices, like some grand inquisitor, saying, "Okay, who started it?"

No one ever likes to admit starting trouble. And asking who started it tempts our children to lie or point blaming fingers at each other. We can learn to ask other questions, and then listen attentively to the answers. By asking "What's going on?" and encouraging them to relate their story, we invite them to express their feelings without accusing someone else. Asking "What can you do to solve this disagreement?" invites them to offer solutions rather than remain focused on blame.

We don't want our children to get into the habit of blaming others whenever they are unhappy or having difficulties. If our response is to judge and scold, we're teaching them that if they don't blame somebody else, we'll lay it on them. When we ask them to examine their own feelings, we're teaching them to be responsible for their feelings and actions.

I won't ask who started it next time my children are causing trouble.

Dreams

· ·

All of us have countless hopes and dreams for our children. We see signs of their enormous potential. Often, as we watch them, admire their innate beauty and delight in their many talents as they work on projects. We cherish their zest for life and appreciate their incredible persistence as they master new skills. As we savor these precious moments of their youth, we also ponder their futures.

Thinking about our children's futures causes us to reflect on our pasts. Have we done what we wanted to do with our lives? Have we followed the dreams of our youth? Some of us have to struggle to remember the promises we made to ourselves in our youth. We haven't always kept our goals in focus, nor have we worked persistently to reach them. There were periods when we lost sight of our dreams entirely. For some of us, there were no bright hopes, big plans, or exciting challenges—only the struggle to survive from day to day. We want our children to have bright hopes, big plans, and exciting dreams that eventually come true.

We encourage our children to live their own lives and follow their own dreams, not our dreams. We focus our attention on our own dreams and are accountable to ourselves—to the benefit of both ourselves and our children.

Today I encourage my children to dream their own dreams.

Cooperation

. . . .

*C*hildren who cooperate with us are real treats. They are easy to raise and fun to be with. They make quick work of household chores by taking part in the effort. At the same time, they are developing a wonderful sense of responsibility. Best of all, they are happy.

Cooperation is such a nice sounding word. It conjures up pictures of smiling children playing well together and eagerly sharing in the chores and tasks around the house. We tend to think of cooperation as the absence of resistance to our authority—pictures that don't seem like reality. Perhaps we're equating cooperation with obedience.

Real cooperation includes our willingness to cooperate with our children. We can't simply demand cooperation from them without being willing to reciprocate. Our children may want us to cooperate by taking time from our busy schedules to read to them, help with homework, play games, or enter into their make-believe world for a few hours. This is our chance to model cooperative behavior by treating them the way we want to be treated. It is a chance to demonstrate that we regard them as persons of equal worth. Cooperation takes place between equals, whereas obedience describes the relationship of a dog to its master. Winning cooperation is quite different from demanding obedience.

Remembering that cooperation is a two-way street,
I teach my children cooperation by example.

Growing Up

. . . .

FEBRUARY 23

*W*hy do our children want to grow up so fast? What
is it about the here and now that they don't like? They seem to
long for the future—when they think they'll be more satisfied,
more free, have more fun. When we see them acting too old,
too grown-up, too serious, we want to stop them in their
tracks, to say, "Slow down! You're trying to grow up too fast."

Perhaps we're setting the example for our kids by chasing
the prize of tomorrow, without pausing to cherish the rich
bounty of the present moment. Some of us grew up in homes
that were more like prisons. Living for tomorrow was one way
to survive. We were all too eager to escape the prisons as soon
as possible. We had no interest in prolonging the oppression
and humiliation of childhood for one more second. We impa-
tiently marked time until we could advance to the freedom and
liberty of adulthood.

Perhaps we should heed the advice we give our children. By
focusing exclusively on the future, we have robbed ourselves
of many special moments we could have shared with them. By
acting as if the important things in life were in the future, we
have treated today as little more than a tedious preparation for
some shining future. This paints a dull and joyless picture of
daily life.

*By enjoying each moment with my children, I can help
them slow down and enjoy their moments.*

56

Lying

. . . .

*W*hen one of our children lies to us, we often don't know what to do. Many of us still remember being severely punished when we were caught lying, and we don't want to treat our children the same way. The first thing we want to know is why they lied. Maybe they are afraid of us, just like some of us were afraid of our parents. We don't want our children to live in dread of our contempt. If they are afraid of us, we may never learn their true feelings, especially if we punish them.

We're learning to respect other people's privacy, and we want others to respect ours. As a parent, however, we hope to teach our children the difference between privacy and personal boundaries and lying. Rather than lie to our children about aspects of our past that we prefer to keep private, we tell them we're not comfortable sharing with them.

We don't want our children to lie in order to cover up their mistakes or to inflate their egos. We can help them tell the truth by reminding them that mistakes can be corrected and misbehavior can be forgiven. Also, we can tell them what we admire about them. We hope taking these steps reduces any motivation they may have to lie to us. Then we will wait to see if the lying continues before we decide if lying is a serious problem.

Today I will not overreact to my children's lies.

Envy

. . . .

*M*ost of us realize our children are lucky to have the love, security, stability, and sane family lives that we did not have. Of course they may not know what it's like not to have such things, so they seem to take it all for granted. We have to bite our tongues to keep from saying things like, "Don't you realize how lucky you are? Do you know how many children don't have parents who support them emotionally? Do you ever think about the punishment and abuse that some children have to endure? And then you complain that you don't get a long enough bedtime story!"

Fortunately, we catch ourselves before we say these things —at least most of the time. We try not to let their normal tendency to take their lives for granted anger us. Of course they don't realize how lucky they are. How could they know the experience of all the abused children in the world? They don't know how troubled our childhoods were, and we shouldn't expect them to.

We are learning to enjoy the security and love our children feel and not expect them to compare their lives with our childhoods. We are learning to turn our envy into joy, and we are working through our grief over our lost childhoods.

I let go of the envy I feel toward my children by working on my own grief over my childhood.

Staying Centered When I Visit My Parents

· ·

*W*e feel good about our relationships with our children, most of the time. We talk, laugh, and share our thoughts and feelings freely. It is different with our parents. Most of us never had this kind of freedom when we were children, and we still don't. We never felt free to be ourselves when we were growing up. They were always finding fault with us for something, and we still feel tense, uneasy, and guarded when we are around them.

When we visit our parents today, we soon feel like powerless children once again. We walk in the door of our childhood homes, and we no longer feel like the grown-up parents we are. Instead, we feel like the children we once were. We keep expecting to be criticized, scolded, or yelled at. This is such a strange sensation when we're there with our children. Stranger still, when we take our children to visit our parents, we sometimes find that we treat them just like our parents treated us. We hate ourselves for being short-tempered and irritable with them for no reason.

We are learning to stay centered in our grown-up, good parent selves when we're in the presence of our parents. The familiar sights and sounds of our childhood homes no longer trigger automatic emotional slides into old behavior patterns.

I can use the tools of my recovery to stay in my power when I visit my family.

Doing It All Myself

. . . .

*B*ecause we grew up in dysfunctional families where others were unreliable, we learned early that if we wanted something done right, we would have to do it ourselves. If we wanted new clothes, it was easier to earn the money and buy them ourselves than it was to hassle with our parents for the money. We were proud of our independence and self-reliance. Many of us got college degrees, good jobs, and careers by following the principle: If you want it done right, do it yourself.

As parents, however, this principle logically leads to our doing everything—and feeling resentful. We also fail to teach our children the sense of confidence that comes from contributing, cooperating, and developing their own skills. Our overresponsibility leads directly to their underresponsibility as they let us do most things for them.

We are gradually learning to be more patient with their imperfect results and with the extra time it takes young children to do tasks that we can do quickly. We are learning to take the time to train our children, knowing this investment will be returned many times over as they contribute more and more to the household tasks. At the same time, we're there for our children when they need our help so they won't become people who do everything themselves and never ask for help.

I am taking time to teach my children to do tasks I could do more easily and quickly myself.

Back Talk

. . . .

We get angry when our children talk back to us when we are trying to discipline them. They interrupt, make excuses, blame others, and try to change the subject. We may be tempted to smack them, especially if we were hit by our parents when we tried to defend ourselves. Most of us were not allowed to talk at all when we were being disciplined. We felt resentful for never being allowed to explain our side of situations. Because we were not allowed to express ourselves, we found other ways to get back at our parents. And we learned very little about respectful communication in the process.

We want our children to respect us and feel respected by us. We don't want them to repress their thoughts and feelings as we did. Mutual respect is not always easy to achieve when we must discipline. We are learning that the best way to teach children respect is to show them respect. We reassure them we are disciplining them for bad behavior, not because they are bad people. We want them to freely express their views without fear of punishment.

We are learning to hold our tempers, listen to our children's explanations, and then follow through with discipline when it is needed. Of course our children continue to protest and explain themselves, but they neither harbor bitter resentments nor act out behind our backs.

By showing my children respect, I am teaching them to respect others.

Learning

· ·

*M*any of our parents, especially our fathers, thought they knew everything. Whenever we told them something we learned in school, they already knew it. As we grew older, we began to see through their intellectual arrogance and to call their bluffs. After many futile arguments, we'd give up, privately conceding only that they were arrogant know-it-alls. We stopped telling our fathers anything about school or about our lives. Although we may have vowed never to do the same thing, we've been surprised, both before getting into recovery and even now, to hear our fathers' words coming from our mouths.

Hearing our parents' words come from us reminds us that recovery is a process, not an instant cure, and spurs us to work harder at our recovery. We practice taking genuine interest in our children's lives and building rapport with them. Instead of competing with them, we shower them with our interest. When we feel the need to test our knowledge, we work a crossword puzzle, read a new book, or find an adult friend to have a lively discussion with.

Now, when one of our children tells us about something they have learned, we let them teach us. We let them explain things to us, and we give them positive feedback. We let them enjoy the spotlight, instead of competing with them for it.

When I let my children share their learning with me,
I get the benefit of learning something new and seeing
their delight in teaching me.

Fighting Reality

. . . .

*G*rowing up with critics and faultfinders taught us to look for flaws in everything. We were never satisfied with the world around us. We built a seemingly endless list of things that ought to be changed. We were always at war with the universe, unwilling to accept any reality that didn't suit us. These attitudes made us negative, unhappy, and irritable most of the time. We rationalized our misery by telling ourselves it was the inevitable result of our high standards.

After we became involved in our recovery, we began to see our incredible arrogance. We'd had acted like self-appointed supervisors of the world, finding fault with the way God ran his universe. We'd had suggestions for everyone and a plan for improving every aspect of life. Our spiritual arrogance was brought to our attention many times before we began to recognize it.

We are learning to accept reality and go with the flow. We adjust our attitudes instead of insisting that God adjust his universe to meet our expectations. Adjusting our attitudes is like adjusting the sails of a sailboat; we can reach our destination regardless of the direction of the wind. We embrace life rather than criticize it. We enjoy life as it is instead of waiting bitterly for things to improve before we let ourselves relax.

Accepting the things I cannot change lets me enjoy life as it is.

Nonintervention

. . . .

We used to intervene whenever our children argued for more than a few seconds. We would command them to stop their arguing immediately. Of course, they would protest their innocence and plead their cases to us. Their arguing was not only aggravating, but we believed it was our duty as parents to control their hostility and teach them to be civil toward one another. Unfortunately, we were unable to keep them from arguing and fighting, no matter how harshly we punished them. Instead of learning civil behavior, they learned to see themselves as victims.

In our recovery, we are learning about codependency. Our codependency kept us overinvolved in managing our children's affairs. Recovering from codependency has meant learning to stay out of other people's concerns, including our children's. Because we were always settling their disputes for them, they were not learning to settle their own disputes. Our recovery involves learning to respect our children by remaining detached from their provocative behavior.

We see the value of letting our children work out disputes and resolve conflicts by themselves. Although they may be resistant to the idea of resolving their own disputes, the number of arguments, as well as the hostility level, has decreased. They are learning to work things out for themselves instead of running to us with each tiny dispute. Best of all, we no longer feel angry and defeated when they argue.

Allowing my children to solve their own disputes makes all of us feel better.

Control What I Can Control

. . . .

*F*or many of us, control was essential for our survival as children. There was so much chaos around us that we did everything we could to maintain some equilibrium in our lives. While control was essential to our survival as children, it doesn't work now. In fact, our need to control everything around us interferes with the quality of our relationships and our emotional well-being.

In recovery, we learned about surrender, letting go, and the futility of trying to control all the outcomes in our lives. Surrender is the key to serenity. In our zeal to surrender, however, we sometimes believed we couldn't control our behavior toward our children. We imagined they were in control of us, that we couldn't stop ourselves from doing or saying the things we did. We may have said, "You kids are driving me crazy!" But we know this was a cop-out.

Sometimes we overcorrect in recovery. We're learning that control is not an all or nothing proposition. There are aspects of our behavior we will always be responsible for—such as everything we say to our children and every action we take toward them. Though we don't always feel like we're in control, we know we can't blame our children for our actions or our words. We are, after all, adults.

I accept full responsibility for everything I say and for all my actions.

Religion and the Program

. . . .

*R*eligion was not enough. Despite the fact that most of us believed in God and viewed ourselves as religious people, we were unable to manage our own lives or the lives of our children. For many of us, religion was so firmly tied up with shame and guilt that it offered no relief from our deep-seated feelings of worthlessness. In fact, this attitude of unworthiness was reinforced by our religious beliefs. We viewed God as an angry, demanding judge, a perfectionist who was impossible to please—just as many of us saw our parents.

Trying to raise emotionally healthy children in an emotionally volatile atmosphere is like trying to rake leaves in a windstorm. Our meager efforts to build up their self-esteem were blown away each time we lost control of our anger. We believed God was judging us for the way we treated our children, and yet we had no tools for dealing with our frustrations.

When we finally admitted that our lives were out of control, we sought the help of a Twelve-Step recovery group. The program has given us tools for dealing with our feelings, especially anger, guilt, and fear. With these new tools, we are gradually learning to apply positive religious principles of love and respect, without losing control when we get frustrated. Without these tools we were unable to apply our religious principles with our children.

I thank God for leading me to my Twelve-Step program where I learned how to live my faith.

Change My Mind

. . . .

*W*e've always had a hard time admitting that we were wrong about anything. Consequently, it was not easy for us to change our minds. Many of our parents were very stubborn, especially after they had taken a position on one of our requests. Once they had taken a stand, they refused to listen to our sides of the issues and were completely closed minded. As much as we disliked their stubbornness, we recognize that we have often done the same thing with our children. It is not easy for us to be vulnerable, admit our mistakes, or change our minds.

The program has taught us that we're not God, we're not perfect, and we can change our minds. We're learning to admit mistakes without losing face and feeling humiliated. As we accept our humanity, we're becoming more spontaneous, joyful, and relaxed. We used to think being vulnerable meant losing control and dignity. We now see vulnerability as a means of connecting with our children.

We are letting our children see our real feelings. Now, when we make mistakes with them, we admit them. We even tell our children when we've changed our minds. We now realize that our fear of losing face came from our insecurity and had nothing to do with our children's views of us. We've learned that being able to change our minds does not mean we're weak or bad.

I'm choosing to be open and honest with my children.

Loyalty

· ·

*M*any of us were easily exploited by our friends because we didn't know what we stood for and we were unable to set our own limits. We avoided taking positions that our friends would not agree with. We were followers who thought nothing of going along with things we didn't agree with. We were too insecure and afraid of rejection to stand up against our friends. We thought it was more important to be popular and have friends than to be honest with ourselves.

In recovery, we have come to understand the difference between loyalty and codependency. While we once thought of ourselves as very loyal friends, we now see that we were people pleasers who were afraid to disappoint others. We are learning to stand up for our values, even when it means disappointing family and friends. For some of us, this is the first time we have experienced genuine dignity and self-respect.

We want our children to be able to identify and walk away from exploitative relationships. We teach them to stand up to their friends when they honestly disagree on some moral principle. We warn them of the subtle dangers in wanting to be popular at all costs. We teach them the proper balance between respect for their friends and respect for themselves and that if they must choose between self-respect and the respect of others, to choose self-respect.

My children and I are all learning that loyalty begins with ourselves.

Making Friends with God

. . . .

*F*ew of us had ever thought of God as a friend. God was ominous and demanding, an unfriendly, perfectionistic scorekeeper. Friends are supportive and accepting, not critical and judging. We felt small and insignificant, of little importance in God's eyes.

Since we began our recovery, our thoughts and ideas about God have been changing. People in our Twelve-Step group talk about God in very personal and ordinary terms. What's more, they talk *to* God, not just about God. Getting to know God as a personal friend has become important to us as we see how God works in the lives of those in our groups. They talk about their spiritual lives as a real and crucial part of their recovery. They experience a type of support, direction, guidance, and serenity for their recovery that we want in our lives.

As we began exploring our own spirituality, we found that we had buried and suppressed our spiritual lives over the years. As we learn to relate to God as our friend, our old fears of being judged slowly dissipate. We can share this new relationship and understanding of God with our children. The God we introduce them to isn't a wrathful parent who rules through fear and the threat of abandonment. We don't want them to go through years of spiritual emptiness but to help them recognize their spiritual needs and encourage them to feel free to go directly to God as a friend.

Making friends with God supports my recovery.

Solutions

. . . .

*M*aking mistakes used to change our moods entirely. If, while having a good day, we made even a minor mistake, the rest of our day was ruined. Making a mistake made us feel small, guilty, and exposed. We raged inwardly and had long conversations with ourselves in which we defended ourselves and our behavior, usually by blaming someone else for our mistakes.

We no longer allow minor mistakes to disturb our serenity. We are learning to overlook our minor errors, as we would those of a friend. Our self-esteem is steadily improving as we continue to work our recovery program. We're no longer as vulnerable to experiencing shame. Although our shame can still be triggered by a simple mistake, we're able to focus on the needs of the situation, rather than on our shame. We are concentrating on solutions, and, if we have injured someone, on amends.

We like the effect our new behavior is having on our children. When we take our mistakes in stride, focusing on amends and solutions rather than on guilt and blame, our children are more relaxed around us. They are able to freely admit their mistakes to us, without adding a long list of excuses. We're also learning to take their mistakes in stride and to teach them to focus on solutions and amends.

When I make mistakes, I focus on finding solutions and making amends.

Lecture

. . . .

*W*e hated it when our parents lectured us. We felt degraded. We tuned them out, for the most part, and endured the harangue until it was over. Consequently, we don't remember anything they said during those lectures. They may have given us good advice, on occasion, but we were so turned off by their hostile tone and criticism that we couldn't learn anything from them at the time.

We don't want to turn our children off with our lectures. We do, however, want to correct them when they make mistakes and to impart our values to them. We try to use a calm, friendly voice when we correct them. Sometimes this means we can't talk to them until we calm down inside. Before lecturing them, we think through our goals. What do we want them to do differently? What do we want them to feel, as a result of our correction? Do we want them to feel ashamed and guilty? Or do we want them to reflect on our words without feeling humiliated?

We are learning to listen to their thoughts and feelings before we speak. As children, we were not allowed to express ourselves when we were being disciplined. Letting our children share their feelings and explain their actions doesn't mean we're letting them off the hook for their misbehavior. We are learning to combine respect for our children's thoughts and feelings with responsible discipline.

I treat my children with respect when I correct them.

Program Carry-Over

. . . .

*O*ur personal recovery has been easier than our recovery as parents. Many of us have found new serenity for our souls, even while we continue to clash daily with our children. Although we may have been in recovery for years, we still react to our children the way our parents reacted to us. We haven't found the cable that connects our new attitudes with the part of our brain that automatically reacts to children. We are, however, always looking for ways to apply the recovery principles to our parenting. "Easy does it" is such a well-worn phrase that we don't often think about how it applies to our kids.

Kids can become hyper over little things, and soon everyone in the family is tense, screaming, and arguing. We are learning to tell them, "Easy does it, kids. Slow down, relax, don't get hyper. Everything will work out." We also tell ourselves the same thing when they are in a frenzy.

We find that when we stay calm and listen to their feelings and concerns, everything goes more smoothly. If we allow their crises to become our crises and become frenzied ourselves, communication breaks down. When we remind ourselves "easy does it," they sense our confidence and security, which has a calming effect on them.

I will remember that "easy does it" works with children.

Raise Children Differently

. . . .

*B*efore we were parents, it was easy to say what we were *not* going to do when we had children of our own. We remembered the things we hated when we were growing up, and we were determined never to do them. Now, however, we are discovering it is not easy to make these changes. Remembering what we hated and knowing how to avoid them are two different things.

We know what we want to accomplish, but we don't know how to do it. We want our children to have good self-images, but we don't know how to provide them. Many of us are particularly confused about how to maintain their self-images when we're angry with them and have to discipline them.

Raising emotionally healthy children is not simply a matter of deciding what we don't want to have happen to them. We're gradually learning to think through the consequences of our decisions before we act on them. We are learning that we can discipline our children without becoming angry or letting our feelings get out of control. We are setting limits without using angry voices or physical punishment. We ask ourselves, "How would it feel if my parents did to me what I'm doing to my child?" before we take certain actions with our children.

I am learning to put myself in my children's shoes in order to be a more sensitive parent.

Normal Is Boring

· ·

Some of us began using alcohol and drugs to numb the pain of our miserable lives as teenagers. By the time we married, we were medicating daily in order to cope with our lives. When we wanted to go out and have fun, many of us needed intense interactions to feel any excitement at all. This cycle of alternately deadening and stimulating ourselves drew us deeper and deeper into the spiral of a chemically controlled existence. Life became dreadfully dull unless we were involved in drama and high-risk activities. This cycle of addiction altered our normal feelings and sensations. Beside chemicals, some of us became addicted to risk, excitement, and stress.

When we quit using alcohol and drugs, some of us still craved excitement, intensity, and risk. We searched for serenity, yet at the same time we were bored to death with quiet, ordinary, daily existence. We craved the rush and thrill of our using days.

Friends in our Twelve-Step groups said this was normal. They assured us that we would gradually adjust to sanity and serenity. Just as they predicted, we gradually began to feel more alive in our recovery. We no longer crave intense interactions or feel attracted to dangerous events. We have learned the joy of spending quality time with our children.

I am learning to enjoy normal peaceful feelings, without craving excitement and intensity.

Self-Reliance

· ·

We love to give advice. Many of us give children advice as if it were a moral duty. In fact, some of us act as if advice giving were our primary mission as parents. We qualified for this mission by enduring the advice giving of our parents. Now it's our turn to play the role of the all-wise, all-knowing, ultimate authority.

When children are confused or struggling with problems, we may feel compelled to enlighten them or solve the problems for them. But are we really helping with this instant advice? Or are we exploiting them to boost our egos, to show them what good problem solvers we are?

Unsolicited advice does not promote self-reliance in our children. In fact, if we give advice too often, they will likely come to depend on others to solve all their problems.

We are learning to be supportive without being invasive and disrespectful. Before giving our children advice, we ask them if they want help. Then we solicit their suggestions on how to solve the problems. We help them explore options and evaluate alternatives instead of handing them our ready-made solutions. In this way, we encourage them to solve their own problems, and we teach them self-reliance.

It's as easy to give my children time as it is to give them advice.

Blame

. . . .

*M*any of us grew up with chronic shaming and blaming. As children, we learned that all disappointments led to blame and/or punishment, and we learned to duck out of the way when someone was upset or angry. We were often blamed just because we were handy, so we learned to think defensively. We were rarely without excuses or alibis and could create them in a flash when we needed them.

These defensive skills often caused problems in our marriages. Our partners felt hurt and misunderstood when we became defensive at the slightest sign that they were disappointed. A simple question such as, "Have you seen my keys?" brought a sharp-toned, defensive response from us. Our defensiveness was automatic, and we felt so justified that we couldn't understand their annoyance. They couldn't understand how we heard criticism and blame in so many of their questions. We, on the other hand, couldn't understand how they could deny that their remarks were critical.

The program has given us insights into our defensiveness. In our belief system, someone always had to be blamed, so we made certain it wasn't us. By learning about our shame, we no longer automatically react to questions as if we are being interrogated for a crime. Our relationships with our children and partners are becoming more open and spontaneous.

I am learning that shame, blame, and defensiveness are habits I can change.

Single Parent

. . . .

*M*any of us were raised by single parents. Although we never planned to raise our children alone, many of us are in the familiar role of single parent. We don't want our children's lives to be blighted as the result of being raised by only one parent. Consequently, we are doing everything we can to ensure that our kids have normal childhoods. We don't want them to feel sorry for us or to stay home in order to keep us company.

In our single parents support group, we are learning to get emotional support from other adults instead of our children. Although it is easy to confide in our children, especially the oldest, it tends to make them feel overly responsible for our lives. We want them to enjoy being children without having to worry about us. We are learning to talk about our loneliness and parenting frustration with adults in our support groups, rather than dumping on our children.

Letting our children be children, instead of little adults, is especially difficult when they seem interested in our lives and eager to listen to our troubles. It's sometimes difficult to resist the temptation to pour out our troubles to them. Even though they act more mature and grown-up than many adults, they should enjoy the freedom of childhood without carrying our emotional burdens.

I use my adult support system and let my children be children.

Enjoying My Kids

. . . .

Sometimes we lie awake in the middle of the night thinking about our children. In the quiet darkness we hear our thoughts clearly. As our children sleep in the next room, we recall how much we love them, how much we enjoy their laughter, thrill in their sense of discovery, and even hurt when they hurt. Sometimes we smile and sometimes we cry softly in the darkness. In these midnight moments of reflection and thanksgiving, we feel a sense of fulfillment that only parents experience.

We like being parents, at least most of the time. It is not all work and worry. But sometimes we have to quiet our thoughts in order to appreciate fully the love and fulfillment our children bring to us. We could not have predicted the changes that our children have brought to our lives. We remember how tiring it was to hear mothers talk for hours about their children. Now we understand and appreciate these mothers.

Being a parent is both a great delight and an awesome responsibility. Fortunately, we're learning to handle the responsibilities one day at a time. We don't always know what to do when our children startle us with surprising behavior. And we don't always know what to say when they share peculiar thoughts or disturbing feelings. But as long as we respond from the deep love we feel at this moment, everything will work out beautifully.

I tell my children how much I enjoy being their parent.

Intimacy

. . . .

*M*any of us were emotionally abandoned as children. This abandonment has had far-reaching affects on us. For example, it has been difficult for us to be emotionally intimate with anyone. We fear that whenever we get close to anyone, they will die, hurt us, or leave. It has taken us a long time to fully accept and completely trust the love and commitment our partners have shown us. We keep expecting that, without warning, they will stop loving us and leave. Once we married, we tried not to dwell on these fears, often with little success.

Our recovery has taught us to face our fears and deal with them, rather than run or hide from them. When we face our fears of abandonment, we begin to enjoy intimacy without becoming unreasonably anxious. We no longer pull away each time our partners approach us with tender initiatives. Our recurring nightmares about being all alone diminish. We continue to stretch ourselves by accepting this risk again and again.

Being emotionally vulnerable is still difficult although we are gradually learning to let our guard down and share our innermost thoughts and feelings. Some of us are experiencing genuine emotional bonding for the first time in our lives. We are experiencing the joy and satisfaction that comes from making a meaningful emotional connection with another human being. We savor the feelings of closeness that result from these intimate conversations.

I build intimacy with my partner (and my children) one day at a time.

Good Company

. . . .

*B*efore we began our recovery, it didn't occur to us that we had a relationship—albeit a neglected one—with ourselves. We thought relationships only involved others, and we were upset because those relationships never seemed to go the way we wanted them to. Now we're realizing that we do have a relationship with ourselves—a very important one that affects all our other relationships. When we're overly self-critical, all our relationships suffer because we're also critical of others. Self-acceptance, we have learned, is the foundation for all positive relationships. When we accept ourselves, we are more accepting of others.

Many of us grew up in families that were hyper-critical, faultfinding, and anything but compassionate. We were taught that accepting ourselves was being conceited, as in "You're no better than anyone else." The message our child-self probably heard was, "You're worse." Self-contempt was only proper humility.

As we become more compassionate toward ourselves, our relationships improve, especially with our children. We no longer feel compelled to criticize them, comment on every mistake, or expect perfection. Our relationship is less strained and more harmonious. Children who used to have chips on their shoulders are less argumentative and more friendly. Children who would never express their feelings for fear of being put down by us are more open and friendly.

When I'm good company for myself, I'm good company for my children.

Ask Other Parents

· ·

MARCH 19

*I*t's hard for some of us to talk with other parents about raising children. Although we want to know how they handle the issues we face, we're afraid to let anyone know how inadequate we feel. We are afraid to ask questions for fear other parents will judge us.

We have very little self-confidence. We always second-guess ourselves when we discipline our kids. We often imagine that other parents know how to discipline, handle fights, motivate kids, and keep them happy—and do it all with poise and self-confidence.

Most of our parents had so many problems of their own that they had little time for raising children. We weren't raised carefully and lovingly, so we don't have role models in our own parents. Even though we've decided to be better parents to our children, we don't always know what to do. We know we can learn from other parents if we can overcome our fears of being judged. We may find we love to listen to other parents talk about how they handle their kids, especially those parents we admire. We'll also probably find that no parent has all the answers and that other parents welcome the chance to have open discussions about parenting.

I resolve to ask those parents I admire to share with me some of the things they know about parenting.

Rejection

. . . .

*W*hen our children feel rejected by their friends, we suffer with them. We see their pain, and we want to rally behind them. We want to shield them from this kind of pain, yet we know we cannot protect them from many of the social slights they will encounter while growing up.

What we can do, however, is pay attention to them and to their feelings. We can listen when they describe how their friends slighted them, ignored them, or spread rumors about them. We can listen without making judgments or giving advice. Over time, we establish ourselves as the kind of parents they can talk to. We can help them accept the disappointments of life by giving them a safe place to talk about their frustrations and sort out their feelings.

We can resist the temptation to lecture them while they are still smarting from the indignity of being hurt by friends. When the initial pain subsides, we can talk with them about friendships, rejection, disappointment, forgiveness, and reconciliation. We might even share some of our own feelings and experiences. In this way, we help our children grow into sensitive young men and woman who are able to recover from rejection, personal slights, and disappointments.

I make it safe for my children to express frustrations, disappointments, and fears by being open with my feelings.

Fun with My Partner

· ·

*I*t is not easy for us to relax and have fun with our partners. We're always afraid our good times will get out of hand, like they often did before we began recovery. Some of us used to party to a point where we neglected our children for hours at a time. Now, although we're in recovery, we fear that if we begin to relax, laugh, and have too much of a good time, we may forget about our responsibilities.

It is especially difficult to let go and relax when we see our partners having fun. Somebody has to mind the store; somebody has to remain serious and responsible. It's as if we are the "designated serious" when we socialize with others. We are afraid of repeating the kind of social and emotional excesses we used to experience when we would do anything to get high, act crazy, and court dangerous risks.

We are learning to have fun together when we go out. We have grown to trust our sobriety, as well as our new feelings of responsibility. We are learning to apply the principle of moderation to our social lives instead of our old all-or-nothing approach. We are learning to have fun when our partners are having fun. We no longer allow our old habits and rigid behaviors to control our new lives.

I can let myself have fun and socialize with my partner.

Act, Not React

· ·

*M*ost of us hate fighting because we endured too much of it when we were children. We vowed never to fight with anyone, especially our children. Our children, however, did not take the same vow. They fight all the time. And when they fight, we immediately become anxious; many of us react by punishing them. We realize this is not a helpful response, so we're trying to break this habit of reacting automatically to their fighting.

One of the big discoveries we've made in our recovery is that we have more control over our emotions than we once thought. We now realize we can decide whether someone else's actions will control our reactions. We no longer feel like victims of other people's behavior. We are learning to practice this freeing discovery with our children. We are learning to stay centered, even in emotionally charged situations. In fact, we're learning to act from within ourselves so we don't react to our children's provocations as often.

We are learning to remain calm and centered when our kids are arguing. We are helping them resolve their conflicts without becoming anxious or being drawn into their hostilities. In doing so, we are also learning to engage in open and honest disagreements rather than avoiding arguments at any cost. Learning to disagree respectfully is a wonderful discovery, both for ourselves and our children.

I am acting from within myself rather than reacting to my children's fights.

Soul Searching with Grace

. . . .

*T*hose of us who use Twelve-Step principles for our recovery found the fourth step extremely difficult. In order to make a searching and fearless moral inventory of ourselves, we had to be completely honest. We had been lying to ourselves for years because the truth was too disgusting and humiliating to acknowledge. We stopped being honest when we discovered that alcohol, drugs, or compulsive behaviors anesthetized us from the pain of living. About the time we drifted away from self-honesty we also drifted away from God. Our lives were so messed up we avoided thinking about God in any but the most abstract way.

When we began our recovery, we couldn't face ourselves honestly. Oh, there were moments of self-pity and remorse, but we extinguished these feelings before they turned into serious reviews of our lives. We discovered, however, that God's grace was indispensable for doing the fourth step. Receiving grace was like receiving the governor's pardon on death row. Leaning on God's grace was like clinging to a life raft while watching our ship sink out of sight.

Once we discovered that honesty did not destroy us, we began recovering our shattered dignity and self-respect. We began making amends with our children. Although they were suspicious at first, they soon embraced our new honesty. This was very encouraging for our ongoing recovery. We received it as a gift from God.

I lean on God's grace in order to face myself honestly.

Changes

. . . .

*W*hen we were children, change usually meant change for the worse. We felt panic each time our parents sat us down to tell us there were going to be changes in our lives. We always had the same feeling in the pits of our stomachs. Change meant a new school, a new neighborhood, and the end of the familiar. What little security there was in our lives was being threatened—again. We prepared ourselves for the worst.

As adults, change still makes us anxious and insecure, although we've learned to hide this. We're learning that not all change is bad. Some changes have actually been freeing rather than limiting. As adult children from dysfunctional families, we never realized we had a role in creating positive change. We always thought of change as something negative that was done to us by others.

We're learning that our attitudes toward change determine whether change will bind us or free us. As we learn to trust God with our lives, we accept the losses from change as opportunities to make way for the new. We are teaching our children to embrace, rather than fear, change. We don't want them to suffer the anxiety and insecurity we have suffered. We want our children to see themselves as participants, with God, in the changes in their lives, rather than as victims.

I'm learning to trust God with the changes in my life by being a full participant in my life.

Self-Love First

∙ ∙

As children, some of us grew up in climates saturated with attention, affection, and nurture, while others learned to survive in emotionally barren climates. Many of us who survived unloving families realize that our parents did the best they could, even though it wasn't enough. We tried many things, including the self-destructive behaviors of compulsions and addictions, in trying to make up for the love we missed out on as children.

We love our children very much, and we want to provide them with the love and security we didn't have. We want them to feel happy, safe, and secure. We are beginning to realize that our desire alone is not enough. Wanting the best for our children does not guarantee that we have the means to provide it. We must first love ourselves before we can love them fully. Love pours from the pitcher of abundance, not from an empty cup.

As we become more accepting of ourselves, our ability to accept others, including our children, is growing steadily. By accepting the friendship, support, and encouragement of others in the program, we gradually fill our own cups. For some, this is the first time we have experienced the unconditional acceptance of others, which profoundly affects our ability to love and accept ourselves. We give up loving our children from a sense of duty and obligation.

I love my children from my growing sense of abundance.

Approval Seeking

. . . .

*A*s teenagers, some of us rebelled openly while others did everything possible to avoid disappointing our parents. When our parents were disappointed in us, we felt terribly guilty. When we knew what they expected of us, we tried to meet those expectations. However, when we faced new situations and weren't sure what to do, we became anxious. We were unable to make decisions for ourselves because we had never developed the ability to think for ourselves or evaluate critical situations. We did not trust our own judgment.

This exaggerated approval seeking followed us into adult life, and we became codependent with those around us. We were loyal and compliant employees but lacked leadership ability because we feared making the wrong decision. In our relationships, we tried hard to please our partners and felt resentful when they didn't meet our needs or show true appreciation for our efforts.

We're teaching our children to think for themselves and develop their own good judgment. When they seek our opinion on choices that clearly belong to them, we encourage them to think for themselves. When they are hesitant to make decisions or choices in new situations, we encourage them to pay attention to their own feelings, preferences, and desires. When they make decisions or choices we object to, we try to discuss these without making them feel guilty for thinking for themselves.

I encourage my children to think for themselves.

Control

. . . .

*A*s children, many of us felt helpless and out of control because of the chaos surrounding us. We learned that we could make our lives a little more predictable if we assumed control. We always felt more secure when we had charge of the things that affected us. Of course, we couldn't control everything, especially our parents' behavior. So we learned to control our feelings—so well that they became frozen feelings. Along the way we lost all spontaneity and became rigid. We also learned to control others, becoming skilled manipulators in the process.

We became afraid of change and afraid to trust others with anything important to us. Because of our need to control and manipulate others, our relationships were superficial and filled with conflict. We were disrespectful to the people we loved the most because we didn't trust them.

Through the program, we came to understand our need for control and learned how to let go of it. By trusting in God for our security instead of in our ability to control everything, we find that freedom and joy replace our fears and anxieties. By putting our trust in God, we also trust our children more. We aren't so worried that they will make us look bad, and we no longer act bossy and try to control their every thought and action.

Trusting God with my life and my future, I have found a new joy and a new serenity.

Falling in Love with Love

. . . .

*N*o one helped us understand the complex emotions of love. For many of us, falling in love was intoxicating. We could not talk about these feelings with our parents, however. Instead, we read romance magazines, moonsick romance novels, or silly self-help articles about how to change ourselves so someone would love us. We were in love with love. We were so addicted to this emotional rush that we paid little attention to the real person we thought we were in love with. He or she was a stand-in for our self-induced emotional high. While we dreamed about our lovers, we ignored any unpleasant reality, such as the way they treated us.

Before we began our recovery, we talked about how our feelings controlled us, confused us, and made us happy or sad. We never considered how we created our own feelings with our minds. Instead, we regarded ourselves as victims of our feelings. We are learning to think about, talk about, and understand complex emotions, including love. We are coming to understand that we create our feelings ourselves. Some of us created the feelings of being in love because we desperately wanted to believe someone loved us.

We are encouraging our children to examine their hearts. We want them to know what it feels like to be loved so they won't have to create the illusion of being loved.

My children are learning what love feels like and what it thinks like.

New Habits

. . . .

*O*ur recovery program teaches us the power of good habits. Before we began our recovery, we probably had very few habits. And the ones we did have were mostly negative. We resented having to follow strict procedures at work. We thought of ourselves as creative types who needed freedom of expression. We prided ourselves for rarely doing things the same way twice. The Twelve-Step program has taught us the benefits of good habits, of doing the right thing over and over until it is automatic behavior. We have learned that good habits will eventually replace character defects with character strengths.

In the past, much of our behavior was mood dependent. We would only do what we were in the mood to do. We were impulsive, unpredictable, and irresponsible although we preferred to think of ourselves as spontaneous and creative. We now realize this was all a cop-out for our irresponsibility and addiction.

Changing a lifetime of bad habits began with changing one single behavior at a time. We practiced this new behavior each day by repeating it—just for the sake of repeating it—whether we felt like it or not. We started with small things like flossing our teeth, reading a daily meditation, or making the bed. Later, we developed more challenging habits like saying a kind word to each of our children before they left for school.

I practice good parenting by repeating loving behaviors toward my children each day, whether or not I'm in the mood.

Review of the Day

. . . .

*T*he fourth step was a painful experience for many of us. We had spent most of our lives in denial, never looking at ourselves and our behavior. At first we thought personal honesty only meant looking at our faults and shortcomings. However, we've come to understand the importance of acknowledging our many good qualities as well. We have also learned to count our blessings instead of complaining about all our problems. We've learned to balance an inventory of our personal shortcomings with an inventory of our personal strengths, not as a rationalization for our faults, but as a way of keeping our lives in perspective.

Each evening we review our day by thinking about our partner and each of our children. We thank our Higher Power as we think of each of them and what they add to our lives. We look for ways in which we are becoming healthier in our relationships. We are content to mark small changes or, some days, to simply acknowledge that we haven't slipped backward.

This new habit of reviewing the positive growth in our family has had a wonderful effect on our outlook. As we go about our days, we are taking notes and preparing mentally for our evening reflections. We are proving the adage that what we look for in children, we will eventually see in them.

When I look for small signs of growth and good things in my relationships with my family, I see an amazing number of them.

Follow Through with Discipline

· ·

*M*any of us were threatened often as children. Whenever our parents wanted to keep us from doing something, they would threaten us with punishment or threaten to take something away from us. Many of us eventually reacted to their threats as if they were dares. We often had no interest in dangerous activities until they threatened to punish us if we did them. Then, we did them out of spite.

Many of the threats our parents issued were so exaggerated that they could not be carried out. Sometimes they threatened to leave us in orphanages, lock us in basements with rats, or beat us senseless. If some of these threats had been carried out, someone would have gone to jail for child neglect or assault and battery. They did not follow through on most of their threats—thank goodness.

When most of us became parents, we believed we had to threaten our children to establish our authority in our home. Now, however, we no longer depend on fear and threats to train and discipline our children. We are learning to be firm and consistent in our discipline. We're learning to use consequences rather than threats. We are learning to select consequences that are meaningful and reasonable—behavior we can, and will, carry out. Our children's respect for authority has increased since we began doing exactly what we said we would do—without raging, blaming, or apologizing.

I follow through with meaningful consequences in my discipline.

Facing Fear

. . . .

*O*ur parents used fear to control us because they believed children behaved primarily out of fear of punishment. They also used the fear of God in their efforts to control us; we were told that God would punish us if we disobeyed them.

For years we did the right thing out of fear. Occasionally, when we felt frustrated because life was so unfair, we did things that were both unethical and immoral. In every case, however, we were confident that we would not get caught. We inwardly rebelled against authority, although we tried to appear cooperative and accommodating to others. No matter how successful or well thought of in our community we were, we lived in fear that one day we would be exposed as impostors.

In our recovery, we learn that fear is not an effective motivator. Living in fear is unhealthy—physically, emotionally, and spiritually. This discovery opened up the possibility of doing what's right because it makes us feel good, it makes our relationships more rewarding, and it makes our lives simpler and more peaceful. Learning to do the will of God without fear is a totally new experience for most of us. We learn that God is a loving God and not someone to be feared. We learn not to use fear to control ourselves or our children. Nor will we teach them to be afraid of God.

Love motivates and fear controls—both me and my children.

Quiet Children

Some of us were painfully shy as children. We were left out, teased, and even regarded as mentally dull. We had few friends and no dates in high school, and we couldn't wait to leave our childhood behind us. We turned to alcohol in vain attempts to overcome our social isolation. We imagined that if we were less inhibited, all our problems would miraculously disappear.

In recovery, we eventually learned to accept ourselves and our quiet personalities. Once we experienced genuine unconditional acceptance from others, we realized we did not have to be social extroverts in order to be okay. As we became more self-accepting, we began relating differently to our quiet children. Because of all the misery we went through as children, we had been determined not to raise quiet children.

We now accept these children and don't project our childhood misery onto them. Quiet children are like deep pools in a hidden forest. On the surface they are placid and beautiful. Beneath the surface they are sensitive, creative, charming, and often deep. We no longer push them to socialize or scold them for staying close to us in public. Instead, we engage them in conversation about their thoughts and feelings. We encourage their artistic interests and pay attention to the many gifts that quiet children have.

I am learning to love my children without projecting my past onto them.

We used to feel guilty whenever our children were disappointed, especially when they were disappointed with us. We lived with the illusion that good parents never allowed their children to experience disappointment for more than a moment and ensured their children's happiness at all times. Because of our codependency, a crying child automatically triggered guilt feelings in us. We imagined that the happy children of ideal parents were never disappointed and never cried.

In recovery, we learn that disappointment is a normal, natural feeling that everyone experiences. The expression of disappointment should not be stifled. As we gradually recover from our codependency with our children, we learn to accept their feelings without trying to fix them. We no longer feel guilty every time they are upset or disappointed. We gradually let go of our unrealistic family ideal—where happy children never cry because they are never disappointed.

Although it seems as if they are disappointed with us, in fact, they are disappointed with our decisions and choices for them. When we accept this, we no longer feel guilty about making tough decisions. Making hard choices is an unavoidable part of leadership and personal responsibility. We want our children to be able to make the hard choices they face without agonizing over the fact that they will disappoint others. By overcoming our codependency with our children, we teach them how to make tough choices.

I gracefully accept the fact that some of my choices will disappoint my children.

Allowance

. . . .

*O*ur parents used our allowances to control and manipulate us. They threatened to withhold our allowances to
gain our compliance. They controlled us further by deciding
what we could spend our money on and how much we had to
save. Not only did we resent this manipulation and control,
but we failed to develop good habits. Some of us have had serious money management problems as adults, spending everything we earn and saving nothing.

In recovery, we discovered we were still rebelling against
our parents through the way we handled our money. When our
partners told us how we should or shouldn't spend money, we
felt like ten-year-olds again. We now identify these feelings
and talk them out rather than acting them out through impulsive spending. We are separating money issues from our self-
esteem. We can make money decisions rationally, as well as
with our feelings, but without acting out in defiance.

We give our children reasonable allowances for their ages,
with no strings attached. If they spend everything immediately and then come to us for an advance because they have
just been asked to go to a movie with their friends, we decline.
Although we give them guidance, we want them to learn from
their own experience, instead of from our lectures. Experience is a wonderful teacher that does not shame them or cause
them to feel guilt or defiance.

*I allow my children to learn money management from
their own experience.*

Restoring My Lost Humor

· ·

*Y*ears of living in dysfunctional relationships have eroded our sense of humor. What semblance of humor remained took the form of cruel sarcasm or put-downs. We chilled our humorous responses until we became numb. Like a frozen stream, our feelings became rigid and unable to flow. We often didn't recognize we felt hurt until hours or even days later. We were too defensive to laugh at ourselves.

Chemical dependency has been called a feeling disease because we don't know how to deal with our own feelings or the feelings of others. In recovery, we are learning to identify feelings and deal with them. We are learning to express our feelings appropriately, without abusing others with them. As we began identifying our long-repressed feelings, we first uncovered sadness, anger, and hurt. As we worked through this logjam, we eventually uncovered happier emotions. We are recovering our emotional elasticity and sense of humor.

Our restored sense of humor is doing wonders for our children. We are laughing with them and even at ourselves, as we make jokes about our mistakes. When one of our children reminds us we forgot to turn off the oven or put out the garbage, we now make a joke about our failing memory, instead of snapping with defensive hostility. Our restored sense of humor is one of the greatest gifts of our recovery.

I enjoy laughing with my family and even laughing at myself.

Small Changes

. . . .

*W*hen we began our recovery, we wanted everything in our lives to change immediately. Most of all, we wanted to start over with our children. We couldn't erase the years of neglect and abuse we'd put them through, however. We hated seeing the emotional scars that our children carried as a result of our problems.

In our eagerness to start new lives with our children, we began doing everything we could think of to build positive memories. We thought that if we provided enough happy activities, these new memories would crowd out all the emotional scars from our prerecovery days. We vowed there would be no more yelling, no more tears, no more physical abuse, no more harsh, punitive discipline, and no more threats of foster homes when they were naughty. Of course, we couldn't create good memories overnight. Nor could we achieve all our vows at once.

We're learning to celebrate small changes in our parenting. We used to get impatient with ourselves, becoming self-critical and depressed whenever we slipped into our old behaviors. Then we began counting our blessings instead of our failures. At first, this seemed corny, but the more we practiced it, the better we felt, and the more consistent we were as parents. We are growing as loving, healthy parents by acknowledging the positive changes in our lives instead of obsessing over our faults and imperfections.

I celebrate the small changes in my growth as a loving parent.

Humility, Not Servility

. . . .

*O*ur parents taught us to be humble as children. Unfortunately, being humble too often meant feeling self-disgust and servility and having a poor self-image. It meant letting others take advantage of us without standing up for ourselves. Our parents believed their subservient attitude toward others was a sign of their superior Christian humility. In reality, it was their low self-esteem, not their Christian humility, that caused them to be weak, self-effacing, and deferential toward others.

Humility only had negative connotations for us, connotations of weakness, submission, and self-denigration. When we began our recovery program, we were extremely resistant to the concept of humility. It took us a long time to realize that humility simply means being honest with ourselves, accepting that we are not God, and that we need a power greater than ourselves in order to get well. We now know that humility means accepting our weaknesses—and our strengths. It means being willing to find and do God's will in the dailiness of our lives.

Our false humility and our rebellious pride interfered with our parenting. We were too concerned about our image as parents to use common sense and compassion with our children. We felt we had to present a flawless image in order to command their respect. Humility heals our wounded pride and enables us to look more honestly at ourselves and our children, on a daily, ongoing basis.

I am learning the healing power of humility to keep me honest.

Amends but No Compensation

. . . .

We used to feel guilty for making even the slightest mistakes with our children. When we mishandled situations, many of us immediately made up excuses to exonerate ourselves. When these didn't work, we begged for forgiveness or bribed our children with special favors. We tried to restore their good will, at all costs, to ensure they wouldn't hate us. We were afraid they would stop loving us if we didn't make it up to them.

When we first heard about making amends, some of us thought we'd been doing this with our children all along. We were wrong. We weren't making amends. We were allowing our children to blackmail us because of our fear of abandonment. It was quite some time before we understood the true nature of our codependence with our children.

We are learning not to be so concerned about their approval. We've come to accept that they love us in spite of our mistakes, just as we love them in spite of their mistakes. We make heartfelt amends, but only when we've done something that has harmed them. Our amends are no longer bribes or negotiated settlements. Instead, they are simple, sincere words of apology. If we have caused them loss, we will repair it if possible. We're learning to let go of mistakes without obsessing about our children's approval.

I make simple amends, when appropriate, and no longer brood about my children's approval.

Gossip

. . . .

*M*any of us hate gossip because our parents gossiped about everyone, including members of our family. As children, we thought everyone around us was mean, selfish, lazy, dirty, stuck-up, immoral, bad, or a heathen, because of the way our parents gossiped. Eventually, we refused to tell our parents who our friends were, so we wouldn't have to listen to them be run down.

Our parents would talk critically about our neighbors behind their backs and later act friendly and cordial toward them when they met in the community. We were puzzled by this turnabout. Eventually, we came to resent the insincerity and two-faced behavior of our parents and vowed we would never act this way.

We now realize that our parents had very low self-esteem and criticized others in order to boost their own egos. We are learning to improve our self-esteem through honesty and self-acceptance. We refuse to put others down in futile attempts to make ourselves feel superior. We are teaching our children not to criticize others when they are feeling inadequate, inferior, or discouraged. We do everything we can to help our children develop and maintain positive self-images.

When I talk about others in front of my children, I am respectful and avoid harmful gossip.

Patience and Self-Esteem

· ·

When our children showed signs of low self-esteem, many of us felt guilty. We felt responsible because of the way we treated them before we got into recovery. We put them down and called them names when we were angry with their behavior. We damaged their self-esteem by shaming them, and we didn't teach them to believe in themselves.

Negative self-esteem works like a cracked lens, distorting everything that passes through it. Sometimes, no matter what we say to discouraged children, they hear criticism. With one harsh reprimand, we can tear down all the positive feelings we have been working to build. Often they can't hear our words because our body language yells too loudly.

Self-esteem has deep roots, and these roots are not always anchored in reality. What children believe about themselves and their abilities or their sense of worth and lovableness may not actually match their abilities or how much we love them. We are working patiently and consistently to build positive self-esteem in each of our children. Their self-esteem is gradually improving. It takes time to rebuild. With patience and consistent effort, we are seeing a gradual improvement in each child's self-esteem.

I show my faith in my children so they will have faith in themselves.

Low Self-Esteem and High Self-Esteem

. . . .

*W*e feel so different as parents than we did as children. Our parents often made us feel small, inadequate, and worthless. Our children make us feel big, important, and worthy of their love and devotion. Who are we? Are we little people with low self-esteem who struggle to feel okay? Or are we all-knowing parents who can do no wrong in our children's eyes?

To see ourselves reflected in our children's eyes is both satisfying and frightening. We are afraid we will let them down. Sometimes we fight the urge to tell them, "Go talk to Grandpa and Grandma, and you'll see that I'm not the person you think I am." And yet, we never want them to think of us the way we thought of ourselves as children. Our self-image used to be rock bottom most of the time.

Now we feel competent most of the time, only occasionally feeling like impostors masquerading as successful adults. There are still a few days when we feel like fakes. However, who we once were and how we once felt on the inside no longer controls our lives. It would not destroy us today if our kids knew we were yelled at and abused as children. We no longer fear they would think less of us.

I pray for the strength and wisdom to be the person
my children look up to and not the person I used to feel
I was.

Surrender

. . . .

*W*e've been stubborn and independent as long as we can remember. We learned early that we couldn't count on others to watch out for us or take care of us. We, alone, were responsible for our survival. We took great pride in our self-reliance. We never cried "uncle," and we never let anyone see our pain.

Soon after we got into the program, we were told that we were very angry and that we would have to surrender before we could expect to get well. This was crazy talk! Surrendering meant giving up, quitting, resigning, and admitting defeat. Why would anyone encourage us to surrender?

Eventually, we began to understand the third step. We learned that surrendering really means giving up our self-centeredness, not giving up the struggle to get well. Surrendering means relaxing and allowing God to direct our lives. Our self-centeredness grew out of our distrust of all those who had broken promises to us. Learning to turn our lives and wills over to God was a huge step for us. We experience inner peace and serenity we have never known. Our inner peace spills over onto our children and our partners. We experience a calm serenity in our households.

I turn my life and will over to God again and again, as often as I need to, in order to maintain my serenity.

Success Without Shame

· ·

*A*s children, many of us took pride in our meager existence. We were poor and proud of being poor. We were taught to look down on rich people, believing they were prideful and not as morally pure and righteous as we were. Our parents accused the rich of dishonesty, insisting they became wealthy by exploiting honest people like us. Now we see this as reverse snobbery, the vain attempt of proud people to elevate themselves by degrading those they secretly envied.

When we began to reap our own success as adults, we experienced shame and guilt. We found ourselves making excuses for our success, as if it were a thing to be ashamed of. We didn't want our parents to condemn us the way they condemned other successful people. We were afraid they would accuse us of being stuck up. Our self-esteem was so low we denied our success and hid our accomplishments.

In recovery, we are learning to accept graciously our talents, abilities, and accomplishments without false modesty. We don't want our children to carry this burden in their lives. We want them to be able to enjoy freely their success without shame or guilt. We want them to feel the proper pride of high achievement and the joy of their accomplishments without slinking around in the shadows hoping not to be noticed.

I am teaching my children to appreciate their accomplishments and enjoy their successes.

Not Alone

. . . .

*S*ome of us are raising our children alone. We felt totally alone and isolated after our divorces. We felt overwhelmed by the task of raising children on our own. We were both too proud and too ashamed to ask for help, especially from our former partners. After all, the reason some of us divorced was to get away from their emotionally destructive influences. However, when our children resisted our authority or challenged our rules, we were filled with self-doubt.

Joining a single parents support group has made all the difference for us. We no longer feel quite so alone, isolated, or different. Hearing other single parents talk about the same problems that we face has been comforting. We gather strength from one another, which enables us to stand our ground when our children tell us our rules are unreasonable, or that all their friends get to do what we have denied them permission to do.

We are becoming comfortable with asking other single parents how they deal with issues—everything from whether they would leave their twelve-year-old in charge of the younger children for a few hours to how to deal with a toddler's temper tantrums to whether their decisions were challenged by their ex-partners. We find ourselves being asked and listened to in the give and take as well. After hearing a variety of opinions and experiences, we feel much more confident in making decisions ourselves.

I am learning how to ask for and receive support from other parents.

Self-Help

*B*ecause our lives were miserable and we longed for happiness and peace of mind, many of us bought self-help books by the dozen. Excited by the hope that we could change our lives into the lives we read about, we dove into change. We dreamed of success, happiness, and peace of mind. We tried everything in these books, but our lives remained miserable. In our despair, we concluded that we were different from others and doomed to lives of quiet depression.

Once we became involved in Twelve-Step recovery programs, we recognized many of the same goals and objectives we had read about. Love, peace of mind, freedom, joy, happiness—all the themes were familiar. Some of the books we read included step-by-step formulas, God and religion, and even suggested getting together with those who shared our needs. None of these self-help strategies showed us where to look for serenity. The Twelve Steps gave us a compass.

The combination of specific, structured steps, the surrendering of our lives to the will of God, and the loving support of others continues to provide us with the help we need to maintain our sobriety and our sanity. Now, for the first time, we can apply principles we learned about in self-help books, one day at a time. We can, for example, apply principles of loving discipline to our children, something we were unable to do when our lives were controlled by addictions.

I thank God daily for my program.

Abandoned by Children

. . . .

*N*ow that our young adult children are leaving home, some of us are in denial while others are in pain. Most of us have experienced so much abandonment in our lives that we are either oversensitive or numb from it. We felt the pain of all our earlier abandonments when our children shut the doors behind them. We don't want to cling to them or treat their leaving home with indifference. We want their leave-taking to go smoothly so they want to come to visit, not out of guilt— like we felt with our parents—but because they want to.

We were reluctant to let our children know we were feeling abandoned. These feelings were so immature and childish that we were embarrassed by them. We wanted to show our children that we were excited and happy for them, now that they were grown-up and independent.

We are learning through our recovery to deal with our feelings as honestly as possible at the time we are feeling them. By admitting we feel embarrassed by our feelings of abandonment, we find that our children are understanding and even flattered that their leaving affects us this way. They were so used to our being in control of everything that our uncommon humility results in a nice warm connection, without anyone becoming gloomy or morbid.

I am no longer anxious about being abandoned by my adult children.

Self-Justification

A P R I L   1 7

We were so good at self-justification that we could have been mistaken for defense attorneys. Seriously dysfunctional families are good training grounds for defense attorneys. As children, we learned to keep mental notes so that we could build a case, at a moment's notice, if our parents questioned us about our activities. Of course, we had little regard for the truth. The truth was not helpful in protecting us from cruel and unusual punishment—our creative imaginations were.

As adults, our self-justification annoyed those around us, including supervisors, coworkers, and family members. They told us we were too defensive. We tended to dismiss their observations. Then, in recovery, we heard the same thing from other members of our Twelve-Step groups. We listened, in amazement, to others talk about overcoming their self-justification. They no longer assume they are being blamed whenever someone asks a question.

When we saw our children developing the habit of self-justification, we decided to address the issue within ourselves. We are working to remove criticism and blame from our inner dialogue. We are also learning to remove blame from our tone, as well as our words, when we talk to our children. We now realize that we were hypersensitive to blame and may have passed this on to our children. As we become more compassionate with ourselves, we are also more compassionate with our children.

*I am learning to talk to myself and to my children
without blame.*

Saying No

. . . .

*W*e hate to disappoint our children. We want them to be happy and content. We become very uncomfortable when they are angry with us for not giving in to their demands. We want them to accept our authority and never challenge our rules. We used to give in to them when they made scenes, especially in public. In the past, our feelings about ourselves as parents were conditioned by whether our children liked us or were angry with us.

We are learning to say no to our kids and to stick to our word. At first it seemed rigid and cold to say no and never yield. Now we're more comfortable saying no, and it has become easier to set limits for our children. We no longer rage at them for trying to get us to change our minds. We are learning to stand firm without punishing them for asking for what they want. Once we've established our limits, we can say no or yes without feeling guilty.

We are helping our children to feel comfortable enough to ask us for whatever they want. They should not have to read our minds to see if we can afford it, have the time to do it, or are in the mood to do what they ask. We are creating a safe and friendly atmosphere where they are not afraid of our anger, as we were afraid of our parents' anger.

I am setting limits with my children without becoming angry.

Accepting Success

*G*ood fortune was something most of us didn't trust as children. More often than not, the promise of good fortune turned out to be a trick. Just as we got our hopes up, they would get dashed by cruel reality. Our lives were so filled with disappointments and letdowns that we grew accustomed to being disillusioned. Bad luck felt more familiar and less threatening than hoping things might change for the better. Life was more predictable if we didn't expect much.

By the time we left home, our self-esteem was so low it was almost nonexistent. Even though we were smart, we had come to believe we didn't deserve to be happy or successful. Whenever we began to succeed at anything, we became anxious and uncomfortable. We don't want our children to struggle with low self-esteem like we did. We want them to expect good things to happen in their lives.

In our recovery, we are working to improve our self-esteem. We are constantly challenging our old, self-defeating, negative beliefs with new, healthy thoughts and beliefs. We're learning to trust God and believe that he has good things in store for us and that sobriety, health, and happiness are not a trick. We are gradually making the transition from old pessimistic beliefs to new expectations of happiness and serenity.

I am beginning to anticipate and savor my successes.

Relaxation

. . . .

We used to feel guilty for relaxing. We associated relaxing with laziness. And laziness was a punishable crime in many of our childhood families. As adults, we lived as if someone were looking over our shoulders all the time, as if we were students in detention hall. If we weren't busy, we learned to look busy. The only way we could relax was with a few drinks. Drinking was an acceptable escape from duty, work, and responsibility. Alcohol (or drugs or food or cigarettes) medicated our anxiety so we could slow down, unwind, and relax.

When we began our recovery, we couldn't relax. Our old familiar crutches were gone. And we felt like we had to make up for lost time with our children. We were trying to start fresh with our lives and do it right this time. We were trying hard to be responsible, and, consequently, we put even more pressure on ourselves. While we longed for the serenity others in our groups seemed to have, we thought the slogan "easy does it" was a cruel joke.

As we grew in the program, we gradually learned to slow down. Putting our trust in God, instead of our frantic efforts to be perfect, was the key that unlocked the door to peace, serenity, and relaxation for us. We can now relax, either alone or with our families, without feeling guilty.

I can relax when I let go and let God.

Facing Conflict

. . . .

*M*any of us grew up in homes filled with conflict. Our parents fought constantly, whether sober or drunk. Often their fights were violent, and we hid from them. Arguing with our parents was futile and could lead to verbal and physical abuse. When we became teenagers, some of us fought back, which only made things worse. We hated conflict and did anything to avoid it, including lying.

Before marriage, we vowed to never argue or fight with our spouses. Unfortunately, we hadn't learned how to handle the difficulties that soon arose in our marriages. We did everything we could to avoid arguments, including lying and hiding things from our partners. Most of the time, we would give in—only to become deeply resentful about doing so. We thought one person had to submit or violence would result. We didn't know that conflict was normal or that healthy couples had ways of resolving conflicts without physical or emotional violence.

In our recovery, we are learning to face conflicts head-on with courage and compassion. We are learning that honesty is the only basis for healthy relationships. We still get extremely anxious when we argue, but we're learning to keep communicating. We keep focused on the issues and avoid name calling and blaming. It is both exciting and satisfying to talk through problems without becoming abusive, frightened, or resentful.

I'm learning to face my conflicts head-on and talk them through.

Amazing Grace

. . . .

*W*e want our children to feel good about themselves. We want them to be free of the despair we felt as children. We were forever trying to prove ourselves worthy, but we never measured up, so we felt ashamed, guilty, and sinful. Our parents reinforced our feelings of unworthiness by their constant criticism and faultfinding. Although we attended Sunday school, we learned nothing about God's grace, only about sin and punishment.

In recovery we met, many of us for the first time, a loving God who accepted us unconditionally. We have experienced the true meaning of amazing grace, which has inoculated us against despair. Now we depend on God's grace, not our own meager efforts, to remove our defects of character. We know in our hearts we will never again have to prove our worth to anyone.

We want our children to experience this same freedom from guilt and despair. We want them to know they are loved even when we are upset or unhappy with them. We do our best to show them unconditional love and we tell them they are loved by God in spite of anything they have done or failed to do. We share with them that God's love is absolutely unconditional. We trust that God will show us how to instill his love in our children.

I am teaching my children the meaning of amazing grace.

Natural Parenting

. . . .

*M*ost of us didn't expect it would be difficult to raise children. We thought it would come naturally, by instinct, and require no special effort. Raising kids, we thought, would be a matter of giving orders, accepting respect, and doling out love and care. We thought we would know what to do and that our children would do whatever we told them. Needless to say, we were unprepared for reality. Once we decided to put our own lives in order, we realized we would have to change the way we were raising our children.

In many ways, our parenting did come naturally. Unfortunately what came naturally were the bad habits of our own parents. Yelling at our children came naturally, as did belittling, humiliating, and teasing them. Some of us, when we weren't verbally abusing them, ignored them, just as naturally as our parents ignored us. We expected our children to know what they were supposed to do and how they were supposed to behave, though we had not taught them proper behavior.

Many of us can't trust our instincts because they were so badly damaged during our abusive childhoods. Most of our tender, loving, trusting instincts were extinguished long ago and replaced by the survival instincts of suspicion, mistrust, wariness, and defensiveness. We're learning to nurture our loving side, to trust ourselves, and to create a different kind of family from the one we grew up in.

I will renew my commitment to be a conscientious parent.

Follow Through on Plans

. . . .

We love to see the joy and excitement on our children's faces when they look forward to something exciting. They talk about it all the time, ask us the same questions over and over, and have trouble falling asleep at night. We want them to experience this joy without the fear of disappointment that we experienced when we were children. Our parents were so unreliable and unpredictable that we could never count on their promises. We couldn't trust them to follow through on plans or promises they made. Consequently, we learned to live without expectations. We learned not to allow ourselves to feel or show any excitement about our future.

We have learned to trust life a little more since we began our recovery. We still find ourselves easily discouraged when things don't work out as we've planned, but we're not as cynical as we once were about being able to experience the good things of life. Now, we actually believe we deserve some of those good things—something we never felt entitled to as children.

We want our children to look forward to the future without constantly expecting the bottom to fall out of their plans and expectations. We are providing structure and routines they can count on. We are learning to give them the stability and emotional security we never had.

I follow through on plans I make with my children so they can experience the joy of expectation.

Telling the Truth

· ·

*I*t's taken most of us a long time to accept our pasts. We're not proud of the years we spent drinking, fighting with partners, and otherwise messing up our lives. We're anxious to put all this behind us. We've completed the fourth and fifth steps, made amends where we could, and worked a good program for the past several years. But we struggle with how much of our pasts we should share with our children.

On the one hand, we want to be honest with them. On the other hand, we don't want them to think badly of us or lose respect for us. We are ashamed of our drinking years, and we still feel embarrassed to talk about the crazy things we did. We don't want our children to worry that they may have inherited our negative traits. We want them to be as worry free as is reasonably possible.

We are learning to be honest about the past without going into all the graphic details and without being overdramatic. We answer our children's questions honestly. We tell them about our recovery, our Higher Power, and the new joy we experience in our lives, joy we never knew when we were drinking.

I am being as honest as I can as I talk with my children about my past and my recovery.

Parenting Goals

· ·

*U*ntil we began our recovery, most of us had no personal discipline or self-control and no particular goals for our lives. We concluded long ago that making New Year's resolutions was a joke that nobody took seriously. We were impulsive and compulsive with no sense of direction for our lives. And we were compulsive in behavior we had no resources to change. Our recovery program taught us that we could change our lives by setting small, workable goals and by taking life one day at a time.

For the first time, we began to feel an exciting sense of mastery over our lives, even in the smallest, most insignificant ways. We made new habits from simple daily routines, like making our beds immediately each morning. (Our compulsiveness often didn't include practical or useful behaviors like making our beds.) Soon, we were experimenting with setting goals that required consistent effort and attention over time. We remember feeling exhilarated when we received our six-month medallion, for example.

Eventually, we began setting goals and objectives for our parenting. We developed structures and objectives to help us stay on track. Otherwise, it was too easy to slide back into old behavior. These goals and objectives have helped us grow into the kind of parents we want to be.

Today I will set goals and objectives for my recovery as a parent.

. . . .

*O*ur children are very impressionable. And we don't want their minds poisoned by vulgar music or offensive television programs. While we don't believe in censorship for adults, children are too immature and impressionable to understand the harmful consequences of filling their minds with mental junk food. Children get their values from their parents. If we allow them to watch terrible programs and listen to disgusting music, they will think of this entertainment as normal and acceptable.

Before we began our recovery, some of us were too busy in our addictions to alcohol, food, work, gambling, or other substances or processes to be concerned with what our children were being exposed to. We were so caught up in our attempts to avoid the pain and emptiness in our lives that we paid little attention to our children. We were happy whenever they were watching anything on television because they didn't bother us then. And we could numb out in peace, often with them in front of the television.

Becoming a conscientious parent is hard work. Monitoring our children's entertainment has not made us popular with them. This is hard for us because we hate conflict, and we don't want them to think of us as old-fashioned or prudish. Although we sometimes feel like giving up and sliding back into indifference, we are learning to handle difficult situations one day at a time.

I accept responsibility for monitoring what my children are exposed to.

Choices

. . . .

*O*ur children make different choices than we do. They don't choose the clothes we would choose. They don't choose the hair styles we would choose. They don't choose the music we would choose. They don't choose the friends we would choose. And they don't always act the way we would have them act. Some of their choices surprise us, while others cause us embarrassment. But, of course, it's not up to us to make these choices for them.

While we have a responsibility to advise them in their decision-making processes, they must learn to make their own choices. Most of us weren't raised this way. Our parents alternated between indifference and overcontrol. They didn't let us decide about the clothes we wore in high school, for example. But they left us alone with no support, help, or guidance when we were harassed by teachers. When we needed their wisdom and experience, they let us down.

We want our children to feel free to come to us for guidance, support, or help without fear of being condemned or ridiculed for their efforts. We are helping our children become responsible, self-reliant individuals. We stand by them when they are struggling with hard decisions. And we help them when they get in over their heads; we don't abandon them when they make poor choices. We respect their right to choose their clothes, music, and hair styles.

I can advise and instruct my children without controlling their choices.

My Witness

. . . .

Some of us feel guilty for the harm we caused our children during our years of drinking. We worry that the negative impact of our drinking years outweighs the positive impact of our time in recovery. We fear our recovery has not influenced our children as much as our drinking behavior did.

We don't know for certain what our children are learning from witnessing our lives in recovery. According to the experts, children are influenced more by who we are than by what we say. We want to be the kind of people our children can look up to. We pray each day that God will help us walk the talk and keep on track with our recovery programs.

Positive changes are gradually appearing in the lives of our children since we began our recovery. For example, a daughter who complained regularly of stomachaches rarely does now. A son who picked fights with his friends is no longer as aggressive and easily provoked as he used to be. When we reflect honestly on our lives together, we see many positive changes. We may never know if the changes in their lives result from our recovery or from their maturing process, but we celebrate these changes in either case.

I pray that God will use my life as a positive influence in the lives of my children.

Retaliation

· ·

"*D*on't get mad, get even!" That was the motto of many of our families. Whenever someone was hurt, humiliated, or put down, he or she would take the first opportunity to return the favor. We learned to be very intolerant of criticism and to never admit our mistakes, errors, or faults. Lies and cover-ups were normal parts of life. The reflex to get even with anyone who embarrassed us is hard to give up.

Old patterns are hard to break. Although we wanted to treat our partners with gentleness at all times, our old behavior burst onto the scene when we felt hurt. We retaliated with sharp words and harsh tones when we felt criticized, embarrassed, or hurt. Our partners were often confused and hurt by these reactions, especially when they had intended no criticism and had no idea we were hurt by their words. Then, partly to justify our defensive reaction, we would insist that they had deliberately put us down.

Our retaliation reflex gradually diminishes as we work our programs and focus on our own recovery. We're not as sensitive to slights as we once were. Now, we try to check ourselves before we fire back at someone. And we usually realize that our defensive impulses are wrong. It is amazing how differently others talk to us since we began our recovery programs. Or is it that we are hearing differently?

I can curb my impulse to retaliate and give others the benefit of the doubt.

Priorities

. . . .

*S*etting priorities enables us to separate important matters from unimportant ones by providing us with a sorting principle. Without priorities, we can't sort out what we should get involved in and what we should ignore. In order to set priorities, we have to get to know ourselves and what's important to us. In our drinking days, we didn't set goals or have priorities. We had little sense of direction and we tried not to think about the future. We lived in the nostalgic past or in the "perfect" future, carefully ignoring the present where all decisions are made.

Once we began our Twelve-step programs, we wanted to put order and structure into our lives. At first, our goals were grandiose and unachievable. This led to self-disgust and feelings of worthlessness until we learned to start with one day at a time and set modest goals we could actually achieve. We structured each day, beginning with a time for meditation and ending with a time for review. This simple structure gave us a tremendous sense of confidence that we could, for the very first time, take charge of our lives by seeking first things first.

We continue establishing priorities for maintaining our sobriety and our serenity. When others challenge our priorities, we stick by them and honor ourselves, instead of giving in to please them. Our priorities help us stay sober. Setting and reviewing our priorities keeps us on track, heading in the right direction.

I honor my priorities, even when others challenge them.

Amends

. . . .

We have not always treated ourselves with respect. Before we began our recovery programs, we didn't even realize what it meant to treat ourselves with respect. We were self-critical, self-abusive, and unforgiving of our mistakes. We would often punish ourselves by wallowing in shame and guilt for making mistakes or for forgetting things. We would sometimes curse loudly or mumble obscenities to ourselves, calling ourselves names like "stupid" when we accidentally hurt ourselves or forgot our car keys. We treated ourselves much worse than we would ever treat our friends.

When we work our recovery programs, we realize we need to make amends for the way we have treated ourselves. We had never thought much about our relationships with ourselves before, but we now realize how vital they are to recovery. Our self-esteem was rock bottom when we came into the program. Recovery remains closely connected to the positive changes in our self-esteem.

We listed the offenses we had done to ourselves. A deep sense of inner healing came over us as we accepted responsibility for our self-abuse. This inner healing helped us accept ourselves. When we accept ourselves as we are, we can accept our children as they are. It is easier to forgive our children when we accept our mistakes, make amends, and forgive ourselves.

I continue to make amends to myself and treat myself with respect—and my children notice the difference.

Overcoming Despair

. . . .

*W*e once thought hopelessness was normal, that everyone felt it. Many of us grew up in dysfunctional families where despair was as common as getting yelled at. We watched our parents despair over losing jobs and alienating their friends and relatives. When we felt discouraged by difficult schoolwork or friends who turned against us, our parents were unable to help us. They belittled us and used our troubles as backdrops to highlight their hopeless lives. We learned it was futile to turn to them for support.

We lived the same kind of despair we grew up with until we began our recovery. The spirituality of the program has enabled us to overcome our despair and hopelessness. Learning about God's love gave us a new outlook. God's love is not dependent on our performance or our perfection.

Once we were able to accept that we are lovable in spite of ourselves, we began to experience genuine hope. We are learning to accept our children just the way they are, especially when they are discouraged. When they come to us with their troubles, we listen carefully, and we don't talk about our own troubles. We don't offer advice unless they ask specifically for it. We have learned that our children's hopelessness is a temporary condition that can best be changed through nonjudgmental, attentive listening.

Experiencing God's love lifts my despair and helps me listen to my children without becoming discouraged.

Sex for Approval

· ·

*M*any of us were so insecure as teenagers that we used sex in attempting to gain acceptance. We believed our dates expected sex and would dump us if we didn't put out. We were so needy we were willing to do anything for acceptance, including having sex when we didn't want to. Some of us were so promiscuous we lost touch with our feelings altogether. Sex became meaningless, devoid of tenderness, joy, and especially commitment. By the time we were married, sex had lost its appeal.

In recovery, we are learning that healthy relationships are based on shared values and mutual respect rather than mutual exploitation. We're learning that true intimacy comes with an honest exchange of feelings and values, not a casual exchange of body fluids. While we can't relive our past, hopefully we can help our sons and daughters avoid the pain and emptiness we experienced as teenagers.

We are talking to our children about sex—something that never happened in our families. We are encouraging our teenagers to respect themselves enough not to use sex for acceptance. We remind them they are wonderful persons who need not barter for acceptance. We encourage them to stand up for their principles. We remind them that having sex when you don't want to is a sign of low self-worth.

I support my children's self-esteem and encourage them not to have sex in order to gain acceptance.

Withholding Affection

. . . .

*S*ometimes we find it difficult to feel warm and friendly toward our children, especially when they annoy us with their bickering. We can easily lose patience with them when their sweet little voices turn shrill and they become crabby. At moments like this we want them to settle down, be quiet, and stop making our lives miserable. It's hard not to react to their irritating behavior. But when we become cool and distant toward them, they don't like it. They get upset, which makes things worse.

Our kids feel secure with us when we are warm, friendly, and emotionally available to them. Consequently, we may be tempted to control their behavior by being cold and unfriendly. They become anxious and frightened when we withdraw from them and try to get us to be warm and friendly once again. We've watched their expressions change when we withdraw. They seem fearful we might reject them. Controlling their behavior by withdrawing makes us feel uncomfortable and makes our children feel anxious and insecure.

We don't want our children to grow up believing that they have to do exactly what other people want in order to get affection and love. We find alternatives to withholding our warmth and affection to influence their behavior.

When my children annoy me, I let them know in a firm but friendly voice.

Name Calling

. . . .

M A Y   6

*A*nger and verbal abuse were synonymous to us as children. When our parents were angry, they showed no restraint in the things they called us—dumb, stupid, crazy. We were never allowed to raise our voices or talk back to them, however. We followed in their footsteps and blew up at our siblings or anyone else who made us mad—except our parents. We regarded outrage as our right when someone made us angry. Some of us moved from verbal outrage to physical rage.

We are learning to recognize and express the feelings of anger without resorting to verbal or physical abuse. We make a distinction between the feeling of anger and the behavior of verbal or physical abuse. We can say, "I'm really angry right now," without losing control of our thoughts or behavior. We describe the behavior that offends us without calling the person names.

We are teaching our children to express their anger without name calling. We model mutual respect when we are angry with our children, and we coach them on how to express their anger. We teach them to say, "I'm angry with you because . . ." We are not always successful ourselves, and our children don't always follow our new rules of fair fighting. But each day, one day at a time, there is much less verbal abuse than there once was.

I am teaching my children to express their anger without name calling.

Honesty, Not Facade

. . . .

"**W**hat will the neighbors think?" We heard this again and again as children. Our families were so concerned with the opinions of others that we never learned to value our own opinions. We did learn that we were not good enough as we were. We learned to create a better impression for others because the impression they might get from actually knowing us would be disastrous. Our parents were always polishing their images, creating facades, and hiding their true selves from others. We learned it was necessary to hide the truth about ourselves to get ahead in the world.

We were not prepared for the level of honesty expected of us in the Twelve-Step program. At first, we thought the members of our groups were telling stories to create a false sense of modesty about themselves. After a while, we realized they were being truthful. Self-honesty is expected of everyone. Anyone who presented him- or herself in the group in an obviously flattering way was challenged by other members.

We are learning that honesty works. There is no point in trying to create good impressions in our groups. We get more support and encouragement for honesty than for appearances. Life is much simpler when we don't have to spend time in impression management. We are learning that we don't have to impress our children either. They accept us and respect us when we are truthful and honest about ourselves with them.

I am presenting myself honestly to myself and my children.

Changing Commitments

. . . .

*A*lthough most of us willingly helped out when asked, we often felt trapped after making commitments. We agreed to help without thinking about the consequences. We didn't always stop to count the costs before we said yes. Once we'd make a commitment, it was difficult for us to change our minds. Our word was our bond, and we felt guilty if we backed out on people. Unfortunately, we didn't always carry out our commitments cheerfully. We often felt bitter and resentful once we realized the extent of our commitments.

The program is helping us learn to admit our mistakes and to recover from them. We used to see life as black and white and to treat all commitments equally. We now realize some are more important than others. It is better, in some instances, to change a commitment than to be dishonest and feel bitter about carrying through.

We used to feel trapped, embarrassed, and angry when we made mistakes. Consequently, we'd put off making the phone calls, trying to escape embarrassment and humiliation by ignoring our mistakes as long as possible. Now, however, if we agree to help at the school carnival and later remember we had planned outings with our spouses, we call immediately and change our commitments.

I count the cost of my commitments and change my mind quickly when I realize I've made a mistake.

Discuss Alternatives

· ·

*S*ome of us grew up without having our fathers around. Consequently, we didn't see dads and moms working together. When we became mothers, we of course wanted our husbands to be involved, to be good dads, maybe even to be the dads we never had. Unfortunately, since parent had always meant mom to us, we thought of the children as ours. We never thought of men as parents. We assumed that men knew little about raising children and that most of them didn't want to be bothered. But our assumptions about men and dads have led to many arguments.

As moms, many of us are strong willed and opinionated when it comes to raising children, and we don't respond well to being challenged or contradicted. We never saw our mothers discuss things with men when it came to their children. So when our husbands want to be involved with their children and expect us to respect them as fathers, we react defensively.

Once we went through treatment together and began working a recovery program, we began communicating better. We treat each other with more respect. Now we make it a practice to discuss alternatives when dealing with our children. We're learning to consider each other's ideas without becoming as defensive as we used to. We're no longer positive that men don't know how to raise children.

I discuss alternatives with my spouse before making final decisions about our children.

Think First

. . . .

*P*atience has never been one of our virtues, especially with our children. Many of us used to decide instantly when our children approached us for favors or for permission. And we usually said no. We were afraid they were up to something mischievous, that they were trying to pull one over on us, especially when they approached us in a group. We often thought of them as adversaries rather than as innocent children. We didn't want them to think we were indecisive or wishy-washy, so consequently, we acted impulsively.

Before recovery, we were paranoid and reactionary. We were suspicious of most people, including our children. In our recovery, we are learning to see the world as more of a friendly place. We no longer think everyone is out to get us. Now we're learning that parental authority does not have to be impulsive. Few decisions have to be made instantly. We are becoming more comfortable with a reasoned and deliberate approach to discipline.

We're learning to apply "easy does it" to our decision-making process, as well as to the rest of our lives. By slowing down decision making, we're learning to take the needs and feelings of our children into consideration. We no longer expect to have instant answers to tough decisions. By taking more time to consider their requests, we are making better decisions and maintaining more harmonious and trusting relationships with our children.

I take my time to consider my children's requests.

Bribes

· ·

*F*or some of us, bribes were a way of life. We believed that no one would associate with us purely by choice. We believed we had to offer something besides ourselves in order to keep the loyalty of others. We were so afraid of being abandoned that we tried to keep people in our lives by making ourselves indispensable. We did this by showering them with gifts, doing favors for them, running ourselves ragged to meet what we thought were their needs, and probably annoying them by being underfoot.

Recovery has shown us what really matters in relationships is honesty and sincerity, not manipulation. As our self-esteem improves, we are taking risks of genuine self-disclosure and sharing. We are shedding our codependent behaviors and daring to believe people will like us because of who we are, not because of what we can do for them. This is a big risk for us.

We encourage our children to share themselves in their friendships. If our young children ask permission to give favorite toys to new friends, we talk with them about their feelings. We explore their generosity to see if it is linked with low self-worth. If so, we reassure them they are wonderful children that anyone would be glad to have as friends. We subtly discourage them from depending on gifts to build friendships. We encourage them to give the gift of themselves.

I am teaching my children to share themselves
in friendship.

Other Parents

. . . .

We used to feel inferior and inadequate in the presence of other parents. We always "knew" they were better than we were and that their children were well behaved at all times. We were especially nervous in church when other parents observed us with our children. We wanted to do everything right, but we felt we were making fools of ourselves. We took our nervousness out on our kids. We had unreal expectations of them and scolded them for not being perfect. This often led to tears. We tried hard to cover up our sense of inadequacy.

The program helps us build our self-esteem and self-confidence. It also helps us realize we're not alone and that most people feel self-conscious at times. We are learning that the low self-worth of most adult children of alcoholics causes them to be especially self-critical. Many of us compensated by being perfectionistic, especially with our children.

By trusting in God for our self-worth, we are no longer driven to prove ourselves worthy with perfectionistic efforts. We no longer take delight in putting others down. The contempt we used to feel toward ourselves has all but vanished. When we stopped judging others, we no longer felt that others were judging us. We are learning to enjoy sharing experiences with other parents.

I enjoy the company of other parents without comparing or judging myself or others.

Meditation

· ·

*S*ome of us have always been high strung. We learned as children that relaxing meant we were lazy. If we stopped to relax, for even a few minutes, we were scolded for goofing off. As adults we find it hard to slow down. When we're supposed to relax, we find something to do with our hands so we're not wasting time. We feel guilty when we're sitting still doing nothing.

When we first heard members of our Twelve-Step groups talking about daily meditation, we thought they were weirdos. Soon, however, we came to admire the quality and serenity we saw in their lives. Sitting still with our eyes closed, doing nothing, felt like such an obvious waste of time that we had to force ourselves to try it. Once we began to experiment with meditation, we uncovered the deep fear of our own inner thoughts and feelings. We had been avoiding ourselves all our lives.

Once we got through the first few minutes of mental quieting each day, without going crazy, we began to enjoy the feeling of peace we experienced. With practice it got easier. Now, when we read a daily meditation after spending a few quiet minutes, we get more out of it. Our minds are more open and receptive. When we begin each day with meditation and reflection, we are more peaceful. We are teaching our children that it is okay to relax, sit quietly, and meditate.

I treat myself to a few moments of serenity and reflection each day.

Criticism

. . . .

*C*riticism can be hard for anyone to deal with, no matter where it comes from. As children, some of us were constantly criticized by our parents. Because we were often criticized unfairly and judged to be "bad," we did anything to avoid it. As youngsters, we believed criticism was something we had to put up with simply because we were children. In our childish understanding, we believed that when we became adults we would no longer be criticized. We thought that because adults made and enforced the rules, they were above the rules and free from criticism.

We were not prepared for the criticism we experienced as adults, especially in our marriages. We felt like children whenever our partners criticized us or even when we simply thought they were being critical, and we responded with anger. When our partners said something like, "Didn't I handle that argument between the kids well?" we heard a criticism of the way we had handled their last argument! We always assumed our inventory was being taken when our partners referred to themselves.

In our recovery, we are learning to separate our thoughts and feelings from our partners' thoughts and feelings and to mind our own business. As our self-esteem has improved, we no longer assume that everyone is scrutinizing us at all times. Now, when our partners do have a criticism, we're more willing to listen thoughtfully before responding.

I listen thoughtfully to genuine criticism and avoid reacting defensively to assumed criticism.

Talking

. . . .

We were surrounded by secrets as children. We were warned not to tell certain secrets to our fathers because they would get upset or violent. We were warned not to tell our mothers certain secrets because they would break their hearts. Much of what went on in our families was secret from our grandparents. Our friends and neighbors never knew what went on in our homes. Our motto was, "We don't hang our dirty laundry in public."

When we joined a parents support group, we were shocked by what others admitted about themselves. Although everyone was encouraged to share struggles and concerns, we were content to listen and keep our horrible secrets to ourselves. While others were reporting significant improvements in their feelings and in their relationships with their children as results of their participation in the group, we were as miserable as ever. We were relieved that no one pressured us into confessing our sins.

Eventually, we opened up and told them we had struck our children so hard that we left marks on them. Although we were prepared to be condemned, everyone seemed to understand and accept us. Once we dared to speak candidly, we no longer felt alone. We had never felt so accepted in our lives. We began to experience changes from the moment we admitted to others the exact nature of our struggles with our children.

I know the healing that comes with honest self-disclosure.

God Accepts Us

. . . .

*G*od was a fierce God for many of us. He was judgmental and punitive. The God of our childhood was neither friendly nor loving. Our parents used the fear of God to control us. They threatened us, saying, "God will punish you for being disobedient to me." God seemed like a powerful extension of our parents' anger and discipline. We wanted nothing to do with this punishing God.

When we began our recovery, many of us resisted any talk of God. We were convinced that a Higher Power was simply a disguise for the angry God of our childhood who was again being used to punish us—this time for our sins of addiction. We were surprised to learn that many others in our groups felt the same way. As they shared their experiences with us, we slowly began to understand God in a new way.

Gradually, we are coming to terms with our spiritual nature. As we acknowledge our spiritual emptiness, we accept spiritual food. We are learning that God accepts us in our brokenness and loves us in spite of our weakness. This understanding of God is radically different from that of our childhood. We eagerly share this loving God with our children, without fear of turning them off. Ours is now a gracious spirituality that cannot be used to frighten children into submission.

I enjoy sharing my loving God with my children.

Handling Conflict

. . . .

*W*e used to believe our conflicts resulted from character defects and our illness. We thought that when we were finally well we would no longer experience conflict in our lives. Conflict had always made us anxious and scared. As children we associated conflict with not knowing what we were expected to do and with being afraid of the punishment we would receive at the hands of our angry parents for not making the right choices.

We were startled when members of our Twelve-Step groups talked about how conflict had become a positive force in their lives. They said it had become very important in their recovery. Conflict had sharpened their thinking processes and heightened their moral and ethical sensitivity. This grabbed our attention. And we wanted the serenity they had discovered.

We had never stopped to feel the feelings of anger, pain, guilt, shame, and fear of punishment, let alone think clearly about the moral and ethical implications of the conflicts in our lives. Now we look for the gift in conflict instead of expecting it to be negative and destructive. We don't react the way we used to when our children have conflicts in their lives. We no longer do their thinking for them, nor do we catastrophize with them when they tell us about their conflicts. We're learning to take conflicts in stride without giving in to anxiety and fear.

Finding the gift in conflict makes me more serene.

Nurturing Touch

. . . .

*M*any of us received little or no physical affection from our parents. As children, we longed to be held, hugged, or patted on the back. Some of us were only touched when we were spanked or beaten. Many of us have suffered depression as a result of not getting the nurturing we needed as children. As a result of this nurturing deficit, some of us were easily sexually exploited by anyone who offered us affectionate touch.

In recovery, we've come to understand the importance of affectionate touch as emotional nurture. We are learning to differentiate exploitative touch from genuine affection and receive comforting touch without sexualizing it. Many of us were afraid to be touched because we had been abused. We are learning to ask for hugs when we want them. We are learning to give hugs to both men and women in our groups without the fear of being misunderstood.

We want our children to receive all the affectionate, nurturing touch they need from us so they won't feel the need to compromise themselves sexually for affection. We avoid using harsh or abusive touch as a means of discipline. We encourage our children to ask us for hugs whenever they want them, and we offer them hugs regularly. We also ask them for hugs when we need them. We all feel happier, less tense, and more emotionally connected to one another since we began hugging more often.

Giving and receiving hugs nurtures me and my children.

Age Appropriate

. . . .

We have had to invent ourselves as parents because we had such poor role models. Consequently, we're not always sure what we should expect from our children. Sometimes our expectations may be too low. At other times, they may be too high. When we were children, our parents' expectations were so high and/or so erratic we could never do anything right. Although we did everything we could to stay out of trouble and do what was expected, we never succeeded.

Some of us vowed we would not yell, as our parents had, "You're old enough to know better!" at our children. We believe that children are only as mature and well behaved as they are taught to be. Without instruction and guidance, children cannot be expected to know how to act.

We're learning what is normal behavior for children of different ages. We used to guess at what was normal and then act as if we were right, when, in fact, we felt uncertain and insecure. In recovery we are learning to accept our limitations gracefully and to ask for help when we need it. We're learning to ask pediatricians, nurses, teachers, friends in recovery, and partners and to consult books to fill in the gaps in our knowledge of children's behavior and development. We no longer feel the need to pretend to be more competent than we are. This is a big relief.

I am willing to ask for help in understanding my children.

Courage, Not Despair

. . . .

*W*e have struggled with despair for much of our lives. We saw our lives as unfolding dramas in which we did not know our scripts, our directors, or how the dramas would end. We saw ourselves as nothing more than bit players who could easily be replaced. We didn't think we could take it any longer. We felt trapped and hopeless and believed no one cared about us or would miss us if we were gone. We felt sorry for ourselves and wallowed in self-pity. The only good to come from our despair was that we eventually hit bottom.

We gave up all pretense and pride and finally asked for help. Since then, we have learned a great deal about ourselves and discovered a new way to live. We gradually turned our despair into hope and our hope into courage. In our recovery, we discovered we could make a difference in our own lives. God is the source of power for our lives, and we now share in this power. We have gone from being bit players to stars in our own life dramas. More importantly, we now have personal relationships with the directors, producers, and playwrights.

Now, when we look at our children, we feel excitement and anticipation for our lives together. The future is filled with promise and hope. We know they love us and support our recovery. We are not alone.

With God's help I am learning to turn despair into hope.

Happiness

. . . .

*H*appiness was a rare experience for many of us as children. Although we occasionally had fun, we were unhappy in our hearts. We felt lonely and alienated from those around us. We failed to develop the social skills needed to relate comfortably with others. Because we were blamed for the unhappiness of others, especially our parents and siblings, we felt powerless over our own happiness. We thought unhappiness was our fate.

In recovery, we discovered a radical notion: Each of us is responsible for our own happiness, and we cannot make anyone else happy. This startling notion contradicted the very core of our codependent beliefs. After all, we had spent our lives trying to manipulate the happiness of those around us and feeling guilty whenever we failed. We felt little or no responsibility for our own happiness but complete responsibility for the happiness of those around us.

We are challenged to practice this new learning with our children. Because we are morally and legally responsible for their lives, it is only natural for us to feel responsible for their happiness. We are learning, however, to encourage them to manage their own happiness. When one of them complains that a brother or sister is making them unhappy, we practice compassionate detachment and resist the temptation to step in. Instead, we share some tips on how they can stay in charge of their own attitudes.

I am learning to detach myself enough to teach my children to manage their own happiness.

Resolving Conflict

. . . .

*M*any of us avoided arguments as much as possible because we hated what they did to us. We became defensive, nasty, aggressive, and threatening in order to intimidate others and win the arguments. All arguments were power struggles. If we didn't win, we were weak. If we didn't win, we felt depressed, beat down, and humiliated. Winning was the only way we knew to avoid deep feelings of worthlessness. Unfortunately, winning always left us feeling lonely, alienated, and ashamed of ourselves.

Inviting God into our lives has changed our lives, both in the way we see things and in the way we do things. We now face conflicts head-on and share our thoughts and feelings freely, without becoming defensive or aggressive. Since we began including prayer and meditation in our daily lives, we are less inclined to take offense at things our children say that once felt threatening. When we feel diminished by our children's angry words toward us, we remember that God loves us unconditionally.

We're learning that conflicts don't have to become power struggles. We can work out solutions without feeling humiliated or beat down. We are learning to resolve conflicts without turning them into win-or-lose contests. We realize that no one wins unless we solve our problems together. Discussing our differences calmly takes determination and real concentration, but it's worth it because we feel less threatened and less vulnerable.

I know that peace and harmony come from resolving conflicts, not winning fights.

Volunteering

. . . .

*M*any of us grew up without seeing our parents volunteer in the community. They were too busy drinking, working, or surviving to give of themselves to the less fortunate or to support social causes. We were not encouraged to volunteer our time for causes either. Their advice was: Mind your own business. Many of us were self-absorbed even before we became addicts. Our addiction only intensified this preoccupation with self. We want our children's lives to be different.

As we come to understand the importance of the spiritual part of our recovery, we discover the joy that comes from volunteering to help others. Most of us had never known this joy until we went along with others on a Twelve-Step call. Now we look for opportunities to volunteer because of what it does for our recovery. Volunteering helps us put our problems in a larger perspective. We learn to break out of our own self-preoccupation by reaching out to others.

We can teach our children the joys of volunteering by taking them with us when we help at homeless shelters, church, school. At first they may be reluctant to go, but once they experience the good feelings that come from helping others, they become eager. The joy on the faces of those they help touches their hearts. They are happier and more outgoing as a result of their volunteer activities.

I love sharing the joys of volunteering with my children.

Emotional Progress

. . . .

*F*or much of our lives, we have felt governed by our emotions, especially anger, guilt, and resentment. We attempted to eliminate painful emotions from our lives by using distraction, denial, repression, and will power. Then we discovered the magic of alcohol, drugs, and other substances to blot out our painful emotions—for a while at least. Using chemicals to cope, however, we found we had to use more denial to block out the reality that our entire lives were out of control.

By the time we started our recovery, we were emotionally dead. Our lives had no zest, meaning, or purpose. Having resisted feeling our feelings for as long as we could, we were scared to unearth our buried emotions. Fortunately, we only have to deal with our lives one day at a time, and the flood turns out to be a steady trickle. Little by little we start to feel again. Step Four was painful the first time we took it, but it opened the door to honesty and renewal.

As we learn to feel our feelings and talk about our inner experiences with others in our Twelve-Step groups, we discover that our painful emotions are manageable and we no longer feel controlled by them. By putting our thoughts and feelings into words, we gradually stop running from them and begin to take responsibility for our lives. This helps us face our children and listen to them without getting angry and defensive.

Honesty is the key to my emotional progress.

Repair Is Possible

. . . .

Dysfunctional families are not in the repair business. They drive cars until they wear out, never bothering with maintenance. When anything breaks, they either use it in its broken-down condition, or they throw it out. Many of us never learned to take proper care of the things we valued. We surely didn't know how to take care of friendships, and we allowed misunderstandings to destroy them. We were too proud to admit our part in misunderstandings, and we didn't have the tools to communicate our feelings.

If we hurt our friends' feelings, we would ignore them rather than try to repair the broken friendships. Rather than face these emotional difficulties, we would hide from them, using whatever means we could to deny our problems. As a result, we had few lasting friendships.

When we began our recovery, our relationships were in tatters, including those with our children. Having never repaired a broken relationship before, we didn't know what to expect when we began making amends. We started with our children, and they were wonderfully accepting and forgiving. Once we experience the healing power of forgiveness from God and our own children, our lives seem hopeful for the first time in years. As we slowly continue to make amends with everyone we can, the love and healing we experience is beyond our comprehension. God's healing love and forgiveness has given us a new lease on life.

I thank God for healing me and teaching me how to heal broken relationships.

Stopping the Old and Starting the New

· ·

*B*efore we began our recovery programs, we'd had little success in changing our self-defeating behavior patterns. Our New Year's resolutions were abandoned after a few days of frustration. We relied on willpower to change, and when that didn't work, we didn't believe we could change. We thought we would have to live with our character defects and self-defeating behavior forever.

In the program we learned that it is not enough to stop old behavior patterns. We must replace them with new ones. Our previous efforts focused exclusively on eliminating character defects, with no thought to new behavior. Eliminating old behavior created a vacuum, and we soon fell back into our old patterns. Now, we plan our new behavior before we eliminate the old. This gives us a positive goal instead of a negative one.

We're finding that eliminating self-defeating behavior starts with action, not contemplation. It is more critical to decide what we are going to do differently than what we will stop doing. While we stopped certain old behaviors, like drinking and running from our problems, we made a list of new behaviors for each one we stopped. Instead of yelling at our children when we are upset with them, for example, we clearly describe the behavior that upsets us and ask them to change to a new behavior that we also clearly describe. This clear, positive approach works much better.

I concentrate on new behavior as I eliminate old behavior.

Reactions

. . . .

We wish we could get well without anyone noticing us until we were all finished. It is difficult enough for us to break our old habits and work on our character defects without others looking over our shoulders and questioning us. We need the support of our families. Yet, when they react negatively to our changes, or even question us about them, we want to run away and hide. Our recovery feels too tentative and fragile to be scrutinized and judged. We're not ready to discuss or explain it, let alone defend it to skeptics.

We have trouble understanding why our families aren't more supportive. Don't they realize how much they have to gain when we get well? The people closest to us are having the hardest time accepting our new behavior. They want us to be the way we were, even though they complained about us before we began our recovery. Those in our step groups give us the most support, even though they've only known us for a short time.

We're learning to concentrate on our own recovery and not worry about the reactions of others. We focus on working our programs, rather than selling our recovery to skeptics. Without our step group, we would have quit—and blamed others for making it too hard for us to continue. We have to trust that our children will one day appreciate our recovery.

I focus on my recovery and not on the reactions of others to my recovery.

Keeping Confidences

. . . .

*W*e feel uncomfortable when one of our children asks us to keep something confidential. Secret keeping is a delicate issue for us. We know keeping secrets can be a bond of trust and loyalty between two people, but it can also be a symptom of denial, sickness, and manipulation. We're not always certain which it is.

Most of us grew up in families that were riddled with secrets. Everyone had secrets about themselves, shared secrets about others, or used secrets for blackmail or as bribes. Personal conversations often began with, "Don't tell anyone we said this but . . ." We can remember feeling close when we shared secrets. We soon discovered, however, the same secrets that made us feel close one day could be used to manipulate us the next.

We want our children to know they can trust us, but we don't want to encourage the kind of secrets that lead to suspicion, manipulation, and alienation. We decided never to ask our children to keep secrets about family members or relatives. Also, we try to discourage them from telling secrets about one another. When one of our children shares something with us they want kept secret, we find out why they don't want it shared and try to reassure them that secrecy is unnecessary. When we are unwilling to keep their confidence, we always tell them, so they won't feel betrayed later.

I find the balance between harmful secretiveness and keeping my children's confidences.

Accountability

· ·

*B*lame played such a central part in our lives as children that we learned to custom tailor alibis and excuses. We focused on the external factors that caused us to do the things we did, rather than on our roles as decision makers. We always had something or someone to blame, and we protected ourselves against being blamed by others. We believed we played an insignificant role in setting the direction for our lives. We felt driven, pushed, and pulled by forces we neither understood nor controlled.

When someone in our group said we were accountable for our actions and choices, we immediately defended ourselves saying they weren't our choices. We had never regarded our actions as choices. We had always felt as though life was forcing decisions on us. And we didn't want to be blamed for the mess our lives were in. We didn't think it was fair to be blamed when we couldn't do anything about it in the first place.

We began learning about personal responsibility for our choices in our recovery programs. At first, we felt like people were saying everything was our fault. We resisted. We had been blamed all our lives, and we were tired of it. Then we learned that accountability is not the same as blame but simply means we own our actions and choices. Accountability is another word for honesty.

I am accountable for my life and teach my children to be accountable without focusing on excuses and blame.

Surrender

. . . .

*M*ost of us have struggled with despair and hope-lessness at one time or another. When we were in the depths of despair, we felt powerless and out of control. We were not only discouraged and depressed, but we were convinced the future would be more bleak and disappointing than the pres-ent. Consequently, we associated the absence of control with despair and hopelessness.

When we first heard about surrender and letting go, we wanted nothing to do with this crazy notion. Surrender seemed like the opposite of what we needed for our lives. We needed to overcome the chaos and disorder that was every-where in our lives. We needed to find a way to gain some con-trol over our despair and hopelessness. Eventually, however, we began to understand the real meaning of surrender as the antidote to despair.

By surrendering our wills to the will of our Higher Power rather than wallowing in despair, we experience a new sense of power. We are learning what Saint Paul meant when he wrote, "My power is made perfect in weakness." By admitting our powerlessness over the things we can't control, we are ac-tually more relaxed with our children. When we struggled to control everything that affected them, we were in a constant panic, never able to enjoy being parents because of our fears and anxieties. Since we learned to surrender, we no longer ob-sess about the things that might go wrong.

When I trust in God, I let go of my constant worry over my children.

Sex Talk

. . . .

We want our children to grow up with healthy attitudes toward sex. We want them to feel good about their bodies and their sexuality. Most of us are struggling to create healthy attitudes from the ruins of our dysfunctional childhoods. Our parents never discussed sex with us in loving, rational ways. Sex was either ignored altogether, or we were threatened with terrible consequences should we or our girlfriends become pregnant. As children, some of us were surrounded by smut, dirty jokes, and sexual innuendos. Others were falsely accused of promiscuity. This abusive treatment left us with deep emotional scars.

As we learn to accept ourselves with all of our feelings, we are coming to accept our sexuality as well. We can only talk openly and lovingly about sex to our children when we can talk openly and lovingly about it to ourselves and our partners. We are learning to accept sexual desires as normal, healthy responses, both for ourselves and for our adolescent children. We want them to feel comfortable with their sexual feelings while respecting their power.

We are learning to talk to our children about their sexual feelings, desires, and attitudes in the context of our love and acceptance of them. We discuss their responsibilities without threatening them or accusing them. Because we listen to them, they are beginning to trust us and share their feelings with us.

As I accept my own sexuality more gracefully, I am able to talk about sex with my children.

Letting Go of Resentments

. . . .

*C*omplaining seemed the easiest and safest way to enter a conversation without exposing ourselves to risk. By complaining about how terrible things were, we established that we were no better than anyone else. Nobody would shoot us down because we were already down in the dumps. Everyone around us complained; it was a way of life. They were either down on their luck or convinced that life was unfair. We felt entitled to our resentments. After all, we were not going to let people get away with mistreating us without voicing our protests.

When we came into recovery we were encouraged to give all this up. Members of our step group shared the freedom they discovered by letting go of lifelong resentments. Although it sounded reasonable that letting go of resentments could lead to peace of mind, it also seemed impossible. Besides, why should everyone who mistreated us get off scot free?

We are learning that resentments do not bring about justice or hold others accountable. Resentments only poison us. The sooner we let go of them, the sooner we recover real joy and spontaneity. We are now teaching our children not to hold resentments or bitterness. We realize that resentments and bitterness add nothing of value to our lives or to the lives of those around us.

I am letting go of my resentments and teaching my children to let go of theirs.

Willing to Turn Our Lives Over to God

. . . .

Rebelliousness is one of the hallmarks of growing up in a dysfunctional family. Some of us expressed our rebelliousness aggressively. Others expressed it indirectly in the form of depression, low self-esteem, and passive-aggressive behavior in our relationships. We inwardly resisted doing anything we didn't want to do, although we put on the people-pleaser's facade and acted as if we were willing to cooperate.

We were living narrow, constricted lives, controlled by our rebelliousness and resistance when we came into the Twelve-Step program. Although our lives were unmanageable, we were not willing to let anyone tell us what to do. Fortunately, no one tried to tell us what to do. Instead, friends simply shared how they had surrendered their lives to the care of their Higher Power and how satisfying the results were.

We are learning that the key to this surrender is willingness. We don't have to understand how God works or will change our lives, we only have to be willing to let God into the driver's seat. In the past, we never trusted anyone to lead us unless we knew exactly where they were going. By trusting God with our lives, we are learning to let go of the anxiety we used to feel whenever our children were out of our sight. A God who can change our troubled lives can also protect our children from harm.

I am willing to have God direct my life and the lives of my children.

Shy

Some of us were so shy as children that other kids teased us, and our parents were ashamed of us. We spent most of our childhood alone. We avoided situations in which we would be called on to speak or perform. We were extremely self-conscious, especially around adults or strangers. As teenagers, we discovered alcohol and soon were dependent on it to reduce our social anxiety and free us from self-consciousness.

In our Twelve-Step group, many of us experienced genuine acceptance for the first time. This has enabled us to accept ourselves. We gradually have become more self-confident and socially at ease. The more self-accepting we become, the easier it is for us to reach out and join in with others. We take initiative to participate in activities we want to be involved in. We no longer wait for others to beg us to get involved.

Because we have learned the importance of acceptance in our own recovery, we don't criticize our shy children. We don't criticize them for spending time alone or push them into social activities. We accept our shy children without reservation. We gently encourage them to stretch and risk in order to go after the things they want from life. We listen very carefully to their interests and desires so we can strengthen these, rather than force our interests on them.

I gently encourage my shy children to take initiative for what they truly want.

Selfish

. . . .

Some of us grew up fighting with the selfish label. We were accused of being selfish whenever we asked for basic things, like clothes or school supplies. We were supposed to learn to get along without things other kids had and we were scolded repeatedly for expressing self-interest of any kind. Consequently, we learned to hide our interests and to disguise our needs in the form of concern for others. Most of us became people pleasers and codependents.

When we came into recovery, we were very bitter. We felt resentful toward all those who had more than we did, whether material things or happiness. We are coming to understand the depths of our codependency and are finding ways to change. We are learning that self-respect includes respect for the legitimacy of our own needs. We have learned the difference between healthy and unhealthy selfishness and no longer feel guilty for asserting ourselves.

We want our children to feel confident and free to assert themselves. We are teaching them the difference between healthy and unhealthy selfishness. We are teaching them to consider their own needs as well as the needs of others. We are able to say no to them without heaping shame on their heads for asking for something they can't have.

My children and I can feel confident in asserting our needs and desires without demanding to have our way.

Power, Not Control

· ·

*M*any of us felt powerless and out of control as children. We believed this was because we were children. We thought we'd feel powerful and in control once we became adults. We were eager to exercise the same power we saw our parents and teachers wield over us. We thought that power and control were one and the same. If we were powerful enough, we believed, we could control others, just like the playground bullies.

As adults, because we never learned the difference between power and control, we created emotional havoc in all our personal relationships by trying to control them. When this same havoc emerged with our children, we began to look at ourselves. We were so convinced that we had to control our children that we were losing our power and authority over them.

In recovery, we are learning that power and control are quite different. We are powerful when we know our own values, thoughts, and feelings and share them clearly and honestly. Real power does not depend on how others respond to us. Control, on the other hand, depends on directing the lives and wills of others. In controlling others, we are calculating our effects on them rather than sharing our views openly and honestly. Our children are more cooperative and less rebellious when we share ourselves with them than when we forcefully tried to control their wills and behavior.

I am enjoying the power that comes with being open
and honest with my children.

Embarrassment and Humiliation

. . . .

We don't want our children to suffer embarrassment when they make mistakes in public performances. Sooner or later, however, all performers have embarrassing performances. When this happens to one of our children, we want to be supportive. Many of us remember our embarrassing performances as children. Our parents minimized our feelings with words like, "You'll do better next time so don't worry about it." Or, they told us we had done a wonderful job when we knew we hadn't.

As we learn to respect feelings, our own and those of others, we no longer minimize painful experiences in order to suppress the pain. When we try to minimize our children's embarrassment to bolster their egos, we actually make things worse. Everything we say to make their embarrassment less embarrassing discounts their real feelings. When they feel awful about their performance and we tell them it was fine, or even great, they stop sharing with us.

We now have the courage to go with our children into the depths of their despair. We let them cry with us as long as they need to without trying to hurry them through the process. We listen patiently and offer comfort in the form of our presence and our gentle touch. We resist the temptation to give them advice or cheer them up with talk about "next time." We let them experience their embarrassment and humiliation until they are ready to move on.

I support my children when they feel embarrassed or humiliated.

Starting from Here

· ·

*M*any of us spent years going in circles. We never got anywhere because we never admitted honestly where we were starting from. We wanted to be someone else and to be some other place in life. We developed this make-believe approach to life as children when our real world was too dangerous and unpredictable for us to manage. We hid our shortcomings in order to protect ourselves from abuse.

In recovery we learned about the power of honesty as the starting point. Having spent our lives pretending, the notion of honestly admitting our shortcomings as a starting place for recovery seemed absurd, overwhelming, and impossible. We were convinced our real selves were disgusting and hopeless. We wanted to get a head start on recovery by starting in the third or fourth grade rather than in kindergarten.

Now we are discovering the power of personal honesty. By admitting our faults and defects, we discover genuine acceptance, new strength, and serenity. Our strength and serenity establish a harmonious atmosphere in our homes. We have more patience with our children because we no longer waste time and energy sustaining false images or creating false impressions. We put our efforts into making small changes in our lives rather than covering up our true selves.

I accept my shortcomings as a starting place for my recovery.

Admitting Mistakes

. . . .

*F*or years, pretense was at the core of our existence. We were so convinced that we were hopeless and disgusting as our true selves that we created and maintained a facade in order to be accepted by others. As children, we suffered for being honest. Mistakes, errors, or missteps brought swift punishment from our parents. Consequently, we never admitted when we were wrong, guilty, at fault, or responsible. Instead, we become experts at alibis, excuses, and stories to get off the hook.

As parents, we continued this pattern of defending our actions, even when we knew we were wrong. We found ourselves lying to our own children rather than admitting we had broken one of their favorite toys or forgotten an agreement we'd made with them. Although we felt guilty about lying to our children, we couldn't stop ourselves.

With God's help and the Twelve-Step program, we are learning to make amends to our children. We could not have overcome our pattern of denial without the help of our recovery program. By learning to accept ourselves, we no longer feel the need to present a false self to our children. We are discovering, much to our surprise, that when we say, "I'm sorry, I was wrong, I apologize" to our children, they actually accept us and show more respect for us than before.

I am learning that honesty is the basis of respect.

Children's Respect

. . . .

We weren't ready to be parents when our first child was born. We were immature and emotionally insecure. Although we wanted our children to look up to us and respect us, we didn't know how to get them to. We were so afraid they wouldn't respect us that we punished them for any signs of resistance to our authority. On the one hand, we believed we had to establish our authority in order to make them respect us. On the other hand, we feared they would hate us. When they withdrew from us, we appeased them in order to get them to reconnect with us. Small wonder they were confused.

In recovery, we are examining our insecurities for the first time. As we are beginning to feel better about ourselves, our relationships with our children are changing. As we begin to feel more confident and secure within ourselves, we are more confident and secure around them. We came to realize they were not defying our authority, they were simply expressing their wants and needs.

We no longer worry about gaining their respect or winning their approval for everything we do. Instead, we respect them as persons of equal worth. We base our parenting on our principles, and not on our popularity with our children. We realize now that if we respect ourselves and respect them, they will respect us.

I respect myself and my children instead of trying to make them respect me.

Impulsiveness

. . . .

*M*any of us acted on impulse, flying off the handle when life didn't suit us. We may have bought things we didn't need, said things we later regretted, and clung emotionally to people we had just met. We've spent much of our lives trying to untangle ourselves from predicaments created by our hasty, shortsighted decisions. We never learned to plan for the future because our lives were too chaotic and unpredictable.

Not surprisingly, some of us became "two-steppers" when we got into recovery. In our impatience, we skipped Steps Two through Eleven and immediately began telling everyone else how they should manage their lives. Fortunately, people who had gone through this same experience gently confronted us and helped us to look at ourselves first. They encouraged us to slow down and trust the process of recovery.

Many of us are learning impulse control for the first time in our lives. We are replacing our impulsiveness with patience and serenity. Recovery is a gradual process involving practice, like learning to play the piano. As piano students, we began by playing the scales with one hand, then the other, and proceeded to scales with both hands together. Then we learned to play melodies and chords. We no longer expect instant changes in our relationships. By learning the recovery scales first, we gradually apply these principles to all our relationships, including the special relationships we have with our children.

I am learning to apply the Twelve-Step recovery principles to my relationships with my children.

Seeking Approval

. . . .

*A*lthough we'd always wanted to be good parents, we didn't know how to tell if we were doing things right. In our ignorance, we acted as if our children knew what good parenting was. If they were happy, we thought we were doing a good job. If they were unhappy, we weren't. Because we depended on their feedback and approval, we tried very hard to please them. They learned to exploit our dependency and soon controlled us with their tears and demands. We were reluctant to set limits with them. Whether they pleaded to stay up late, or begged for a treat at the grocery store, we gave in. Eventually, of course, we got fed up and angry. Then we punished them severely, felt terribly guilty, and started the cycle over again.

In the program we're learning that our children are not responsible for our self-esteem. By depending on our children for approval, we abdicated our role of providing guidance and direction for them. We'd turned our families upside down.

Now we base our parenting decisions on principles rather than on their tears and pouting. We set limits, make requests, and calmly hold them accountable without worrying about being rejected by them. We are learning to manage our own self-esteem needs without being dependent on our children's approval. We feel much better, and our children are calmer, more respectful, and less confused.

I value and approve of myself.

Sharing

· ·

*M*any of us were stingy as children. Hoarding was the rule in our families. Our parents kept money from each other, and our siblings had secret stores of comic books, candy, and toys. We were not encouraged to share. Consequently, we continuously fought and bickered over possessions. We did learn to manipulate others into sharing with us, and then we regarded them as fools and suckers.

Before we began our recovery, we lived in a stingy world marked by scarcity and greed. The Twelve-Step recovery program has taught us the concept of abundance, a radical concept for those of us who were convinced the good things of life were in short supply and everyone was our competitor. We've learned that God is infinite and has all the good things any of us need, if we only trust. We've begun to share what we have without fear of emotional or physical starvation.

Because we want our children to live in a world of abundance, rather than scarcity, we encourage them to share what they have with their friends. One way to do this is by sharing our abundance with them. Sharing what we have with others is evidence of our faith in God's providence. By trusting in God's abundance, we no longer feel as anxious about our survival. Our serenity affects our children in a positive way.

I enjoy sharing the secret of an abundant universe with my children.

Forgive Myself

· ·

When we began our recovery we were so steeped in shame and guilt that we couldn't imagine not hurting. For many of us, shame and guilt were deeply embedded in our self-concepts from childhood. We were raised in perfectionism—with high standards, unrealistic expectations, and/or stiff punishment. What little leniency we received was accompanied by shaming words like, "You certainly don't deserve this break, so don't think we're letting you get by with anything here!" Forgiveness was often just a word we heard in church that had no meaning in our lives.

As adults, we inventively devised a series of cover-ups to hide our shame and guilt. We used alcohol, food, or work to shield ourselves from the pain of these feelings. When we weren't medicating, we used denial to cope with our shame and guilt. We invented lies to cover our lies. We were frauds. We put on a mask of respectability and Christian pretense to hide our deceptive and irresponsible lifestyles.

Learning to forgive ourselves, while a difficult challenge, has been enormously healing. Taking Step Seven made all the difference. We realize that if God could forgive us, we could forgive ourselves—not because we deserved it but because we were willing to accept it. Self-forgiveness softens our armor and diminishes our perfectionism. We can forgive others, especially our children, more easily and without carrying resentment.

I know I can forgive myself as many times a day as
I need to.

Forgiveness

· ·

Some of us were forced to forgive siblings who hurt us, broke our toys, took our things, or wore our clothes without permission. We associated forgiveness with phony reconciliation and unfairness. When we became adults, we were both judge and jury. Holding onto anger and resentments until offenders qualified for our forgiveness made us feel powerful and righteous. Some of us even made our children squirm before we forgave them.

In recovery, we learn about a totally different understanding of forgiveness. Step group members talk about the power of forgiveness to restore us to sanity and free us from the poison of resentments. They talk of forgiving others, not because the offenders qualified for forgiveness, but because the act of forgiveness liberates them from their mental anguish. Others said forgiveness helps them repair broken relationships, that by forgiving others, they emotionally decontaminate old memories. The memories are still there, but forgiveness flushes away the emotional pain.

The prospect of being free from the emotional pain of old memories is so appealing that we practice this new understanding of forgiveness whenever we become aware of a resentment we're holding. We release ourselves from the grip of old slights, hurts, and emotional wounds. We are happier, more cheerful, and less moody. Our children seem happier too, because the emotional poison we were carrying affected everyone in our household.

I am learning to forgive others for my sake, not theirs.

Beyond Ourselves

· ·

At one time, we were so obsessed with our problems and concerns that we had no time for other people. We believed our problems were more serious than anyone else's. We were impatient with others and refused to listen when they talked about their personal concerns. We, however, complained to anyone who would listen. Complaining was such a part of our lives that we felt out of place, and a little annoyed, with cheerful, lighthearted people.

In recovery, we are learning to face our problems and deal with them constructively, instead of complaining endlessly while making no effort to change. Our old habit of complaining to anyone who would listen didn't go over well in our step group. Group members soon confronted us by asking what we were going to do. When we tried to deflect their challenges by declaring our helplessness, we were challenged to change ourselves.

Now that we are changing the things we can, we are also learning to get outside of ourselves by taking a genuine interest in others. We no longer obsess over our problems. Instead, we reach out to others by listening to their concerns and sharing our recovery experiences with them. This strengthens our recovery more than we could have imagined. By sharing our story with others, we reinforce our own commitment to continue our recovery.

Listening to others and sharing my recovery with them lets me get outside myself.

God and Manipulation

. . . .

*M*any of us learned to hate God because our parents used the fear of God to manipulate and control us. They told us God was angry at us for not obeying them and he would punish us if we ever lied to them. Sometimes they told us we were going to burn in hell because we did something wrong. We did not know how to free ourselves from the guilt and fear that bound us, so we turned to alcohol, sex, drugs, or other people for relief.

Through the Twelve-Step program we have come to know a loving God who accepts us unconditionally. Now we embrace our spirituality and no longer run from God. The old punishing God from childhood may still lurk in the corners of our minds and we constantly remind ourselves that this is a carryover from our dysfunctional pasts.

We want our children to know only the God of love. We never use the fear of God as a moral club to punish them but we teach them that God loves them unconditionally. We are careful not to tell them God will be pleased if they eat their peas, do their homework, clean their rooms—or even read the Bible regularly. We avoid all temptation to manipulate them in God's name.

I share my loving God with my children and avoid the temptation to use God to control them.

Facing Fears

. . . .

*M*any of us never learned to face our fears as children. Instead, we learned avoidance, denial, and redefining. We became experts at redefining our feelings in order to cover up our anxiety and cowardice. We still remember the jeers and taunts we faced on the playground when we showed fear. We learned to repress these feelings. When we couldn't repress our fears, we turned them into rage. Nobody challenged us or called us cowards while we were raging. Later, many of us turned to chemicals to medicate our fears.

One of the important things we are learning in our recovery is how to face our fears. It was difficult to admit, even to ourselves, that we were ever afraid. We'd spent years hiding our fears from ourselves and others. We were surprised we weren't humiliated the first time we admitted in group that we were afraid. Instead, several other members said they, too, struggled with fears daily. Once we expressed our fears, they lost their power over us.

We are teaching our children to face their fears. We avoid scolding or ridiculing them for showing fear, even when their fears seem exaggerated or irrational. We encourage them to talk about their fears and accept these feelings as normal. Teaching them to face their fears is like inoculating them against dishonesty and denial. Hopefully, these inoculations give them less reason to abuse alcohol and drugs.

When I face my fears I teach my children to face theirs.

Longing

. . . .

J U N E   1 8

O the balmy, sweet, wistful feeling of falling in love. For many of us, falling in love was a bittersweet experience associated with a deep hunger for warmth and solace. We knew we were in love when we felt this powerful sense of longing, this feeling of helplessness and total dependency. These feelings were always strongest when the person of our dreams was remote and distant. The more remote the possibility of fulfillment, the stronger our feelings of love.

In recovery, we have come to understand our confusion about love. Growing up in a dysfunctional family that did not provide consistently nurturing behavior led us to associate love with emptiness and longing. We associated the absence of loving behavior from parents and our deep desire to be loved with love itself. Consequently, we felt most powerfully in love when we experienced a strong desire for recognition and comfort from someone who was remote or emotionally distant from us.

We're learning to be emotionally available and supportive to our children so they associate love with actually being loved and getting their needs met, rather than with loneliness and longing. We want to provide our children with a mature understanding of love. We want them to be attracted to partners who are both available and loving toward them.

I make it a point to show my children love by being available to them and listening to their needs and feelings.

Asking for Help

. . . .

Some of us were raised by fiercely stubborn and independent parents. Many of us turned out the same way. We find it difficult, if not impossible, to admit when we are wrong or to ask for help when we need it. We have missed many opportunities and made unnecessary mistakes simply because we were too proud to ask for help when we needed it. This foolish pride costs us dearly because it interferes with harmonious relationships as well.

The first step was difficult for us, and we still wince at the thought of admitting our powerlessness. We are, however, learning to let go of our foolish pride and seek the help and support we need. Not only are we learning to get our needs met more effectively through asking, but others report finding us easier to relate to now that our arrogance is gone. We may feel close to others for the first time in our lives.

We're teaching our children to feel secure enough within themselves to ask for help whenever they need it. We don't want them to feel ashamed of needing help or of asking for it. When they are stuck with a problem in their homework, we encourage them to talk to their teachers, even if it means calling them at home. We model our new sense of interdependence with our children. They now witness us asking for help when we need it.

I encourage my children to ask for what they need.

Overwhelmed

. . . .

*M*ost of us grew up without emotional support from our families. When we faced new challenges, such as starting school, learning to drive, beginning to date, or starting new jobs, we had to find support from others. Our parents were either too busy, not interested in us, or trying to control us or do things for us. We want this to be different for our children.

In our recovery groups, we are learning about a new way of giving support called empowerment. We used to think of parenting as being in control of our children and telling them what to do and how to do it. Empowerment means giving people the power to do things for themselves. Empowering our children means giving them encouragement, support, and guidance so they can meet the challenges of life for themselves, instead of doing things for them.

We are learning to empower our children when they are discouraged or overwhelmed by the demands of life. Instead of making decisions for them and telling them what to do, we ask questions and help them discover their own solutions. Through this process of dialogue, they feel much more self-confident. We help them break big problems into many little ones that can be managed. We remind them to take small steps rather becoming overwhelmed with giant steps.

Empowering my children when they are discouraged or overwhelmed empowers me.

Fun

. . . .

When we were in the depths of our addiction, life seemed pretty grim. Things felt tedious and boring when we weren't in crisis. We found little to laugh about, especially at home with our children. The only time we laughed was when we were high. We were grouchy, irritable, and easily annoyed by the tiniest hassles from our children. They were often hurt and confused by our unpredictable, abusive behavior.

When we began our recovery, we gradually crawled out of the darkness of our despair into the light of hope. We actually started looking forward to life once again, especially life with our children. We began planning events with them. We were no longer living from one crisis to the next. As our lives have become more stable and predictable, our children are more relaxed with us. We've begun to laugh again, as we've gradually recovered a sense of optimism about the future.

We love hearing the sound of laughter in our home once again. We are more relaxed with our children because we are less anxious ourselves. Our worry and anxiety used to block us from seeing the lighter side of things. Now we can even laugh about how crazy and bizarre our behavior used to be. When we relax with our children, they open up and become more spontaneous with us. Everything has become lighter and brighter since we sobered up.

I love the laughter that surrounds my family once again.

Fourth Step

· ·

JUNE 22

*W*e were so steeped in shame and guilt that we painstakingly organized our lives so we wouldn't be overwhelmed by these feelings. Some of us became conspicuously well behaved, while others escaped into alcohol, drugs, sex, work, or food in order to keep our mental demons at bay. Eventually, these strategies quit working, and our demons began to haunt us daily.

When we sought refuge in the Twelve-Step program, we didn't think we would ever be able to face our dark thoughts and fears. The fourth step—making an inventory of our failings—seemed like it would start a cascade of mental garbage that would bury us. Much to our surprise, this step was enormously cleansing. It was like pouring the garbage through a filter that separated the impurities from normal thoughts and feelings. We still had to dispose of the impurities, but at least they were out in the open.

We want our children to be free of the mental garbage we carried. We are learning to listen to our children and help them deal with their inner feelings. We are working to provide them with a means for making amends, healing hurts, and correcting mistakes so they won't have to carry guilt and shame with them. We have explained the fourth and fifth steps—sharing our sins and offenses with others—to them and the relief we experience from using this process.

I am learning to use the fourth step in my own life and to help my children.

1 7 6

Boundaries Without Anger

. . . .

J U N E   2 3

*M*any of us were yelled at so often we thought yelling was the way parents talked to their children. When we became parents, we followed in their footsteps. We yelled at our children whenever they annoyed us. When they begged for candy in the grocery store, pushed and poked one another in the car, or asked to stay up late, we yelled at them. Whenever they forced us to set limits or deny them something, we got angry. Deep down, we hated to disappoint them and resented them for making us do so.

By the time we began our recovery, our relationships with our children may have deteriorated to the point where they yelled at us as often as we yelled at them. We were losing our authority over them and were taking more drastic measures to punish them. This only increased their defiance. The tension in our home was so great that we turned to the bottle more frequently, acted out, avoided coming home, buried ourselves in work, or sank deeper into despair.

In our sobriety, we learned to talk to our children without yelling at them. We began to not feel guilty or uncomfortable when we set limits for them. Amazingly—at least that's how it seems to us—our children don't get as upset with our rules and limits when we calmly explain them.

When I calmly set limits, my children calmly respond.

Greed

· ·

Some of us felt invisible as children because our parents were more interested in their possessions than they were in us. They had more pictures of their prized possessions and exotic vacations than of their children. They were greedy, materialistic, and totally lacking in spiritual values. As adults, some of us became even more driven by greed than our parents, until we became exhausted and destroyed our relationships. We could no longer function without alcohol, drugs, sex, and many, many goodies.

We were looking for love in all the wrong places. In recovery, we put people and feelings before things. Our possessions did not bring us love, serenity, security, or happiness. Now, however, we discover these things by relying on our higher power, the support of our group, and the principles of the program. We are learning to base our lives on honesty, integrity, and compassion instead of greed.

We are teaching our children to value people more than things. We make a point to consider their needs and feelings before material things. We no longer concern ourselves with social status, and we avoid conspicuous consumption. Our sobriety and serenity is far more important than what others think of us. We bring our teenagers when we volunteer at homeless shelters or nursing homes. We encourage them to join church work-camp projects. This helps offset the materialism of their peers, especially in affluent high schools.

I am putting people and their feelings ahead of material things and encouraging my children to do the same.

Courtroom

. . . .

*W*e've all been drawn into our children's arguments at one time or another. When they fight, one of them comes to us complaining about the others, hoping to get us to intervene on their behalf and to punish their siblings. We often feel compelled to do something—anything—to stop their bickering. We get tired of their arguments and disputes, especially when they carry on in the room where we are reading, watching television, or talking with someone.

We used to get angry when they involved us in their courtroom dramas. We couldn't resolve their disputes in a way that they all would accept. No matter what we did, someone ended up crying. Out of our frustration, we often punished everyone equally, hoping this would discourage them from involving us the next time. Our responses were sometimes unreasonable and excessive, especially if we felt out of control.

We are learning to be more detached and less reactive to our children. We can act, not react. We no longer allow them to draw us into their disputes against our will. We manage to stay out of their disputes while helping them learn to resolve their issues themselves. We empower them when we refuse to enable their helplessness. They argue less and less since we made this change in our response.

I am teaching my children to resolve their own disputes.

Peer Pressure

· ·

*M*ost of us felt like outsiders as teenagers. We didn't fit in. Although we wanted to be popular in high school, we lacked the social skills and self-confidence to relate comfortably with our peers. We didn't invite our friends over because many of us were ashamed of our homes and had too many family secrets. We often paid high prices in order to feel socially acceptable. We hung out and got involved with drinking, drugs, and sex in vain attempts to feel accepted.

We want our children to fit in. We want them to feel comfortable and relaxed with their peers. Because we were socially isolated as teenagers, we want them to be popular. We realize, however, that the price of popularity is often too high. Our teenagers are discovering that some popular kids are into drugs, alcohol, and promiscuous sex.

Although we hope they're popular, we also want them to get good grades and avoid alcohol, drugs, and sex. We can help our children deal with peer pressure by listening to them and helping them clarify their values. Popularity is very seductive, especially for junior high students. The desire to be popular is related to the desire to be loved and accepted. We regularly reassure them of our love and acceptance of them. We talk to them about the balance between being popular and maintaining self-respect. We help them trust themselves and stand up for their values.

I am learning to help my children deal with peer pressure.

Order

· ·

*M*ost of us grew up surrounded by confusion and disorder. There was so little order in our lives that we became accustomed to chaos. Our rooms were a mess, and we were forever losing our schoolbooks, papers, or car keys. Our parents' occasional attempts to introduce order were autocratic and chaotic. They usually created more stress than they relieved. Within a few days, life returned to clutter as usual.

When many of us began recovery, our lives were not only unmanageable, they were literally messes. Our homes, our finances, and our children's lives were messes. Putting our lives in order has meant finding a new respect for personal discipline and daily routines. We take a little extra time each day to maintain order. We take time each day to read and meditate in an effort to restore order to our once chaotic inner lives, as well.

We want our children to experience the pleasure and benefits of orderly lives. We are learning to help them appreciate order by taking time to teach them to put their things away each day and keep their rooms neat. The new sense of order in our family has brought a sense of peace and harmony. When our home was disorderly and chaotic, it was easy to escape into work, television, alcohol, or other distractions. Now we all enjoy being at home together.

I enjoy helping my children appreciate and maintain order in their lives.

Flexible Rules

. . . .

*M*any of us grew up with rigid rules that were unevenly applied. Because we never knew from one day to the next if the rules would be ignored or strictly enforced, we were always anxious. Our parents never sought out middle ground during conflicts. They either locked us in our rooms or threw up their hands in despair and told us to do whatever we wanted to since we wouldn't listen to them anyway. We felt awful when they did this.

We can learn to look at life through flexible, multicolored lenses. Life is not black and white. There are exceptions to every rule. We are learning to think more flexibly about rules, taking into account circumstances, feelings, and relationships. Rules are intended to provide security, order, and continuity in family life. Rules are not meant to humiliate, threaten, or dominate children. When we uphold reasonable rules in a consistent, appropriate manner, our children rarely defy them.

We can learn to apply our family rules with flexibility without making them unpredictable. For instance, our children have a fixed bedtime, but we gladly allowed them to stay up to watch the last game of the World Series with us. This flexing of a family rule did not undermine our authority, create anxiety in our children, or begin a dangerous slide into anarchy. Instead, it pulled us closer together and created a friendly feeling in the family.

I apply our family rules in a consistent but flexible manner.

Sexual Boundaries

· ·

*A*lthough it is difficult for most of us to talk with our teenagers about sex, we are determined to do our best. Those of us who grew up in dysfunctional families struggle with a "no talk" rule that makes honest conversation about sex difficult. We didn't understand our sexual urges or know how to manage our sexual boundaries when we were their age because nobody talked to us about sex. Those of us who were sexually exploited as children didn't realize we had rights to our bodies. We want our children to know they do not have to let others—peers, friends, or adults—exploit them.

We're learning how to recognize our sexual boundaries and how to be in control of our sexual contacts. We used to feel totally powerless concerning our bodies. We were afraid to tell anyone, especially someone we liked, that we did not want to have sex or to be touched sexually. We were afraid we would hurt their feelings or that they might get rough with us.

We can teach our children that it is okay to talk about sex by doing so. They'll get the message that it's okay to ask for help when they are scared, confused, or worried. We can teach them how to be in control of their sexual contacts. We can help them develop scripts of what to say when someone touches them in unwanted ways.

I am talking to my teenagers about sex.

Courage to Be Imperfect

. . . .

J U N E   3 0

*M*any of us were so penalized as children for making mistakes and doing things imperfectly that we became timid, shy, and unwilling to take normal risks. We did everything possible to avoid mistakes: We refused to speak up in classes, offer our opinions in discussions, or take stands with friends. Being above reproach became an obsession with us. Little did we realize the price we paid for our quest for perfection.

In recovery, we learn that perfectionism is more of a curse than a virtue. Perfectionism interferes with our creativity, spontaneity, and healthy risk taking. Perfectionism causes anxiety so overwhelming that it can interfere with our memory, clear thinking, and physical performance. When we let go of our perfectionism, we begin to enjoy life. We experiment with activities we had once dreamed of but were afraid to try because we feared we might fail or look foolish.

When we have the courage to be imperfect, we can teach it to our children. We encourage them to try things they may fail at in the beginning. We do not overemphasize perfect scores, perfect grades, or perfect performances. We focus attention on the process of life instead of placing all the emphasis on the outcome. We encourage them to take risks, and we support them for going all out with effort, regardless of the outcome.

I encourage my children to take risks and live with enthusiasm.

Healthy Boundaries

. . . .

*W*hen we leveled with our children by accepting responsibility for our mistakes and making amends for our past behavior, some of us experienced healing forgiveness from our children. Others, however, experienced the opposite. Some children saw our new openness and vulnerability as opportunities to blame us for their own disappointments and problems. We were confused and uncertain about how to respond to these blaming attacks. We vacillated between accepting all the blame and going back to our old defensive positions.

In our recovery, we learn the importance of maintaining personal boundaries. Boundaries are the invisible fences that surround each of us. Just as pasture fences keep neighbors' sheep from grazing in our pastures, our boundaries keep our children's problems and disappointments from wandering into our souls and eating up our serenity. When we began our recovery, our fences were so broken down that everyone in our lives could graze on our serenity.

Now we teach our children to accept personal responsibility for their own lives. While we are sensitive to their problems and concerns, we resist taking the blame for them. As tempting as it may be to accept all the blame and lay it at the feet of our addictions, it's not helpful to our children to do so. When we don't take blame that doesn't belong to us, we are modeling honesty, self-respect, and dignity for our children.

I maintain an appropriate boundary between myself and my children's problems.

Overcommitment
. . . .

*M*any of us have a very difficult time saying no. As a result, we easily become overcommitted, harried, and frazzled. In our codependence, we never learned how to say no, establish our own boundaries, or set limits. As teenagers, we hated staying home, wanted to be included in all the social action, so we said yes to every opportunity for outside involvement that came our way. When we became too stressed from this pace, we medicated with chemicals in order to keep going.

Recovery has taught us that serenity involves learning to say no to some of the activities and involvements that interest us. Although many of these activities are wholesome and beneficial, we cannot maintain our serenity unless we slow down and manage our time commitments differently. We learn to grieve the losses that result from making responsible choices. We accept responsibility for our choices without complaining or blaming others for the limits we set.

When we manage our own time commitments, we teach our children to manage theirs, to say no, and to set reasonable limits. Some of our children want to be involved in everything, just as we did. Without cheating them of the opportunity to learn from their own experience, we encourage them to listen to their bodies when they are exhausted and make appropriate changes in their schedules. We help them weigh their choices by acting as sounding boards—without giving too much advice.

I am teaching my children to manage their commitments.

Convictions

. . . .

As children growing up in dysfunctional families, many of us felt insecure and afraid of being abandoned. We were codependent with our friends and we lived in fear of alienating them. We went along with them, even when we were scared to death of the adventures they took us on or knew what they were suggesting was wrong. We never said a word. We were too afraid of being teased or rejected. We have many regrets about the things we did because we were too timid to speak up.

Recovery has changed us. As we develop a relationship with our Higher Power, we become less dependent on the approval of our friends. We develop new standards of moral conduct. We can now stand alone because of our values and convictions without falling apart emotionally. It has become more important to sleep at night and face ourselves in the mirror than to please our friends.

We want our children to be able to stand their ground with their friends. We share with them what we have learned about the importance of moral courage and the benefits of a clear conscience. We assure them that we will always stand behind them, no matter what their friends say. We are creating a new trust level with our children in which they feel free to discuss some of their moral dilemmas with us.

I support my children in standing up for their convictions.

Doing Everything Ourselves

. . . .

*M*any of us became fiercely independent as the result of living in dysfunctional families we could not count on for love and support. We learned to do without things that required us to depend on others. We took pride in our independence and self-reliance. We believed we had developed a means of protecting ourselves from disappointment and heartache. When we realized we had created lives of loneliness and stress, we medicated ourselves with booze or drugs, drowned ourselves in work, went on eating binges.

By the time our do-it-all-myself program collapsed in ruin, we were mentally and physically exhausted. Fortunately, we found a group that introduced us to a recovery program. We did not have to do it alone. Although we were suspicious of a method that required us to depend on others, we were too exhausted to fight any longer. We had nearly killed ourselves by stubbornly clinging to our independence. We were finally willing to learn from others how they used a support system when they needed help.

We are learning to relax, let go, and accept our human limitations. Letting go of the need to be totally and ridiculously independent was like allowing ourselves to be pulled from icy waters by a rescue helicopter. We are asking for help whenever we can benefit from it, rather than waiting until we are drowning before we reach out for help.

I reach out for help when I can benefit from extra support.

God Is Love
. . . .

*M*ost of us knew nothing of God's unconditional love before we came into the Twelve-Step program. God had been presented to us as a stern, demanding, punitive judge. God's love, like all other love in our family, was always conditional. "God loves you when you clean your room." Our parents made promises to us, but their promises were always conditional. "If you are good boys and girls, I will show you I love you by buying you . . ." When they failed to keep their promises, they always blamed us for not keeping up our half of the bargain. And we soon learned we couldn't live up to everything they said God would love us for.

In recovery, we no longer have to bargain for love and acceptance. We are accepted just the way we are. We have finally discovered a God who loves us totally and unconditionally, with no bargains or preconditions. We have come to joyously depend on God's unconditional love for our healing and as the source of our growing self-acceptance.

We want our children to know this unconditional love, and we are learning more and more to model the love of God, however imperfectly. We don't bargain with our children to get them to do things. We keep our promises, and we expect them to meet their responsibilities without bargains or threats.

When I know God's unconditional love, I can teach it to my children.

Failure

. . . .

We want our children to be relaxed and self-confident about their performance and achievement. We want them to be able to enjoy stage performance, sports, games, and competition without being concerned about hurting our feelings when they make mistakes or don't win. When we were growing up, our parents got angry when we failed, so we hid the truth from them. Their good feelings were linked with our performance in school and sports. If we did well, they took the credit. If we failed, they berated us, yelling things like, "How could you do that to us? How could you let us down? You embarrassed us!"

In recovery, we are learning how to take failure more lightly. We used to believe that failure was a sin. Now we realize that everyone fails at times and that failure is a necessary part of learning and growing. We are discovering that we are best able to succeed when we are the least anxious about failing. We can admit our mistakes, acknowledge them to others, and then go on with life.

We are letting our children know they are free to fail. We don't humiliate them when they fail. We base our good feelings about ourselves on our own accomplishments, and we do not depend on our children's performances to bolster our egos. We are letting go of the demand that our children be perfect for us.

I am teaching my children to take failure lightly.

Detachment

. . . .

*B*ecause we want our children to have the things we never had, including good educations, we insisted they study hard, do their homework, and take college prep courses. Eventually, some of them became angry, defiant, and acted out in every way possible. We were not prepared for their rebellion. We responded by tightening our control over their social lives and applying more pressure for grades. They reacted with more defiance, perhaps including drug or alcohol abuse.

We were willing to do anything to help them, including attend parent meetings while they were in treatment. Here we began learning about our codependence. We were emotionally hooked by their defiant behavior and became codependent when they got involved with drugs or alcohol. When we first heard other parents in our groups talking about letting go of their children's acting out behavior, we were dumbfounded and very leery. It seemed these parents didn't really care about their children or were giving up. Eventually, we began to see the destructive impact of our overinvolvement.

Detaching was extremely difficult for us to do. Because we grew up with parents who were preoccupied with their own problems and had no time for us, we were determined to give our children the attention we never had. But what we had thought was attention was really pressure and control. We were creating resentful children rather than grateful ones. By detaching from our defiant children, we help them become personally responsible.

I am learning to detach from my defiant child.

Prisoners

. . . .

*M*any of us described our former lives with words like trapped, stuck, helpless, bogged down, and imprisoned. Although we are enjoying a new sense of freedom, we remember how terrifying it was to be the prisoners of our addictions and compulsions. We craved alcohol, food, drugs, sex, or work—whichever addictions imprisoned us. We had difficulty keeping our lives focused and productive because of our obsessions.

In our recovery, we eventually realized the true nature of our imprisonment. We were prisoners in an unguarded cell. Although we believed we could not escape from the grip of our compulsions, in fact, we had only to reach for the key that would eventually free us. Although it was in plain sight, it was invisible to us because we were looking for a different kind of key. We were desperately looking for a key that would strengthen our willpower and increase our control. We overlooked the unlikely key—surrender.

As we continue to use this key of surrender, we break free of our destructive patterns. We embrace our children without trying to control their thoughts, feelings, and actions. We learn to love and accept others as they are, not for how they can help us. We are learning to go with the flow instead of resisting everything that doesn't meet with our approval.

I gladly surrender my life to the will of God and walk through the open door of my prison cell.

Clean House

. . . .

*M*ost of us became independent at very early ages because we could not depend on anyone to help us. We had to look out for ourselves. We had to learn how to protect ourselves from exploitation and abuse. Unaccustomed to looking to anyone for help or assistance, we learned never to count on anyone but ourselves. Counting on God was a bad joke for most of us. Where was God when we were being abused?

Consequently, many of us found the spiritual part of the Twelve-Step program hard to swallow at first. We would have dismissed it entirely, were it not for the testimony of persons just like us. We were very cautious about trusting in anyone, let alone someone we didn't know and couldn't check out first. However, we were so desperate we had nothing to lose.

Eventually, we were ready to ask God to remove our shortcomings. For some of us, this was the biggest step of trust we had ever taken. We are learning that asking God to remove our shortcomings is like asking a doorman to open the door for us. That's what doormen do. That's why they stand next to the door waiting for us to approach. God is waiting for us to come to him so he can heal us. That's his job. That's why he is standing at the door waiting for us. Now we can walk through to healing.

I am trusting God to heal me.

Perfectionism

. . . .

As children, many of us became perfectionists in attempting to avoid being criticized and humiliated. We may have won some protection, but we limited our experiences. We were so afraid of making mistakes that we failed to take normal risks or try new adventures. The fear of appearing less than perfect inhibited our creativity and our social lives. Because we regarded most situations we faced as tests of our adequacy, we treated trivial tasks as if they were life-and-death situations.

In recovery, we're learning that perfectionism is a curse, not a virtue. Not all situations we face in life are of equal importance. We take responsibility for sorting out the significant from the insignificant. We don't have to invest maximum effort in every enterprise we undertake, nor do we have to win every game we play. We take new risks in expressing our thoughts and feelings and in experimenting with activities we had once only dreamed of trying.

We are helping our children discern what is important and what is unimportant, by talking about values and the big picture. Values include the importance of feelings, education, morals, and relationships. By helping them see the big picture, we encourage them to let go of petty details like fastidious neatness, perfect appearance, and people pleasing and concentrate on the things that are related to their larger values.

I'm teaching my children the difference between perfect and well done.

Denial

. . . .

As children, we had no say in our lives. Our parents refused to listen to us and never acknowledged that we knew anything. Although we hated being discounted, we thought it was normal to discount children. After all, grown-ups have more experience and are smarter than children. When we became parents, it was easy to assume that we knew everything and our children knew nothing. We believed that we knew what they needed, wanted, or ought to have. We acted just like our parents had with us.

We used denial to maintain our faulty belief system that children do not know what is best for them. When one of our children told us he was afraid of us because we yelled at him, we told him he was all mixed up and didn't know what he was talking about. When one of them told us she was sick, we accused her of making it up to avoid school.

In recovery, we've come to understand that each of us is the expert on our own experience. Our children know what they feel and what they want. Now when our children tell us what they are feeling, we take them at face value. We no longer use denial to maintain our faulty belief system that children don't know what they feel or need. When they tell us things about ourselves, we no longer discount them or criticize them for confronting us.

I acknowledge my children's feelings and do not deny them their experiences.

Self-Honesty

· ·

*O*nce we were old enough to see through their dishonesty, many of us lost respect for our parents. They lied to cover up their broken promises, lack of initiative, and all the inconsistencies in their desperate lives. Although we'd lost respect for their moral authority, we avoided doing things that would unnecessarily provoke them. We were determined to be better parents with our children, although we were not certain what that meant or how we'd earn their respect.

By the time we began our recovery, our children were already losing respect for us. In spite of our determination to be better parents, we had failed to realize the importance of self-honesty. Self-honesty is like looking in a crystal clear mirror that shows us everything about ourselves. Once we look and acknowledge what is there, we can begin to regain our self-respect.

We now realize we couldn't expect our children to respect our authority until we were honest with ourselves. When we were lying to ourselves, they saw through us, just as we had seen through our parents. We are learning that self-honesty is the foundation for integrity, and integrity is the basis for moral authority. When we admit our mistakes and make appropriate amends, our children respect us. When we lie and cover up our mistakes, they lose respect for us. They are not easily deceived.

I am learning to be honest with myself.

Self-Forgiveness

*M*any of us grew up with parents who never admitted their mistakes, errors, or faults. Even when they were clearly and absolutely wrong, they refused to apologize or admit their mistakes. We vowed we would not do this when we became parents. Because of our addictions, however, we lived in denial and did not keep this vow. How could we honestly admit mistakes we didn't recognize we'd made?

Now that we're involved in recovery, we're painfully aware of our many faults and character weaknesses. It was difficult for us to do the fourth and fifth steps regarding what we'd done to our children. Many of the things we did while we were using and abusing, such as leaving them unattended for hours at a time, had harmful effects on them. We have learned the freedom and peace that comes from owning and admitting our faults and errors. We no longer struggle with overwhelming guilt while trying to support a pretentious lie.

We acknowledge our faults and accept responsibility for having caused harm to our children. By coming clean with ourselves, we are free to change, grow, and do our best without wallowing in our guilt. The benefits of honesty and self-forgiveness include courage and serenity. Now when we see insecurity in our children, we do our best to give them emotional support and reassurance.

I accept responsibility for causing harm to my children without wallowing in guilt about it.

Respect for Children

R*ecovery* has dramatically changed our lives. While many of us once endured lives of emotional and spiritual poverty, we now have found purpose and the means for getting our emotional needs met. Finding a Twelve-Step recovery program was like finding the secret code.

One of the biggest challenges for us as recovering parents is sharing our new lives with our children. Now that we have discovered the secret for overcoming our own unhappiness and despair, we want to share this secret with them. Because we suffered for years before we learned how to live, we can't stand the thought of our own children wasting their lives on the low road to despair and misery when we know the way that leads to serenity. In our fondest dreams, our children are looking up to us, begging us to share our knowledge, experience, and wisdom with them. In reality, however, they ignore our teaching, especially if they are adolescents. They assert their identities and independence by challenging or resisting our recommendations.

Sharing our recovery experience with them is one thing. The challenge comes in resisting the temptation to force it down their throats. It is often difficult to respect our children's rights to live their own lives. However, mutual respect is a far better example of recovery principles than excessive force.

***Respecting my children's rights to think for themselves,
I share my recovery through the example of my own life.***

Making Mistakes

· ·

*W*e did everything possible to avoid making mistakes while growing up. When we did, we hid the evidence and covered up with lies in order to protect ourselves. Making mistakes was dangerous; we were often beaten for making simple ones. We were regularly degraded and humiliated, often in front of others, for making mistakes. Some of us avoided risks altogether, while others of us lived incredibly risky secret lives away from our parents' sight.

In recovery, we are learning that mistakes are not sins. Making mistakes is a normal, natural part of living, especially for children. They are important to the creative learning process. In order to discover and learn, we need to be free to experiment with untried ideas. We gather useful information from our experiments.

We are helping our children to value their mistakes instead of feeling ashamed of them. We no longer punish them for their errors. In order to respond graciously, we practice our patience. When we find that our children have made mistakes, we first attend to their feelings, reassuring them if they are anxious or frightened. Once they are calm, we have them share their decision-making process. Often they discover for themselves what to do differently next time. If they are unable to see alternative approaches, we point them out. Teaching them how to learn from their mistakes lifts a burden from their shoulders.

When I help my children accept their mistakes without fear, we both learn from the experience.

Positive Activities

. . . .

JULY 16

*A*lthough many of us have been in recovery for a long time, we still have lots of things to learn. And some of our old dysfunctional parenting habits die hard, especially when we are tired or irritable. Although we try to be gentle with ourselves, we sometimes become easily discouraged when our negative character traits appear. In our discouragement, we often berate ourselves unmercifully. After all, we chide ourselves, we've been in the program long enough to know better.

We are learning to focus, not only on our character defects, but on our strengths. We focus on what we can do for our children today, rather than on what we should be able to accomplish. When we do what we can instead of brooding about what we should be able to accomplish, we are spending quality time with our children. We encourage them to share their feelings with us, especially when they are upset, even though we do not always share our feelings calmly with them when we are upset.

We can learn to celebrate small victories while continuing to acknowledge our needs for growth. Taking positive action is more important than contemplating future perfection. At one time we may have believed it hypocritical to teach our children to share their feelings when we were not yet able to share ours completely. We now do what we can today and trust that our progress will continue tomorrow.

I do what I can today while I continue to grow as a parent.

Fear of Abandonment

. . . .

*M*ost of us believed that we were accepted only because we did things that pleased others. We lived in the fear that if we disappointed others, we would be rejected and abandoned. Because we feared rejection, we had a hard time asserting our own beliefs and expressing our own opinions. Whenever our ideas or beliefs were challenged, we caved in. Our personal relationships were very insecure.

When we began our recovery, we decided to be honest about our thoughts and feelings and express them directly. This was a frightening risk for us, and we prepared ourselves for rejection. We feared that if we dared to stand up to our children and our spouses, we would end up alone. Much to our surprise, they did not reject us. Having always thought of ourselves as peacemakers, we now realize that we were simply people pleasers with low self-worth.

The Twelve-Step program has helped us face this fear and deal with it. By facing our fear of abandonment, we're learning to trust the truth. We now believe that truth is the best policy, especially in family relationships. Although the truth may cause initial distress and tension, in the long run when our children know where we stand and what we expect of them, our relationships are healthier. And we don't use our new commitment to truth to verbally batter our children.

Speaking my truth honestly and openly helps me let go of my fear of abandonment.

Through the Eyes of Children

. . . .

*A*t one time, we had little patience with our young children. We regarded their words as idle prattle. Now that we are taking time to listen to them, we are astounded by their observations of life and the world. They see the world from a fresh, innocent perspective. Taking time to carefully listen and look at the world through their eyes opens us to spiritual renewal.

Sometimes we forget what recovery means. We are recovering the lost innocence, awe, and wonder of our own early childhoods. We are recovering our lost trust in God. We are reconnecting with the child within us and letting this inner child inform us and guide our hearts. Recovery is learning to see and trust the world through the eyes of an innocent child again.

Letting our young children correct our faulty vision keeps us humble and tutors us in serenity. They can teach us a whole new way of being if we are open to their delightful influence in our lives. By looking at the world through the eyes of our young children, we can see with the eyes of God. Following my four-year-old on a nature walk is more inspiring and satisfying than taking a hike in the woods with my knapsack packed with my worries and burdens.

I am learning to receive the gift of serenity from my young children.

Amends Without Shame

- -

We knew absolutely nothing about making amends when we began our recovery program. We were so poisoned with shame from years of struggling with low self-esteem that we refused to consider making amends to anyone. To make amends meant admitting we were inferior. We hid behind denial, pride, and stubbornness in futile attempts to shield ourselves from the anguish of our shame.

Making amends was the last thing we wanted to do because it forced us to acknowledge our faults, both to ourselves and others, and to call attention to them. We wanted to hide from our sins, not announce them to others. We certainly didn't want to remind anyone that we had injured them. We wanted to erase the memories of the many people we had hurt, not dig them up. Eventually, we realized that our method for finding serenity wasn't working.

Old-timers in our Twelve-Step group said Step Nine would help us to put the past behind and bring us serenity. At first, this sounded like nonsense. Step Nine seemed like an impossible task that would only lead to more shame. When we made amends with a few people, much to our surprise, we felt real peace for the first time. We went on to complete our list of amends. Not all our efforts are successful in healing relationships, but we find a new peace replacing shame in our lives.

I continue to make amends whenever I have harmed anyone, including myself.

Trust, Not Fear

. . . .

We are chemically dependent (or dependent on relationships or work) in part because we never learned to depend on or trust anyone for support, including God, until we began our recovery. We were fiercely independent and didn't want *anybody* giving us advice on how to live. We found comfort in our addictions, not in honest relationships with our Higher Power, ourselves, and others. We were cut off socially and spiritually, and we took pride in not needing anyone.

When we first got into the program, many of us used fear to keep us straight. While we were scared enough to stop our addictive behavior, we were as determined as ever not to depend on anyone. We were going to lick our dependency, even if it killed us. Fear, it turns out, is not a good motivator. We needed the positive motivation that comes from listening to others who have learned to live sober, healthy lives.

We are gradually learning to depend on God to remove our defects of character—something we cannot do for ourselves. As we began to trust God and depend on him more and more, we also start to depend on others for some of the support we need to stay sober. We find that we are depending on others and they are depending on us—in a two-way street to peace and recovery in our lives.

I am learning to trust God, my program, and other people to keep me sober.

Laughter

. . . .

As our family lives deteriorated during the years we were active addicts, laughter became increasingly rare for us and for our children. We didn't tell stories or make jokes. Table conversation consisted of, "Pass the salt and pepper please." What little conversation remained was limited to one-word answers to questions we asked our children. The children kept low profiles to avoid being yelled at, and the atmosphere was tense most of the time. Harmony was the absence of yelling.

As we regained our sanity through recovery, we also regained our emotional responsiveness. One of the welcome signs of the spiritual renewal in our lives is the return of laughter. When we were emotionally depressed in our illness, we could find no goodness or joy in our lives. Everything looked bleak and dismal. The future was dark, the present was intolerable, and the past was a blur.

Recovery has brought us back into the light of God's love. Without God's love and forgiveness we would still be locked in the tiny dark cell of our emotional prisons. Now we live again in the healing sunlight of his love. We are learning once again to laugh at ourselves and with each other. Laughter refreshes our spirits and lightens our loads. Laughter is the sure sign of harmony and healing in our families.

I welcome the return of laughter to my life and to my family.

Feelings

. . . .

*M*any of us remember hearing our parents say to us when we were children, "You don't feel that." Or, "You shouldn't feel that way." They refused to accept certain feelings, especially strong anger, fear, or sadness. We learned to hide these from our parents and/or to repress them from our own consciousness. When we became parents, we said the same things to our children. When one of our children reported feeling vengeful, rageful, or furious at someone else, we were quick to tell them they shouldn't feel that way.

Our recovery teaches us that we all have a right to our feelings, even children. When we are not allowed to feel our feelings, or express what we feel, we are deprived of an important part of our humanness. Unless we are omniscient—and we're not!—we cannot know with certainty what someone else's inner feelings are. Feelings may not be logical or follow the rules of evidence.

Respecting our children's rights to their feelings teaches them both to feel them and to take responsibility for what they do with them. When they express anger, hurt, or fear, we resist the temptation to say, "You shouldn't feel that way." Instead, we encourage them to make a distinction between what they feel, what they think, and what they plan to do.

I let my children feel their feelings and express them while holding them accountable for their behavior.

Performance

· ·

We want our children to be well motivated and disciplined. Sometimes we get too involved in their performance, however. We remember how our parents criticized us when we failed to score enough points in a game, get the lead in the class play, or bring home all A's on our report cards. Everything we did was for them and not for ourselves. We worked so hard to please our parents that we lost ourselves. We couldn't separate what we wanted from what they wanted for us. We went to the colleges they chose and dated people we knew they'd approve of, even though we weren't attracted to them.

With the help of our codependency support group, we practice letting our children take responsibility for their lives. We're coming to understand we had too much of our own self-esteem invested in their lives, especially in their achievements. We're learning to base our good feelings about ourselves on our own achievements rather than on theirs.

Because we're encouraging our children to follow their own interests and standards of excellence, they are becoming more responsible for their own lives. They are more involved in their choices and less dependent on our approval for the things they do. We don't neglect them, though. We ask them to share with us what they are involved in, and we offer help and support when they need it.

I encourage my children to perform well, but I no longer base my self-esteem on their performance.

Trusting Children's Judgment

Some of us have had difficulty making decisions as adults because we were never encouraged to develop good judgment as children. We did not receive support from our parents for making our own decisions. Instead, we heard about how stupid we were and what poor decisions we made. We want our children to trust their judgment and feel confident in their decision making.

We realize that in order to develop good judgment, our children need lots of opportunities to make decisions. Allowing children to make their own decisions is difficult for most recovering parents. Because we were so accustomed to trying to control our children's lives, it is hard for us to allow them to fail. Failure, of course, is a necessary part of learning to make good decisions. No one can develop good judgment without making mistakes—lots of them.

We can encourage our children to make decisions for themselves, beginning early in their lives. A four-year-old can choose what to wear, for example, even if the colors don't always match. The more practice they get, the better they will be at making good decisions. We can provide guidance without imposing our final choices on them. Although this requires a great deal of restraint on our part, the payoff is worth it.

I am helping my children develop good judgment by letting them make decisions and mistakes.

Reading Between the Lines

. . . .

*S*ome of us grew up in families filled with intense conflict, chaos, and bedlam. We came to accept our chaotic surroundings and never complained about personal slights, hurt feelings, or wounded pride. But we didn't know from one day to the next if there would be food to eat, a roof over our heads, or parents around. Consequently, we focused on our survival. We coped by filtering out the chaos and intensity to keep from feeling overwhelmed. Although this filtering enabled us to survive, we failed to detect or appreciate the subtleties of interpersonal communication.

In recovery, we are gradually learning to pay attention to the subtle nuances of emotions and feelings. We were so accustomed to ignoring our personal feelings that we didn't recognize when people put us down, exploited us, or treated us disrespectfully. When we were out of touch with our own feelings, we ignored the emotional needs of our children until they acted out or screamed at us.

Now that we recognize our feelings we are learning to tune in to the subtle nuances of our children's expressions. We can recognize their slightest signals as well as their blatant signs of emotional distress. Now we respond to their subtle, nonverbal signals before they get frustrated and act out to get our attention. We can read between the lines with our children.

I am learning to read the subtle signals in my children's nonverbal communication and respond to their emotional needs.

Divcorcing

*M*any of us remember our parents' divorces as if they were yesterday. We remember where we were standing when we found out, who told us, and how devastated we felt. No one told us what we could expect, and our fears kept us awake at night. We felt responsible for their divorces. For years we were afraid to ask our parents why they divorced. Our families lived by the no-talk rule.

In recovery, we've learning to tell the truth, even when we know the truth will disappoint and upset others. Breaking our families' no-talk rule is an important step in our recovery. Our commitment to honesty had always been a conditional commitment before our recovery. We only told the truth when it would not upset those close to us. We're learning that the whole truth works, even in our most intimate relationships, even within ourselves.

We're learning to talk to our children honestly, even when they are angry with us. If we are divorcing, we can tell them why as truthfully as possible and answer their questions at a level they can understand. We don't berate their other parent in our explanations, nor do we lie about facts, like outside involvements. We accept responsibility for our choices and we don't make excuses or hide behind blame. We want them to know they can come to us for the truth.

I tell my children the truth, even when I know it will upset them.

Action

. . . .

As children, many of us were too afraid of making mistakes and getting in trouble to risk taking initiative. Some of us are still handcuffed by this fear as adults. When the moment for decisive action is upon us, we hesitate. We worry about what others might think, whether they will judge or criticize us. By the time we review all the potential risks involved, the golden moment of opportunity has passed—once again.

In recovery, we're learning to take action, even when we cannot predict perfect outcomes. Our hesitancy has cost us too many lost opportunities. Our reluctance to take normal, appropriate risks has resulted in a life of dull, depressing monotony. We were socially inhibited and depended on alcohol to relax and loosen up enough to engage in normal social interaction. Now we learn to reach out to others and stop obsessing about personal slights.

We are encouraging our children to prefer action to perfection, especially when they are afraid of making mistakes. "Mistakes are not sins. Mistakes are often creative ways of doing things," we tell them. We reassure them that we will not penalize them for making mistakes in honest attempts to solve problems or while trying something new. By lifting the curse of perfectionism from their shoulders, we unshackle their initiative. They are now more energetic and creative.

I encourage my children and myself to be proactive instead of hesitant and reactive.

High-Spirited Children

. . . .

J U L Y   2 8

Some of us live with high-spirited children. It's like living with perpetual motion machines. We often feel overwhelmed by their constant movement and activity. We've tried to slow them down and control them in order to calm our nerves, but their constant activity level can leave us exhausted, cranky, and irritable. We've often felt guilty and ashamed of the way we treat our high-spirited child. Most of us are impatient with our children at times, especially when we are tense or exhausted from a long day at work.

Some of us remember reading our parents' moods and staying clear of them when they were irritable or angry. We could usually tell the moment they crossed the threshold at the end of the day what kind of moods they were in. We certainly weren't allowed our own exuberance, especially when they were exhausted or in a bad mood.

We are learning to accept our high-spirited children. We have learned that their energy level is natural for them and not a sign of ill-temper or misbehavior. We're learning to respect the diversity of life and not expect everyone to act the same way. We don't want our high-spirited children to be afraid of us. We're learning to love and appreciate their incredible energy and practice a measured detachment so we don't become anxious around them.

I love my high-spirited children and stay calm in their presence.

Enjoy Process

. . . .

*W*e used to pride ourselves in being results oriented. We were interested in the bottom line, the final outcome. We rushed through our lives as if we were in a hurry to reach old age. We took shortcuts whenever possible to save time and get results more quickly. We were competitive in everything we did, making contests out of everyday activities. Winning was everything. Home became a boot camp for our children to learn to hurry and compete.

By the time we started in recovery, our lives had become joyless and totally unmanageable. We were burned out and completely devoid of a sense of meaning and purpose. In recovery, we've developed a calmer way of life in which serenity replaces frenzy and competition. We've learned to stop and smell the roses. We are learning about the importance of process. How we live our lives, day to day, has become as important to us as the bottom line used to be.

We now teach our children to enjoy each day of their lives, to enjoy the process as much as the outcome. When we help them with a project, like a pine box derby car, we go slowly and work patiently while talking with them about the enjoyment of each step along the way. We talk about looking forward to returning to the project the next day and make the process itself fun.

I enjoy teaching my children to be patient and enjoy the process.

Sharing Troubles

. . . .

"We don't hang our dirty laundry in public, after all, what will the neighbors think?" Many of us heard this repeatedly as we grew up. Our parents were closed and secretive about what went on in our homes. We were forbidden to talk to anyone about our problems. We now see that they were ashamed, and in some cases, probably afraid of being charged with child abuse. We learned the no-talk rule so well we talked to no one. Even today, we feel anxious and guilty when we talk honestly about certain details of our childhoods.

Most of us continued the no-talk rule as adults. We didn't want anyone to know that we lost our tempers and sometimes treated our children exactly as we had been treated. After all, we thought, what would the neighbors think?

In recovery we learn that the no-talk rule undermines children's self-esteem and keeps them and us from growing. We learn to be honest with others about our struggles. In fact, we discover that by talking with others about the problems we have with our children, we put things in perspective, gain confidence, and find new ways of dealing with our children. The more we share our problems, the smaller and more manageable they become.

Sharing my parenting problems with friends I trust helps me accept my limitations and reach out to others.

Projection

. . . .

*L*ike all parents, we worry about our children and how they will turn out as adults. We want them to be happy, well adjusted, and successful. We worry they will be adversely affected by our mistakes and failures. In an effort to be more conscientious, many of us overreacted to our children's choices. We projected our fears onto their future by imagining that their normal childhood behavior would continue into adulthood. We worried about sons who played with dolls or daughters who climbed trees or worked on cars. We feared that childhood choices could lead to gender confusion. Some of us worried that our children might never learn responsibility or earn social acceptance.

In recovery we're learning that our compulsive efforts to become perfect parents have often resulted in negative projection. We become anxious and uptight when we fret about the smallest details of their behavior. We can become too conscientious, too concerned, and too worried for our children's good. We practice "easy does it" to calm our fears and trust our children's normal development.

We admire parents who are relaxed and easygoing. We're learning from them to enjoy our children while they are children. Our worry and negative projections interfere with our ability to enjoy the present moment. We are learning to make the most of the present moment with our children, instead of trying to live so we will have no regrets.

I am enjoying the present with my children and trusting God for their future.

First Romance

. . . .

"I'm in love!"

Our teenagers make the big announcement, maybe not in so many words. They are giddy with excitement and want us to be excited too. But because of the many painful memories we have of our teenage romances, we struggle to keep from projecting our fears on them instead. Our impulse is to warn our teenagers of the terrible things that can happen to adolescents in love. However, we manage to smile and say something neutral, for the moment.

When we bring up our fears and negative projections with our friends in recovery, we are relieved to hear from other parents that they, too, have struggled with this issue. We talk about the dangers of negative projection and how to keep from reacting to our children on the basis of our fears. We remind ourselves that our children are not us as children, and we're not our parents.

We're learning to keep our fears under control and to avoid projecting them on our teenagers. We support them by opening conversations about their romantic interest. We resist our temptation to fill these conversations with warnings, sermons on sex, or the odds of their breaking up in two weeks. We calmly listen as they talk about imagining being married to their new friend in the future. We remind ourselves that these fantasies are normal and harmless.

I'm learning to resist projecting my negative fears on my teenagers.

Smarting Off

. . . .

*N*obody likes a smart mouth. As parents, we bristle when our children smart off to us. Their behavior reminds us that we were never allowed to express anger to our parents, no matter what they said or did to us. As a result, we used sarcasm, withdrawal, and other indirect ways to express our feelings. Many of us were slapped, grounded, forced to "wash" our mouths with soap, or otherwise punished.

As we've learned more about feelings in recovery, we've discovered that anger is often a cover-up for deeper emotions. We're learning both to express our anger appropriately and to explore our deeper emotions when we're angry. We are coming to realize that sorrow, fear, or hurt usually lie beneath the anger. The more we can identify and express the underlying feelings, the easier it is for us to let go of the anger.

Now when our children smart off to us, we're learning to listen for the deeper emotions, which are often hurt or feeling misunderstood. By listening for the feelings beneath their anger, we can help our kids articulate their feelings. We can open up a productive conversation, even when it starts with their smart-mouth remark.

I am helping my children express their deeper feelings when they are angry.

Temper

· ·

Some of us had temper tantrums as children. Others of us learned to repress our angry feelings and consequently became depressed or acted out in destructive ways. None of us who grew up in dysfunctional families learned to deal with anger in healthy ways. Anger is a powerful emotion that easily threatens family harmony when it is not understood. Many of us alternate between stuffing our anger and letting it control our behavior.

In recovery, we're learning the importance of dealing with our angry feelings before our feelings deal with us. Stuffing our feelings leads to problems such as depression or psychosomatic symptoms like headaches, backaches, stomachaches, or hives. Dumping our angry feelings on others produces hostility and conflict. We are learning to recognize our anger before it gets too big to contain. We acknowledge that these feelings belong to us and no one else. Then we talk about how we feel, without blaming others or dumping on them.

Helping our children recognize their angry feelings before they explode in temper tantrums is challenging. We're doing everything possible to encourage our children to talk about their angry feelings before they give up self-control in tantrums or repress their anger and then act out in other ways. We no longer appease them when they have tantrums, even in public. Instead, we ignore the tantrums and continue to relate calmly to them until they calm down.

I am teaching my children to express their anger without using tantrums.

No Teasing

· ·

*S*arcasm and put-downs passed for humor and play-fulness when we were growing up. Although we may have laughed a lot, the laughter was always at someone's expense. This kind of humor was most apparent when everyone in the family got together. The key to survival was knowing how to dish it back as fast as it was dished out and never letting any-one know your feelings were hurt.

In our recovery, we've begun to feel our feelings rather than hide them from ourselves and others. Once we acknowledged our feelings and expressed them honestly, sarcastic put-downs lost their appeal as a source of good-natured humor and fun. Although this was one of the few ways our family had fun to-gether, it no longer appeals to us. We are learning to laugh with, not at, others. We no longer enjoy having to armor our-selves emotionally just to be able to spend time with family members.

We are teaching our children to be playful without hurting other people's feelings. We laugh and play together in a spirit of silliness that is caring and free of sarcasm. We all let our hair down when we play charades, for example. Abusive teas-ing is not tolerated, whether between siblings or adults. Our humor is lighthearted and friendly now that anger and bitter-ness no longer simmer just below the surface in everyone's lives.

I enjoy laughter and playfulness that is not at someone's expense.

Arguments

. . . .

*O*ur parents argued and fought much of the time. As children we laid awake at night listening to them. We were often afraid they were hurting each other or that they were going to divorce. When they argued in front of us, they tried to get us to take sides. We hated having to choose between them because one of them was always mad at us. We don't want to put our children through this.

Before we got into recovery, we tried to avoid arguments. This only worked when we stuffed our feelings. When things boiled over, we exploited our children by arguing in front of them just as our parents had done. In recovery, we're learning to be honest with our feelings and to talk out our problems before they build up inside and we lose control. We are even learning to schedule time for arguments.

We're teaching our children to stay out of our arguments. We try to discuss our problems when they're not around. This is not always possible, however. Sometimes when we argue, they will interrupt and say, "Mommy, Daddy, don't fight!" We both reassure them that everything is okay. We explain that we need to talk out our differences and they need not worry about us or about their security.

I am keeping my children free from my arguments with my partner.

God as Security

*W*e suffered so many broken promises as children that we came to ignore promises altogether. We refused to cooperate with others because it involved trusting them. We felt more secure when we trusted no one but ourselves. What little security we experienced was the result of our own doing; security came to mean self-sufficiency.

Our recovery program introduced us to a new understanding of security based on faith and trust in a Higher Power. This struck many of us as insane. After all, we didn't even trust those we knew and could confront when they let us down. How could we trust an invisible, spiritual being we'd never seen and couldn't confront? The unpretentious testimony of persons like ourselves got us to look at this notion of security.

Counting on God for our security is like counting on gravity to keep our feet on the ground. We trust gravity, even though we have never seen it. Gravity is always there for us, whether we choose to believe in it or not. Gravity does not betray our trust, even when we accidentally fall and curse the ground for hurting us. As we learn to rely on God's grace for our security, we are becoming more dependable parents.

I trust God as the ultimate source of my security.

What If?

. . . .

*O*ur parents were professional worriers. They worried about everything and warned us about every conceivable danger. We want our children to be free to live without these unnecessary anxieties. As parents, it is easy to let our minds wander into the land of "What if?" Once we begin asking what if questions, our thinking moves from observation and reason to the realm of fearful speculation.

In recovery, we turn our worries over to our Higher Power. In the serenity prayer, we ask for the wisdom to know the difference between those things we can change and those things we can't. We have come to accept that we can't change the universe to make it free of all danger for our children. We can, however, ask God to watch over our children and to free us from our anxious worries.

When we put our trust in God to watch over our children, we are better able to change the things we can change. We now teach our children how to avoid reasonable dangers. We teach them to look before they cross streets, avoid talking to strangers, make their own decisions about behavior free from peer pressure, and so on. Although we cannot possibly protect our children from all harm, we do give them certain practical precautions.

I entrust the safety and welfare of my children to my Higher Power, while giving them practical precautions.

Moral Purpose

. . . .

We want our children to base their decisions on moral principles and not on what may be popular at the moment. Many of us have struggled to figure out what we believe is right and wrong. Our moral sense of right and wrong was skewed by the years we spent in dysfunctional relationships. We were so preoccupied with survival that we didn't think about morals. We had the capacity to feel guilty and ashamed without having a moral foundation to base these feelings on.

Recovery introduced us to the concept of moral purpose. We're learning to base our decisions on something other than expedience, pleasing others, or personal pleasure. At one time, we saw little difference between doing the right thing and doing what placated others. We confused morality with popularity and being above reproach. We have since discovered that living with a sense of moral purpose will often put us at odds with those around us.

We help our children develop moral purpose when we show them they have something to live for besides materialism and popularity. When they talk to us about their fears of standing up for an unpopular friend, we encourage them to do what's right rather than what's popular. We discuss moral principles with them in terms they can understand and ask them how the golden rule applies in their specific situations.

I love helping my children develop moral foundations for their lives.

Appreciation

. . . .

*B*eing appreciated feels a lot like being loved. When someone tells us how much they value us, we feel wonderful. Many of us cannot remember ever hearing our parents express appreciation for anything we did. We can, however, clearly remember being scolded, ridiculed, teased. Because we never heard praise, we never learned to express appreciation to our parents either.

In recovery, we're experiencing the importance of expressing our positive feelings to others. We can bask for hours in the inner glow we feel when someone in our group expresses appreciation for a personal experience we've shared in group. When we have a positive feeling about someone, we make it a point to tell them. Giving and receiving appreciation has become both comfortable and natural for us.

By expressing appreciation to our children, we let them know they are loved and we teach them to express themselves as well. Young children respond quickly to our efforts. Teenagers, however, seem to find it more difficult to express appreciation to their parents. It must conflict with their need for autonomy and independence. We don't let their reluctance to express themselves get in the way of our telling them how much we appreciate them, however. We trust that our efforts will make a difference in their lives someday.

I enjoy expressing appreciation to my children and teaching them the wonderful benefits of expressing appreciation to others.

Attractive

· ·

*S*ome of us have obsessed over our physical appearance. We have been extremely self-conscious about our looks, especially as teenagers. We've constantly compared ourselves with others and felt inferior. Maybe we dieted all through high school, even though we were not obese. Or we entered beauty contests, read beauty magazines, and watched every beauty pageant on television. Some of us lifted weights and took steroids to make ourselves more attractive and competitive. This obsession caused us a lot of distress and led some of us into eating disorders, steroid abuse, and various addictions.

Developing a spiritual perspective has helped us overcome our obsession with physical appearance. We are learning to see ourselves in a larger, more spiritual context in which physical appearance is only a small part of our total being. This spiritual awakening brings us a serenity we had never known before. We spent most of our lives chasing the illusion that physical beauty would make us happy and give our lives a sense of meaning. We don't want our teenagers to waste their lives chasing this illusion.

We are teaching our teenagers to broaden their horizons to include spiritual values. We want them to put appearance, athletic performance, and popularity in their proper perspective. We share the stories of our struggles with physical appearance and its consequences—eating disorders, steroid abuse—in the hope it will help them avoid our mistakes.

My teenagers and I put physical appearance in the larger perspective of spiritual values.

Small Changes

. . . .

*M*ost of us have raised our children using the same methods that our parents' used. Although we wanted better relationships with our children, the means and methods we used were essentially the same. If our parents were loud and expressive in discipline, we were loud and expressive. If our parents used corporal punishment, we used corporal punishment—even though we may have vowed we would never strike our children. We unconsciously absorbed our parents' methods without intending to.

When we came to the point in our recovery where we began setting goals for our new life, we wanted to change our relationship with our children. Many of us seriously neglected or abused our children while we were abusing ourselves with alcohol, drugs, sex, food, work, or other means. Once we took an honest look at ourselves, we were ashamed of our past and overwhelmed with the task of repairing our damaged relationships with our children.

Changing our methods of parenting is like replacing all the bricks in a wall without letting the wall fall apart in the process. We take things one small step at a time in order to prevent the wall from collapsing and our lives from becoming unmanageable once again. We quietly replace many of our harsh methods of discipline with consistent, respectful approaches, rather than avoid discipline altogether until we learn to do it perfectly. This transition is tricky but the wall remains intact.

I improve my parenting one tiny step at a time.

Humor

. . . .

*M*any of us grew up with the message that life is serious and hard—no laughing matter. What little humor there was often came at someone else's expense. In the family photographs from our childhood, we look pretty somber. Life was not pretty, and we didn't know how to cover up our pain when pictures were taken. As teenagers, our approach to humor was sarcasm and put-downs as we tried to keep up with our siblings. Humor was usually painful, although we would never acknowledge that we felt the jabs.

What a wonderful discovery it was to meet people in the program whose use of humor was warm, caring, and light-hearted. We have come to appreciate those who use humor to lighten tense situations and to laugh at themselves, especially when they're taking life too seriously. Humor has become a cherished resource for maintaining a healthy outlook and a light attitude. Laughter around the family table no longer feels strident or shrill. Now, it feels friendly and warm, like a tropical breeze wafting through the air.

As we learn to accept ourselves and our children, we also learn to laugh at situations that, in the past, would have caused an argument or a tense, unpleasant encounter between us and our children. As we learn to laugh at ourselves, we're learning not to take life too seriously. And we're teaching our children that important lesson as well.

I thank God for showing me the leavening effect of humor.

Prayer

. . . .

*M*any of us learned to pray in a rigid, impersonal, and formal way. It seemed easy to make mistakes. What if we forgot the right words? Our parents did not pray spontaneously. Some of them recited memorized prayers at mealtime and bedtime. Prayer was more often an empty ritual than a conversation with God. Most of us left prayer behind when we left home.

Recovery opens up a new understanding of spirituality in our lives, making it easier for us to pray. Prayer is no longer an empty ritual of reciting memorized, scary words like "If I should die before I wake." Prayer is now a conversation with our Higher Power. We no longer worry about getting our words just right to please an angry father. We trust that God understands us better than we understand ourselves. We practice meditative prayer, in which we listen for God's responses in the stillness of our hearts.

We teach our children to pray by praying with them at mealtime and bedtime. We create prayers in common language that reflect events happening in our lives together. We want our children to know God as their loving friend. Teaching our children to pray has lightened our load as parents. Now we have a backup system to help when we are overwhelmed. We ask God to help us to be good parents and help us through our tough times.

I like teaching my children to pray in their own words.

Self-Absorbed

*A*lthough many of us became people pleasers in trying to get others to accept us, others of us were taught to look out only for ourselves. We were on our own, emotionally and socially, from a very early age. No one taught us the social skills of cooperation and consideration of others. We regarded others with suspicion. There seemed to be a limited supply of goodies in life, and we were competing with everyone else for them. Needless to say, we did not develop close relationships.

In recovery, we are belatedly acquiring the social skills of consideration and cooperation. We are learning to consider the feelings of others. As we come to understand our common humanity and the benefits of sharing our struggles with others, we are dissolving the painful social isolation that we once maintained with pride. We balance concern for ourselves with concern for others.

We're teaching our children to consider others and helping them put the Golden Rule into practice in their lives. We remind them that they feel better when they are emotionally close and connected with others. We help them show consideration for others, including their brothers or sisters, and we encourage them to wait for one another and help one another. Rather than scold them when they act selfishly, we remind them of how much better they feel when someone is considerate to them.

I enjoy teaching my children to be considerate of others.

Participation

. . . .

*M*any of us have gone through our lives like children with our noses pressed against store windows. We feel like outsiders looking in. We never felt we were a part of the action, that we belonged, fit in, or were part of the crowd. We did not join clubs, groups, organizations, or causes. We never ran for class office or the student council. We sat on the sidelines of life like a wallflower at the school dance. We even felt like outsiders within our own family.

As we grow in our recovery, we learn to take initiative and reach out to others. For the first time, we make connections, beginning with others in our Twelve-Step group. We experience the satisfaction that comes from being a part of a mutual support group. We feel more and more connected as we accept responsibility for something more than our own immediate well-being. We're becoming good citizens and good neighbors.

We want our children to be active participants in life. We encourage them to get involved in organizations, clubs, or causes. We expose them to many types of activities—sports, recreation, music, and religious groups. But we know that simply joining won't make them feel like they belong, so we don't force them into activities they're not interested in. We pay close attention to their curiosity and applaud their enthusiasm.

My children and I can learn to participate in activities and experiment with leadership together.

Solitude

. . . .

*O*ur parents scolded us for spending time by ourselves. They told us we would never learn to make friends if we spent time alone. They made us feel like there was something wrong with us for wanting solitude. We felt guilty for going on long solitary walks or staying in our rooms to read or listen to music. We were forced to socialize when we didn't want to, and we never took time to search our own thoughts or get to know our inner selves.

When we began our recovery, we didn't know ourselves. We had been running from ourselves since childhood. We'd never gotten acquainted with our own inner thoughts and feelings. So taking a searching moral inventory was uncomfortable and difficult. As we developed the habit of daily meditation and personal reflection, however, we became more comfortable with ourselves. We enjoy our own company.

We want our children to be comfortable with themselves. We don't want them to feel strange or guilty for enjoying solitude. We recognize that our teenagers want to spend time in their rooms away from the rest of the family. As long as they relate to us and manage their responsibilities, we are not worried about the time they spend alone. We encourage them to enjoy their own company, take time for daily meditation, and keep journals. We want them to be comfortable relating to themselves.

I encourage my children to enjoy time alone.

Insecurity

. . . .

*M*any of us wanted to have children so we could feel needed by someone. We felt important to our children, even if the rest of the world didn't recognize us. Our babies were especially dependent on us, making us feel indispensable and significant. As our children grew older and less dependent on us, we insisted that they follow our rules and guidelines. We felt it was important for our children to have a firm code of conduct to guide them. The more important our role was in their lives, the more secure we felt.

In our parenting support group, we are discovering that depending on our children for our security is not healthy—for either them or us. The more we did to direct and control their lives, the more discouraged they became. They felt insecure because we warned them about everything. They felt resentful because we controlled their every move. They felt helpless because we would not let them try things on their own.

We can deal with our insecurity by examining our lives and using the tools of the Twelve-Step program. We had lost ourselves in our children, needing them to make our lives meaningful by being perfect children. We recognize that as we let go of our children, we discover ourselves. And now that we are lifting the pressure from their shoulders, our children are responding responsibly.

I do not expect my children to make my life meaningful and secure.

Trustworthy

. . . .

When we began our recovery, we were eager to establish better relations with our children. We made amends for all the times we had broken our word and let them down. We asked them to forgive us immediately and trust us from now on. They didn't, of course. As time passed, we became more and more frustrated with their continuing mistrust of us. We began trying to persuade them of our trustworthiness with examples, evidence, and logical arguments. They were not moved.

In our Twelve-Step group, we've learned that the rebuilding of trust takes time, and we cannot force anyone to trust us. As much as we want others to trust us, they have their own reasons for remaining skeptical and cautious. In our codependence, we want everyone to accept us and see us the way we see ourselves. We're learning to let go of our compulsive need to control other people's impressions of us.

We make a sincere effort to follow through on all our promises and commitments. We no longer try to force our children to trust us. Now when they tell us they don't believe we will keep our word, we don't take it personally. Instead, we focus our efforts on being trustworthy and let go of the demand that they trust us.

I do all I can to be worthy of my children's trust and let go of my expectations of them.

Overwhelmed
. . . .

*M*any of us remember asking our parents, "Is it all right if I . . . ?" and hearing, "No!" before we finished our requests. They had an automatic response to all our requests, whether we were asking permission for an overnight with our friends or asking them to buy us a new bike. They did everything they could to discourage us from asking for anything. They seemed overwhelmed whenever we needed something from them, whether school supplies or permission to do something. Many of us decided to respond more positively to our children's requests. To our surprise, we felt overwhelmed because we couldn't say no when we needed to.

In recovery we're overcoming our people-pleasing behavior. Once we learn to say no, it becomes easier to listen to and consider our children's needs and requests without feeling overwhelmed or manipulated. We used to be so afraid of disappointing them that we avoided taking them shopping with us, even to the grocery store. Now we can go anywhere with our children without fear that their begging will spoil our time together.

By carefully considering our children's needs and requests, we help them to feel secure in their neediness and not to disguise their needs or feel guilty about them. We want them to acknowledge their desires and feel comfortable asserting themselves to get what they want.

I listen carefully to my children's requests and respond according to my values and resources, without feeling guilty, overwhelmed, or manipulated.

Envying My Children

. . . .

*S*ome of us envy the maturity of our children. Some of them are much more mature than we were at their ages. They understand and accept their feelings and know how to cope with them better than we did. Many of us were acting out at their ages. When our feelings were hurt, we raged, broke things, or withdrew into silence. In contrast, our children talk freely about their anger and disappointments.

In recovery, some of us faced our competition with our children for the first time. If they were more mature, we resented them for making us look bad in comparison. Now that we are able to identify these feelings, we can stop acting on them. We admit to ourselves that we feel envy and competition, but we keep ourselves from acting on these feelings.

We can support our children's growth and maturity, even when they act more maturely than we do. We no longer think of our children as threats to our self-esteem. Instead, we see in them the positive results of our hard work in recovery. Some of the best fruits of recovery are to be seen in the lives of our children. We may not be able to take all of the credit for their maturity, but we can surely take some of it.

I delight in the maturity of my children and accept some of the credit.

Blaming

. . . .

*M*any of us grew up with parents who whined and complained about the burdens and obligations of having children. We felt we were the cause of our parents' financial problems and unhappiness. If it weren't for us, they would have been rich and personally fulfilled. They reminded us of all the money they spent for our clothes, doctor bills, braces, school supplies, sports equipment, and lessons. They talked about careers they might have had or trips they might have taken if they didn't have children. We felt they resented having us.

Through sharing stories in our parents support group, we see that children are very sensitive to feeling unwanted and unloved. They easily misinterpret casual remarks we make to other adults. We remember how painful it was to listen to our parents complain about us, and we refuse to do this to our children. When our children are listening, we avoid complaining about them to other adults.

We affirm our children by telling them frequently how much we enjoy being their parents. We never complain to them about the costs involved in raising them. When we discuss the cost of hockey skates, musical instruments and lessons, prom dresses, class rings, class trips, college, and so on, we deal with the financial facts and the reality of our budgets, without blaming our kids for the high cost of these things. We tell them what we can and cannot afford without blaming anyone.

I let my children know that they're worth far more to me than money.

Evil

. . . .

*B*eing raised in dysfunctional families was different for each of us. Oddly enough, many of us had at least one parent who saw to it that we led sheltered lives in a fairy tale world where all stories had happy endings. Evil didn't exist in our world. (Or, at least, no one admitted it did.) We were exhorted to live by the golden rule. Our codependent parent taught us to believe we could reform mean and cruel people by showering them with kindness.

Some of us were long exploited in abusive marriages before we realized that our partners were basically evil and beyond the reach of generosity and healing kindness. We eventually faced the limits of our love and patience and chose to save ourselves before we were destroyed. We are coming to understand that evil does exist in the world. We are learning to recognize the evil some people commit and respond accordingly.

We are teaching our children that all stories do not have happy endings, and that some people will never return the kindness that is shown to them. We don't want our children to become cynical and mistrusting, but neither do we want them to be easy marks for charming cons who will exploit their kindness and generosity. We are teaching our children to be able to recognize the presence of evil and to get away from it as quickly as possible.

Facing the world honestly, for me and my children, means, in part, acknowledging evil.

Divorce

Some of us remember terrible fights between our parents before and after their divorces. We were frightened and confused by their anger and the terrible things they told us about each other. They tried to force us to take sides in their power struggles. Some of us were coerced into spying when we spent time with one parent or the other. We learned to lie and cover up facts and details to try to keep peace between them.

Those of us who get divorced are determined to protect our children from the abuses we experienced when our parents divorced. We accept responsibility for our choices without feeling responsible for our children's feelings. We recognize the dangers of feeling sorry for our children or feeling guilty about our divorces. We watch for things that trigger our guilt so we can change our attitudes about them.

We are helping our children accept the reality of our divorce without trying to compensate them for their loss. We allow them to express their anger and sorrow without stifling their feelings and without trying to make it all better. By listening to their feelings of frustration and loss, we help them adjust to their new reality. We never ask our children to spy on their other parent or to give us details about their visits.

Helping my children adjust to my divorce without feeling defensive or guilty helps my recovery.

Obligation

. . . .

*M*ost of us wanted to have children. Once we had them, however, we often longed for the freedom we enjoyed before they were born. We sometimes felt trapped by our children. We wanted to experience the joys of children without the burdens and responsibilities. Some of us left our children unattended for hours while we got high. Or we resented what having children made us do—work regularly, lead reasonably scheduled lives.

In recovery, we realized that our lives are the result of our choices. We have no obligations, only choices. We used to manipulate ourselves by calling our desires and choices obligations. In this way we could complain about them and feel resentful. It was our desire to have children. We made choices based on that desire. Now we are aligning our daily lives to reflect our desires and choices. And we focus on what we have chosen instead of what we don't have.

We cheerfully arrange our activities to reflect our desires and choices. Because we freely chose to be parents, we no longer compare our lives with those who party every night. Instead, we associate with other parents who spend time with their children, who take their children to church, soccer practice, Little League, piano lessons, youth choir. For many of us, this is a radically new way of looking at our lives.

Seeing my parenting as a choice makes me a more joyful parent.

Golden Rule

. . . .

*M*any of us become codependent caretakers and people pleasers in futile attempts to keep our parents sober and ourselves from being abused. Although we were unsuccessful on both counts, we nonetheless continued in our codependent behavior patterns. In our adult relationships, we tried to control others by using our generosity, kindness, and consideration to manipulate them into meeting our needs. Because we didn't say no to their requests, we expected them to say yes to ours.

In recovery, we are learning to both ask for what we expect in a relationship and to maintain our boundaries. We no longer try to manipulate others with generosity. If we need something, we ask for it. If someone takes advantage of our generosity, we readjust it. We are learning when to make exceptions to our rule of doing unto others as we'd have them do unto us. We don't allow ourselves to be taken in by those who would exploit our generosity.

We are teaching our children that the general rules of generosity and kindness have exceptions. Some people will try to take advantage of their generosity. We let them know that it is okay to modify their behavior when someone takes advantage of them, while encouraging them to continue living by the rule that one person's kindness and generosity brings out the kindness and generosity in others.

I encourage my children to be up front in their kindness and generosity and clear about asking for what they need in return.

Demanding Appreciation

. . . .

*B*efore we began our recovery, we often manipulated our children by demanding signs of appreciation from them as conditions for meeting their needs. When they needed a ride to ball practice, money for the school carnival, or help with a project, we manipulated the situations by demanding they express appreciation for everything we did for them. We thought we were teaching them respect. We controlled them by refusing to help them until they conformed to our expectations.

When some of our older children got in trouble, perhaps ending up in treatment and recovery, we could not understand why our children were so resentful and defiant toward us. We saw them as demanding, spoiled kids who had to be taught to respect their parents. In our parents support group, we learn the importance of meeting our children's needs without manipulating them for our ego needs.

We've learned to resist the temptation to manipulate our children whenever they make a request of us. Now we listen to their requests and respond on the basis of principle. If their request is a reasonable one, and we are able to fulfill it, we do. If it seems unreasonable, we tell them so. If, for any reason, we are either unable or unwilling to fulfill their request, we tell them so, without blaming them for our decision.

I no longer manipulate my children when they ask for my help.

Noncompete

· ·

*W*hen we were first divorced, we were overly sensitive to comparisons between ourselves and our former partners. We did everything we could to be perfect parents. We were determined to be all things to our children so they wouldn't miss their other parents. We tried to make them happy every moment and distracted them whenever they talked about their other parents. We became so obsessed with being better parents than our exes that we eventually became anxious, irritable, and depressed.

In our single parents support group we're learning to trust ourselves and avoid making comparisons. We discovered that all divorced parents have at least some competitive feelings with their exes about parenting and that this is normal. We've begun to keep our competitive feelings in check so we don't become obsessed with proving our worth to our children. We've experienced a great sense of relief in being able to talk about these feelings with other parents who know what we are going through.

We no longer compare our parenting or our financial means with that of our former partners. Instead, we are learning to be with our children, enjoying the wonderful privilege of having them as a part of our lives. By focusing on what we have together, instead of envying others, we keep things in a healthy perspective.

I no longer compete with my former partner for the parent of the year award.

Addicted to Love

. . . .

*S*ome of us were so addicted to love that we could not function. We went from one broken heart to another and from one broken marriage to another. Because our addiction was an obsession with romantic relationships, and not a substance addiction, we went for years without recognizing our problem. No one could satisfy our craving for mood altering, romantic interludes because our fantasies had little connection with reality. All relationships eventually fell short of our romantic scripts and failed to sustain the emotional high we craved.

When the shell of our denial finally crashed into the wall of reality, we could no longer deceive ourselves. We began attending a Twelve-Step recovery group where we learned we were not alone. We heard others describe the hell they'd gone through and the losses they'd sustained while pursuing the perfect love affair. We began tearing down our walls of silence and sharing our pain and loneliness.

We're finding courage to feel our feelings and not run from them. We're facing our loneliness and actually talking about it with group members instead of running out to get a fix from a new romance. When we feel the craving for romantic attention and touch, we look inward to identify the feeling that we are trying to medicate. Once we uncover the feeling, we talk about it rather than act out.

Accepting my need for honest intimacy, I selectively share my inner thoughts and feelings rather than chase after a magical romance.

Approval Seeking

. . . .

*M*any of us have been overly dependent on the approval of others for most of our lives. As children, we were so afraid to disappoint our parents that we did as we were told and carefully patterned our lives after their expectations. As teenagers, we transferred this approval seeking to our peer group. Our parents were scandalized when we began following the crowd, especially when it meant violating their morals. They did not see how their demand for obedience contributed to our dependency.

In recovery, we begin to understand the price we paid for our dependency on the approval of others. Our dependency drove us to mistrust and abandon ourselves. We automatically discounted our own feelings, needs, thoughts, and opinions and overvalued those of others, especially people who were important to us. As different people became important to us at different times in our lives, our behavior, and even our values, changed. As adults, we were codependent with our partners and our children.

We are teaching our children to value their own needs, feelings, thoughts, and opinions at an early age so they will be able to deal with pressure from their peers when they become adolescents. We are careful not to praise them for conforming to our views or being too eager to please us. Although it is flattering to have obedient children, we prefer that they develop appropriate boundaries and personal integrity.

I gently discourage exaggerated approval seeking in my children.

Spare the Rod

. . . .

A U G U S T   3 0

*A*lthough we hated being beaten by our parents, many of us did the same thing to our children. We believed that "spare the rod, spoil the child" meant we needed to spank our children to teach them respect for our authority and to keep them from becoming spoiled brats. We didn't know how else to control them, and we couldn't stand the thought of bratty kids talking back to us.

As we have grown in our recovery, we have come to better understand our feelings and the feelings of our children. We no longer believe in corporal punishment, or physically abusing our children, in the name of discipline. We are now learning to manage our frustration without taking it out on our children. Although we used to justify hitting our children by claiming we were following the authority of the Bible, in fact, we ignored all the biblical teachings about patience, love, and respect.

Now we discipline our children with firm words and consistent behavior. We no longer use abuse or threats of abuse to control them. Instead, we explain the consequences of disobedience and calmly carry out these consequences if they disobey. Now we realize the biblical proverb referred to the shepherd's rod, which he used to guide and protect his sheep but not to beat them.

I protect my children with the guiding rod of discipline.

Negative Thoughts

. . . .

We used to poison our minds with negative thoughts and feelings about our children. We began by dwelling on minor incidents in which they were upset with us. We mentally projected these incidents into huge blow-ups in which we imagined our children screaming, even threatening to get even by running away from home or filing abuse charges. These negative thoughts disturbed us so much that we were angry and resentful toward our children.

In our recovery, we learned that dwelling on negative thoughts and feelings is a common experience among alcoholics and addicts. We are learning to recognize these thoughts and feelings, and deal with them immediately, before they take over our minds. We name them as a part of our old addictive way of living. We take responsibility for our thoughts by keeping our minds focused on reality, and not on the negative projections of our imagination.

We refuse to dwell on negative thoughts and feelings about our children. If there is an issue we need to face with one of our children, we talk it over immediately. If we are scaring ourselves with anxious and fearful thoughts about our inadequacy, we use our recovery program to help us deal with these feelings. We talk about these feelings with our partners and other group members and turn it over to our Higher Power.

I refuse to poison my mind and my life by dwelling on negative thoughts and feelings about my children.

Serendipity

· ·

*M*any of us used to feel that if we didn't have bad luck, we wouldn't have any luck at all. We felt that God's providence was a joke, and we saw no signs of good fortune in our desperate lives. Some of us actually felt as if we lived under a curse of some kind. Others developed a kind of negative superstition in which we expected bad things to happen to us and dared anything good to happen.

When we began our recovery, many of us were not interested in the spiritual part. The notion that a benevolent power was at work in the universe seemed like a cruel joke. All of our experiences told us the universe was impersonal, at best, and, more probably, a hostile place. However, the witness of members of our step group finally opened us to experimenting with the concept of a Higher Power. Once we opened our minds the least bit to God's love, startling things began to happen. We began experiencing surprising coincidences. Good things began happening to us in most unexpected ways.

When we described these events to members of our step group, some of them smiled knowingly, as if they were not the least bit surprised. Now we are encouraging our children to expect good things and positive outcomes in their lives. We discourage them from making the kind of negative projections we used to make.

I thank God for the providence that surprises me daily.

Admiration

. . . .

*W*e used to feel uncomfortable when people gave us compliments. We insisted we were undeserving, or we did our "Aw shucks, it was nothing" routine, which was supposed to distract attention from us and quickly change the subject. Compliments made us self-conscious, especially about our conduct. We carried so much guilt about our behavior from our pre-recovery days that we didn't want anyone to pay attention to our conduct.

As we grow in our recovery, more and more people are giving us compliments, especially members of our Twelve-Step group. They also confront us immediately if we blow off compliments. We are learning that compliments are gifts, and the proper response is to say thank you, even if we believe the gift is the wrong size and doesn't fit us perfectly.

We're learning to be gracious receivers. It has not been easy to accept the admiration of our children. While we want them to admire and look up to us, we are uncomfortable being on their pedestal. What if we slip or let them down? We're learning to gracefully accept their admiration, just as we accept compliments from adults. We resist the temptation to shock them with horror stories from our past. By accepting the reality that we will disappoint them at times, we no longer drive ourselves to be perfect.

I gracefully accept the admiration of my children.

Inner Resources

. . . .

*O*ur parents did everything they could to keep us dependent on them for advice and support. They tried to make themselves indispensable in our lives. We don't want to keep our children chained to us the way our parents did. We want them to develop independence and self-reliance. We intend to gradually work ourselves out of the job of parenting rather than perpetuate it, like many of our parents. They still try to tell us how to run our lives and raise our children.

We have grown in self-reliance through our recovery, and we want to share this gift with our children. As we break the chains of codependency with our parents, we become aware of our codependency with our children. In recovery, we have found powerful inner resources that we want to share with our children. The most important of these is our Higher Power. Now we can stand up to those who would enslave us with their conditional demands because we know we are loved unconditionally.

We are helping our children develop their self-reliance by introducing them to their own Higher Power. By feeling this unconditional love, they, too, can resist those who would seek to enslave them with conditional demands. As they become stronger in their self-confidence and trust their inner voice, they can take care of themselves in all their relationships.

Sharing my story of liberation, through the help of my Higher Power, with my children helps them develop their own inner resources.

Battle of Wills

*M*any of our parents tried to control us, forcing us to do things we didn't want to do. We resisted as much as we could without getting beaten up, physically or emotionally. For some of us, the physical abuse stopped the day we stood up for ourselves and successfully fought back. For others, the abuse only changed forms as we got older. We don't want to engage our children in a battle of wills this way. We want to have relaxed and friendly relationships with them, not ones based on power, domination, and threats.

With other parents in recovery, we are learning to keep our egos out of our parenting. We used to look at every discussion with our children as an opportunity to show them who was boss and to make them mind us. We were obsessed with controlling them. After all, good parents had children who were under control, well-behaved, smart, and more. However, our children were becoming defiant and emotionally closed.

We are learning to influence our children by example and gentle persuasion rather than through domination and control. We go out of our way to avoid a battle of wills. We encourage them to eat well-balanced meals through our example, not by engaging in mealtime battles. We recommend vegetables, for example, and gently encourage our kids to try them, without forcing them to.

I avoid power struggles with my children by keeping my ego out of my parenting.

Letting Go

· ·

When we complained to our parents that someone called us names or said something nasty to us, we were told, "Just ignore it. Let it go in one ear and out the other." We were taught to repress unpleasant feelings. We learned this so well that it became automatic, and soon we were out of touch with ourselves. We didn't know what we felt, what we liked, what we didn't like, or when we were being abused.

In recovery, we gradually regained our self-awareness, and learned to identify our feelings. As we learned to listen to our inner child, we uncovered years of buried pain and sorrow. We are feeling the feelings, naming the feelings, and letting go of the past. We are re-parenting ourselves by giving ourselves permission to experience all our feelings before we name them and let them go.

We are careful not to teach our children to repress all their unpleasant feelings. When they are upset, we encourage them to express their feelings through their tears and their words. Only after they have gotten all their hurt out and experienced emotional relief do we help them let go and move on. We are teaching them to let go of their resentments in order to be free, but only after they have owned them and expressed them.

Encouraging my children and myself to express our unpleasant feelings helps free us to move on.

Favors

. . . .

Whenever we asked our parents for favors, they would get something from us in return. They had counter-demands on the tips of their tongues. They never did anything for us without extracting promises or favors from us first. The more important our requests were to us, the more they demanded in return. They took advantage of our dependence on them to barter for their ego needs. Of course, we stopped asking them for anything as soon as we could do for ourselves or get help from others.

With our recovery, we are learning to respond to our children's requests without thinking they will take advantage of us the way our parents did. We say no to unreasonable requests without feeling guilty. We review each request on its merit, instead of reacting to the number of requests they have made or to our fatigue at the moment. We are letting our kids be kids and acting like adults ourselves.

We don't barter favors with our children. When we want favors from them, we ask them politely and respectfully. If they refuse, we may express our disappointment, but we don't retaliate by refusing to consider their next request. We only request favors when we are open to their refusal. If they don't have a choice in the matter, like going to school, we insist rather than ask.

I respond to my children's requests directly, without bargaining with them for things I may need.

Honesty

. . . .

*M*any of us were lied to so often as children that we learned to believe our parents only when we could verify what they told us. They seemed to tell the truth only in situations where there was nothing to be gained by reshaping the story to make themselves look better. We want our children to be able to both trust that we are telling the truth and tell the truth themselves.

We were not exactly devoted to the truth when we began our recovery. Now honesty has become a very important part of our lives. As we grow in our recovery, we continue to uncover subtle aspects of our lying, like denial. Many of us, for example, have an automatic tendency to deny our true feelings when our children ask us if we are angry or upset. In the past, we had never thought of this as dishonesty.

We help our children develop the habit of telling the truth when we respond to them in ways that reinforce truth telling. When they tell us the truth about feeling sad or angry we acknowledge their truth. When we know they have lied to us, we confront them on their lie. When they tell the truth about something they have done wrong, we first acknowledge that they told the truth. Only then do we consider consequences for what they did wrong.

I am making it as easy as I can for my children to develop the truth habit.

Experience Mistakes

. . . .

We want our children to learn from their errors. We don't want them to be so afraid of making mistakes that they are unable to take risks. We remember being humiliated by our parents for making mistakes. They laughed at us and told our relatives about what we'd done. They seemed to enjoy our humiliation and claimed that it taught us lessons. The only lessons we learned were to avoid risks and avoid letting our parents know what we were doing.

In our recovery, we understand the terrible toll humiliation took on our spirit. When humiliation was used to discipline us, something within us was destroyed. Our spirit was crushed, and we retreated into a shell of cynicism. We associated humiliation with making mistakes and learned the wrong lesson. We didn't learn that mistakes are a normal part of living.

We don't force our children to grovel or wallow in their mistakes. While we do discuss their mistakes with them, we do not talk to other family members about them or call attention to them. We never laugh at them when they make mistakes or use them in our storytelling. We are sensitive to their feelings when they mess up and, at the same time, impress on them that making mistakes is normal. We tell them about similar errors we made at their age.

I do not deliberately embarrass my children when they make mistakes.

New Models

. . . .

*M*any of us who are raising our children alone grew up in traditional two-parent families. Much of what we learned about parenting from watching our parents raise us does not apply to our situations. We can't turn on the auto-pilot and drift through our parenting years, like some of our friends seem to be doing. We are juggling career demands with parenting responsibilities—all too often finding our-selves exhausted and resentful. We have no time for ourselves.

Our single parents support group provides us with some very good models that we didn't have before. We're hearing how other single parents get together for weekend outings with their children to get support and companionship for themselves, as well as to give their children a richer social ex-perience. By talking with others about time management and balancing priorities, we are learning some of the tricks others use to maximize their efficiency.

We are learning to invent ourselves as single parents through reading, discussions, and observing those single par-ents we admire. This learning process is no different than learning any other skill. It takes dedication, patience, and the willingness to learn from mistakes. Finding new models was an important beginning. We no longer feel inferior to married parents. We have come to see the single parent experience in a positive light and not as a poor substitute for the real thing.

I am enjoying my new role as a single parent.

Viewpoints

. . . .

*M*ost of us experienced little or no respect for our viewpoints as children. Our parents did not respect us or our ideas. Our teachers were more concerned with teaching their ideas than listening to ours. We were ignored, put down, or scolded when we tried to express original thoughts. We came to expect that our thoughts and opinions would be ignored until we became adults.

Once we became adults, the respect we longed for did not automatically occur. By then we were too easily discouraged to support our ideas in conversations with other adults. We were quickly defeated and easily talked out of our viewpoints because we lacked the necessary self-confidence to stand up for ourselves. We learned to avoid discussions where ideas were disputed, even when we held strong viewpoints. Some of us felt intellectually inferior just because we lacked self-confidence.

We want our children to be self-confident. This includes confidence in their ability to think and arrive at their own conclusions. We help them develop self-confidence by encouraging them to express their ideas. We can respect their viewpoints, even when we don't agree with them. Listening respectfully to their views is like looking at the world with an open mind and fresh eyes. We encourage them to express their thoughts. We enjoy watching them develop the ability to think for themselves.

Respecting my children's viewpoints encourages them to express themselves and opens up new perspectives for all of us.

Compassion

. . . .

*W*hen we first began our recovery, we tried too hard to do everything right. We became so impatient with ourselves that we increased, rather than decreased, our guilt. We wanted to experience all the benefits of sobriety immediately. We misunderstood some of the steps and misapplied others. For example, we failed to understand the purpose of a searching moral inventory and abused ourselves with this step by using it for self-punishment.

As we grew in our recovery, we came to understand that all the steps were designed to free us from our feelings of worthlessness, shame, and guilt. We made amends with ourselves and gradually ended our old pattern of self-punishment. We came to see our perfectionism as a disguise for self-hate. Where we once took pride in our high standards, we now take pride in the compassion we feel toward ourselves. Our inner dialogue has now become gentle and peaceful, instead of harsh and punitive.

As we grow in patience and compassion toward ourselves, we feel more spiritual. Our spirituality has blossomed in our recovery. We feel closer to God and closer to those around us. As we become more compassionate toward ourselves, we are less critical and faultfinding with members of our family. We are happier each day, and more optimistic about the future. We finally understand the meaning of the slogan, "easy does it."

I am becoming my own best friend by treating myself with compassion.

Learning to Help Others

· ·

We were not encouraged to reach out to help others when we were growing up. Our parents maintained that we should stay at home and help around the house. They did not reach out to others in need. When we talked of helping those less fortunate than ourselves, our parents remarked that charity begins at home. They felt we should mind our own business and let people help themselves.

Most of us were loners who felt we had nothing to offer others. We were uncomfortable around people we didn't know because we'd been taught to mind our own business and not to go looking for trouble. In recovery, we discovered the joy that comes from reaching out to others and sharing the freedom and renewal we have found in the program. This kind of connecting and sharing with others was a new experience for many of us.

We're helping our children experience the personal enjoyment that comes from helping others. We want them to have the sense of satisfaction that comes from getting outside their own problems and concerns by helping others. We encourage them to get involved in things like tutoring, visiting shut-ins, or painting houses for the elderly. We're pleased to see them becoming more mature, sensitive, and less materialistic.

My children and I are discovering the sense of satisfaction that comes from helping others.

Pressure

· ·

*M*any of us have habitually put tasks and projects off as long as possible. In school, we wrote all our term papers on the nights before they were due. Eventually, we became addicted to the adrenaline rush we felt when we were under extreme time pressures. We created a lifestyle of crisis management in which we were unable to motivate ourselves to do anything until the very last minute. Our performance suffered as we struggled with incompletes, shoddy results, and serious motivation problems.

A crisis-management lifestyle, not uncommon among alcoholics, is related to self-esteem. Those of us with low self-esteem often fail to act until it is too late, perhaps because we aren't sure we deserve to succeed. People with good self-esteem organize their time to avoid crises. We are learning to think of planning as a way of being kind to a future state of ourselves.

We want our children to learn to plan ahead so they won't become addicted to crises and deadlines. We want them to have good self-esteem. We're helping them develop good study habits while they are still young. We encourage them to think about that future moment when their assignments are due and to make friends with that future person. As they begin to think differently about themselves, they're developing better work habits.

Helping my children plan ahead builds their self-esteem.

Serenity

. . . .

*S*ome of our parents were so easily overwhelmed that we learned not to tell them about our crises. When we did, they hit the panic button, making things worse. Then we had to calm them down as well as deal with the crisis. We learned to handle things for ourselves, though often badly because of our inexperience. We either become overly cool and detached or hysterical in crisis.

In recovery, we are learning how to deal with our feelings in critical situations. We neither deny our feelings and act in heartless ways nor act on our hysterical impulses. We ask, in the words of the serenity prayer, for the courage to change the things we can, serenity to accept the things we can't change, and the wisdom to know the difference. The Cool Cucumbers among us may need more wisdom while the Chicken Littles may need more serenity.

We can keep our feelings in check when our children come to us with crises. Even though we often feel anxious and scared on the inside, we do everything we can to give our children our undivided attention. We share the principles of accepting what we can't change and courageously changing what we can with our children so they can begin to sort out their own crises without becoming withdrawn or overwhelmed. And we don't forget to help them ask for wisdom to keep their thinking clear.

The serenity prayer is a major resource for myself and my children in times of crisis.

Accepting My Body

. . . .

*S*ome of us have been self-consciously disappointed with our bodies as long as we can remember. As children, we may have been teased about being fat and forced to go on diets or about being skinny and compelled to eat "fattening" foods. Consequently, we have struggled with weight, appearance, and self-acceptance ever since. We have struggled to accept our physical appearance as good enough. We fail to realize that our bodies are perfect and beautiful in their function and efficiency. We want our children to be free from the curse of self-consciousness and physical perfectionism.

We came into recovery in desperate need of serenity. We discovered a serenity that involves acceptance of our bodies as a gift from God. It was impossible to be self-accepting when we were self-conscious, embarrassed, and ashamed of our bodies. By accepting our physical selves, we have become more accepting of ourselves as a whole. This liberating discovery lets us experience a new joy and freedom. We no longer obsess over our physical appearance.

We're teaching our children to accept their bodies gracefully, rather than obsess about weight and eating. We are careful to avoid calling attention to their weight or their physique. When we take them shopping, we give them positive strokes about their appearance as they try on new clothes. We gently challenge any negative remarks they make about their appearance without discounting their feelings.

When I accept my body, I teach my children to accept their bodies.

Responsible

· ·

"*T*his hurts me more than it does you," our parents said over our loud screaming protests as they proceeded to spank us. They told us they didn't want to spank us or punish us in other ways, but we had given them no choice in the matter. They blamed us for making them punish us. They refused to accept their responsibility or authority as parents. They wanted us to believe they preferred being friendly but, instead, our behavior forced them to be punitive.

In our parents support group we are learning to accept our roles as disciplinarian. We no longer apologize for setting limits for our children or for holding them accountable for their behavior. We are learning to administer discipline calmly and firmly, without abusing them or blaming them for our actions. When we administer consequences that were previously agreed upon, we do it without a long speech defending our actions. By carrying out discipline without words, we avoid verbal escalation that used to end in abuse.

We accept the unpleasant parts of the parenting role. We no longer act as if our self-esteem depends solely on whether or not our children like us at the moment. We are doing the hard tasks of setting limits, holding our children accountable, and administering appropriate discipline when it is needed. We take full responsibility for our actions, and we don't blame them for making us do something we don't want to do.

Accepting my parenting responsibilities helps my children grow responsibly.

Asking for Support

. . . .

*A*s children we learned to expect nothing. We learned to look out for ourselves and never rely on others. We ignored our needs as much as possible, especially our emotional needs. Appearing needy exposed us to disappointment, rejection, and ridicule. We regarded needy people as suckers, fools, and weaklings.

Hiding our needs did not eliminate them, however. In fact, we were exceptionally needy because of the chaos and uncertainty we lived with. We developed ingenious denial mechanisms to hide our needs, both from ourselves and others. Although we successfully buried our needs from our consciousness, they reappeared in inappropriate behavior, such as promiscuity, abusing alcohol, working eighty-hour weeks.

In recovery, we've begun to see that our dysfunctional behavior patterns are indirect ways of getting our emotional needs met. As we become more honest with ourselves concerning our needs, we make direct requests for emotional support. We ask for hugs from our partners, children, and close friends. We ask for words of reassurance when we feel distant. We teach our children to accept their needs and ask directly. They learn this much more quickly than we are able to. The ease with which they ask helps us stay on track in our lives. We notice that we are less irritable with our children when our emotional needs are being met.

When I need emotional support, I ask instead of act out.

Changing Commitments

. . . .

S E P T E M B E R   1 8

*W*e were not allowed to change our commitments as children. Once we agreed to join a club, work on a project, accept employment, or go with friends to a concert, our parents would not allow us to change our minds or back out of our commitments. They indoctrinated us on the hazards of being quitters. We often felt trapped by our commitments. We became overly cautious and devoid of all spontaneity.

In recovery, we're learning the importance of listening to our inner voice. When prior commitments we made feel wrong, or no longer seem in our best interest, we renegotiate them. We are learning to review our choices and decisions and to change the ones that no longer fit. While we take our commitments seriously, we respect and honor our feelings when they tell us something no longer feels right.

Now we are teaching our children how to carefully review their choices and to listen to their own inner voices when something doesn't feel right. Although we don't want them to become impulsive and unreliable, we do want them to respect their feelings and develop good judgment. By allowing our children to back out of some of their commitments, we encourage them to develop their own review processes. When they know they can review their choices, it is easier for them to be spontaneous.

I support my children's rights, as well as my own,
to review commitments.

God's Will

. . . .

SEPTEMBER 19

Some of us were oppressed by parents who used religion as a form of mind control. They taught us that if we really wanted to do something, this meant that it was our will and not God's. And if we really hated to do something, this meant that it was God's will. They also threatened us with God, saying he would punish us if we disobeyed their authority. By the time we learned to ignore their religious threats, we were alienated from them and from God. We did not know God's love and did not seek his will for our lives.

In recovery, we discovered a Higher Power that loves us and supports our happiness, serenity, and fulfillment. We found people who are deeply spiritual, without being controlling and judgmental. We seek God's will without fear that he will command us to do things we hate. We are discovering that God wants us to have abundant lives, not depressing, joyless lives filled with shame and guilt.

We tell our children about God's love and acceptance of them. We teach them to seek God's will in their lives, knowing that his will for them will always be loving and just. We tell them God wants good things for their lives. We never tell them that God wants to punish them. We will never abuse religion the way our parents did.

Together my children and I are learning to seek God's will in our lives.

265

Fear of Parenting

· ·

*W*hen we began raising children, we had many fears, including the fear that something awful would happen to them because of our sins. We were afraid we wouldn't know what to do when they were sick. We were afraid they would electrocute themselves in an outlet, drink poison, or get run over in the street. We tried to cover up these fears by distracting ourselves and denying our feelings. One of our darkest fears was that we would pass on to them our own insecurities.

In recovery, we're learning to be honest and humble about our fears. We no longer wish to hide our humanness from others. We began by openly admitting that we're afraid of many things regarding our children. We discovered we were not alone. Most parents have had similar fears from time to time. When we admitted our fears, they began to subside and lose their power over us.

We're learning to accept our humanness and relax with our children. We put our faith in our Higher Power and not in ourselves or our ability to provide our children with perfect security. As we share more honestly with other parents, we no longer feel strange and different. We can face a teacher's conference without undue anxiety. We no longer obsess about being blamed by school officials for being terrible parents.

I am learning to trust myself as a parent.

Detachment

. . . .

*O*ur children used to provoke us to anger on a daily basis. We were always yelling at them or spanking them. They drove us crazy with their constant bickering, haranguing, and whining. By the end of the day, we were totally exhausted and very crabby. We felt ashamed of the unloving thoughts and feelings we harbored toward them and guilty about our harsh words and rough behaviors. We promised ourselves that we would do better tomorrow, but tomorrow was always the same.

In recovery groups, we began to learn how to manage our feelings and moods, no matter what was happening around us. We began to find serenity in the midst of chaos. We were introduced to the concept of emotional detachment. Although we already knew how to check out mentally, we did not know how to detach from someone's provocative behavior without withdrawing completely. We're learning how to detach from our children's annoying behavior without withdrawing from them emotionally. We can talk to them while ignoring their behavior.

When our children are overly demanding, we tell them no, give them one reasonable explanation, and refuse to let them draw us into long arguments. We simply smile at them and refuse to answer their demands. We think about all their precious qualities while we tune out their voices. When they are unable to engage us in arguments, they stop. We feel better about ourselves and better about them.

I practice compassionate detachment from my children's annoying behavior.

Needs

. . . .

*M*any of us have difficulty recognizing our needs. As children we never discovered our own needs. Our parents told us what we did and didn't need. We weren't allowed to think about them ourselves. When we were told we didn't need a new skirt or shirt we had asked for, we learned three things: (1) we weren't capable of perceiving our own needs, (2) our needs weren't worthy, and (3) not to ask to have our needs met. As adults, it is difficult for us to recognize our needs or feel entitled to get them met.

Our recovery makes us aware of how little we have expected for ourselves and how much we have given to others. Many of us, in fact, became supposed experts at knowing what our spouses and children needed before they knew themselves. But we were so accustomed to ignoring our own emotional needs that we were not in touch with them. Now we're learning to monitor our feelings in order to recognize our own needs.

We don't try to tell our children what they need or don't need. We want them to recognize their needs and tell us what they are. If they ask us for something unreasonable or something we can't provide, we may not give it to them, but we won't scold them for asking. We never tell them the reason is that they don't need it.

Knowing my own needs helps me respect my children's knowledge about what they need.

Depression

· ·

*M*any of us were not allowed to express our feelings as children, especially anger. In fact, we hardly knew anger was a feeling. To us, anger meant enraged behavior. Only adults were allowed to rage. We stuffed our feelings of anger and became depressed. Some of us suffered from serious, clinical depression, while others experienced chronic, low-level, undiagnosed depression. We were labeled as shy, quiet, or moody kids.

Recovery teaches us the importance of owning and expressing our feelings. At first, we were afraid of acknowledging or expressing our feelings because of the pain involved. As we gradually learned to identify our feelings, we uncovered a reservoir of anger that had been festering for years. We are learning to let it out a little at a time. In our group we heard the slogan, "Name it, claim it, and tame it." As we name our feelings and take responsibility for them, they lose their power over us.

We're teaching our children that it is not only okay, but healthy, to express their anger appropriately. We teach them to recognize their anger and help them find words to express it. We don't tolerate verbal abuse in expressing anger. We teach them to speak for themselves and not blame others for their anger. As they learn to own and express their angry feelings, they have more energy and vitality and fewer signs of depression.

I can help my children recognize and express their anger when I recognize and express my own.

Long Arguments

· ·

We used to get drawn into long-winded arguments with our teenagers in which tempers flared and fights erupted. We felt set up by them and often lost control of our temper. They seemed to enjoy getting us riled up. They loved to draw us into silly arguments, especially about rules and expectations. We usually felt guilty after losing our temper in these arguments. We hated feeling out of control, especially around our children.

In the process of our recovery, we've learned to control our temper by dealing with feelings before they build into destructive forces. We also practice impulse control. Where we used to explode when we were upset, we now let out our feelings in more moderate ways. We are also more aware of the specific situations that tend to make us boil. We've learned to change the things we say to ourselves in these situations and thus reduce our inner stress.

We're learning to avoid being drawn into futile arguments with our teenagers. We say, "I can see that on this issue we will not agree." This puts a respectful end to silly arguments as well as disputes that have no possible resolution. Teenagers are rarely open to being persuaded when they argue with their parents. They fear losing face if they back down. We can refrain from unnecessary conflicts with our teenagers without assaulting their dignity.

I am avoiding long-winded arguments with my teenagers.

Feeling Trapped

. . . .

*B*efore we came into the Twelve-Step program, we felt frustrated by situations in which we felt we had no choice. Disciplining our children was one big one. Although we felt guilty about spanking them when they wouldn't mind us, there seemed to be nothing else we could do, short of ignoring their disobedience. Spanking only made them more defiant and aggressive, however.

In recovery, we've discovered that God is able to show us a way when there is no way. He turns our dead ends into living opportunities for amazing growth and discovery. In the past, we were too arrogant to look beyond ourselves to a Higher Power and too proud to ask for help. We were often overwhelmed, not only by the serious problems we faced, but by the normal demands of life.

We are learning to trust our Higher Power for direction and help. Now, when we feel frustrated and out of options for dealing with our children, we ask God for help. We stop trying to do everything ourselves and turn the situation over to our Higher Power. Trusting our Higher Power to help us cope with everyday challenges lightens our load. Once we turn our dilemmas over, we feel an inner peace. We no longer feel helpless, and we're able to ask others for help.

I am learning to let go and let God when I'm frustrated with my children.

Freedom of Religion

. . . .

*T*here was no religious freedom for many of us as children. We were expected to accept our parents' religious beliefs and practices without question. Although some of us were severely punished, even beaten, for daring to challenge our parents' religious beliefs, many of us still rebelled. Others were cut off from the family, both physically and emotionally. Most of us, however, took our religious protest underground. We conformed on the surface but secretly held to our own beliefs underneath.

Recovery has shown us a totally new respect and openness in the area of religious beliefs and spirituality. People talk openly in our Twelve-Step groups about faith and spirituality, and no one gets angry or tries to control the conversation. People actually disagree without arguing. For the first time in our lives, we share our private beliefs without fear of being contradicted, criticized, or condemned. This has been a very healing experience for us.

We extend this freedom to our children. We want them to feel free to talk openly about their religious beliefs, doubts, and problems, without fear of shame or judgment. While we share our beliefs with them, we also tell them their faith is their personal response to the love of God, as they experience it. We are careful not to insist, or even suggest, that our way is the only way.

I respect the religious rights of my children.

Accepting My Partner

. . . .

*W*e wanted to provide our children with a perfect home. We wanted to give them all of the love and security we never had. We wanted them to be happy, well-adjusted, and perfectly behaved at all times. When this didn't happen, we looked for someone to blame—other than ourselves, of course. We blamed our partners for failing to create this storybook family. We criticized their parenting and accused them of causing all the problems in our family.

In recovery, we let go of both our grandiosity and our perfectionism. We begin to accept that we are all human. The more honest we become in accepting ourselves and our shortcomings, the more accepting we are of our partners and their shortcomings. We no longer hide our shame and guilt by criticizing and blaming our partners. When we are disappointed in our children's behavior, we take our own inventory instead of our partners'.

We are learning both to accept and appreciate our partners as team members in parenting. We have come to respect and appreciate the unique gifts we each bring to parenting, instead of feeling a need to apologize for our partners. We let go of the possessiveness we once felt toward our children. We now accept that our partners have the same right to develop a unique parenting relationship with our children as we do.

Accepting the differences my partner and I each bring to parenting enriches my family.

Proof

. . . .

S E P T E M B E R   2 8

At the height of our codependence, we were doing everything we could to prove to our children that we loved them. They, in turn, were naturally doing everything they could to exploit our insecurity. They blamed us for all their problems. They said we didn't love them. In our desperate efforts to prove that we loved them, and to win their favor, we asked them what they wanted from us. The younger ones likely responded with frequent requests for toys, later bedtimes, and other privileges. The older ones gave us a list of demands including concessions on curfews, driving privileges, and a shopping list of the latest fashions. We felt trapped. If we didn't meet some of their demands, they said we didn't love them. On the other hand, when we yielded to their demands, we felt blackmailed.

In recovery, we're learning to resist our children's exploitation. We discover that trying to prove that we love them is codependent. We ask God, not our children, to judge our hearts.

Expressing our love in caring behavior is not the same as proving to them that we love them, however. We're learning to show our love by setting limits, meeting their needs, and enjoying their company. We determine the shape of our love. We have taken our power back, and reassure ourselves that we love our children—not that we always like their attitudes or behaviors.

I no longer try to prove to my children that I love them.

Control

· ·

*W*e used to believe it was our duty as parents to control our children's behavior. We thought well-behaved children were signs of good parenting. We did not respect parents
who could not control their children in public. We felt smug
that our young children did not act up in public. We used
threats and physical punishment to keep them in line at all
times. Needless to say, we were unprepared for their hostility
and defiance when they became adolescents.

By believing that it is possible to control children, and
realizing we could not, we became abusive. Some of us
abused our children for resisting us. Others of us abused ourselves for being spineless, ineffective parents. We abused ourselves with depression, alcohol, food, or other compulsive
behaviors. In our parents support group, we took a first step
with our children. We admitted we were powerless over their
behavior and that our lives had become unmanageable. In recovery, we came to realize that it's a dangerous illusion that
parents have a duty to control their children.

Now we realize that parents cannot absolutely control their
children's behavior unless they handcuff themselves to their
kids' wrists twenty-four hours a day. But we do have a tremendous responsibility to respect them, influence their behavior,
and cultivate their moral development so they will make
responsible decisions for themselves.

*Giving up the illusion that I can, or should, absolutely
control my children frees me to influence them.*

Maintaining My Own Disposition

· ·

Whenever people were upset in our childhood families, they blamed somebody else. If someone felt sad, angry, afraid—somebody else must be at fault. Blame was the response to all negative emotions. We're learning to accept responsibility for our own emotions without blaming others. For instance, we've actually experienced disappointment without wondering who we could blame for making us feel that way.

We're also learning to maintain our own emotional center when others around us are upset. Before we started our recovery, we didn't even know this was a possibility. We believed our feelings and emotions were the direct result of the people or the events around us. It seemed obvious that certain people made us feel bad, and others made us feel good. When we were happy, we knew someone else deserved the credit. When we were upset, we knew that someone else was to blame.

Now we're learning to stay centered when our children are irritable and upset. Their arguments and irritable behavior provoke us more than anyone else's. We get annoyed, impatient, and crabby when they are in bad moods. We're learning to keep ourselves in stable when they are cranky and irritable. We're learning to detach ourselves from their moods without becoming detached from them. We're learning that we're not responsible for their bad moods and vice versa.

I am working to remain in my own good mood, even when my children are crabby.

Promises

· ·

*B*roken promises have been a source of heartache for many of us. We've suffered from broken promises and have caused others to suffer when we broke our promises. Many of us have struggled to overcome the deep suspicion we feel whenever anyone makes a promise to us—whether a boss, clerk, family member, or friend. It was much easier to ignore promises than risk disappointment by getting our hopes up.

When we asked God to remove our defects of character, we made a commitment to be honest with others, including keeping promises. At first, we avoided making promises to others. Eventually, as we gained self-confidence, we began making commitments to others—and keeping them. We soon learned that mutual accountability made our relationships more satisfying and enjoyable. As we repaired the broken trust in our relationships, we began to feel more trusting of others as well.

Now we emphasize the importance of keeping promises with our children. When they fail to keep promises, we confront them by reminding them of the importance of keeping their word. We explain that others feel hurt and discounted when we break our promises. We are careful to model this with our children. When we cannot honor a commitment we have made to them, we acknowledge it immediately and make alternate arrangements. Or we make amends.

I keep the promises I make to my children and encourage them to keep theirs.

Responsibility

. . . .

*M*any of our parents never gave us chances to try our hand at something new if there was a chance we might screw up. They said we had to prove ourselves before they would give us chances to try. Consequently we learned to cook in school, rather than at home. We learned to drive, work on cars, use power tools, bake, sew, fish, and hunt with the help of other adults—relatives, teachers, or our friends' parents.

From our parents, we learned the lesson that it's our job to keep our children from making mistakes. Even though we had to learn lots of things by trial and error, we still saw it as the worst possible way to learn something. In our recovery, we focus on learning from our mistakes and on helping our children learn from theirs. We are creating an atmosphere where they can make mistakes without fear.

Like most parents, we want our children to take on more responsibilities as they grow older. We are learning to downplay the shame of mistake making and encourage our kids to learn by trying. We ask our teenagers to drive the family to church when they get their learner's permit. We ask them to bake, check the oil in the car, split firewood, and barbecue burgers for the family.

I give my children opportunities to learn and grow within the family, with no penalty for making mistakes.

Abuse

. . . .

*E*motional abuse was so common in our childhood families that we took it for granted and thought it was normal. In many cases, our parents were raised in strict homes where verbal abuse, shame, humiliation, and physical punishment were used as training methods. Harsh training methods were not uncommon in past generations. Children were often whipped, beaten, forced to labor in harsh conditions, shamed, humiliated with dunce caps, and called hurtful names.

In the process of our recovery, we've begun to recognize emotional abuse. As we begin to understand the importance of good self-esteem, we realize how damaging harsh words can be. Comments we once regarded as humorous, we now recognize as abusive. We now recognize certain belittling gestures and remarks, which we used to try to ignore, as abusive. We recognize passive behavior, like being ignored while speaking, as emotional abuse. As we learn to respect ourselves and others, we no longer tolerate abuse of any kind.

We can now recognize emotional and verbal abuse within our families. We teach our children to express their feelings in ways that do not involve verbal abuse. When our children call each other hurtful names, we intervene, telling them in no un-certain terms they may not call names, no matter how angry they are. We reassure them they are entitled to their feelings, whether anger, hurt, or frustration, and we explain ways of expressing feelings without name calling.

I am teaching my children to express their frustration without being verbally abusive.

Pity

. . . .

*M*any of us have suffered from low self-esteem for most of our lives. We felt so inadequate and self-conscious that we had difficulty socializing and developing close relationships. The only people we felt we could get close to were those we felt sorry for or looked down on. We took comfort in knowing there were persons more pathetic than we. We were drawn to others with low self-esteem. We confused pity with love, and many of us attracted emotionally crippled partners.

In recovery our self-esteem has improved to the point that we no longer feel beneath others. We regard ourselves as equals and relate more gracefully to all people. We understand the difference between compassion and genuine love on the one hand and feeling sorry for people on the other. We no longer feel drawn toward people with serious emotional problems. We enjoy the company of self-confident people who treat us with dignity and respect.

We are teaching our children to feel good about themselves so they won't limit their social contacts to people with serious emotional problems. We want our children to be sensitive to the needs of others without becoming caretakers who attract emotional cripples. We are teaching them to treat all people with respect, without looking down on anyone. When they fall in love, we hope they fall in love with someone they respect as equals.

Helping my children feel good about themselves helps them develop compassion and love.

Patience

· ·

*M*any of us have struggled with impatience all of our lives. Too often we have snapped at our children, yelled at our partners, and cursed other drivers on the road. Those of us who lived with alcoholics were especially impatient and irritable. We always seemed to be waiting for others to shape up, make decisions, get out of our way, and stop complaining. We were forever saying, "You're driving me crazy!"

When we began attending Al-Anon meetings, we came to see that our impatience was causing us to suffer needlessly. We began to look more closely at our attitudes toward life and others. Members pointed out that our blaming attitude was interfering with our serenity. As we learned to take responsibility for our feelings, we began to relax and go with the flow. We are learning to detach ourselves emotionally from the behavior of others.

We are learning to live in the moment. We no longer prod and poke our children to hurry up, make up their minds, or get out of the way. We let them take as much time as they need to choose a video or a new pair of jeans. We savor stopping on a walk to count ants. And we no longer rush through dinner. We are learning to enjoy spending time with our children, rather than seeing them as intrusions in our busy schedule.

Patience begins with me and nurtures my serenity as well as the serenity of my children.

Tears

· ·

We don't want our children to be afraid of showing tears as many of us have been. We were teased, ridiculed, and shamed for crying when we were children. No emotion was openly expressed in our family. Every emotion was repressed, stuffed, or denied. We soon learned to hide our feelings, no matter how much we hurt on the inside. We even took pride in our toughness. We bragged that our parents couldn't make us cry by spanking us or screaming at us. Little did we know the price we were paying.

It took several months in a Twelve-Step recovery group before we began to see the mental and emotional damage that was done to us by living in such repressive families. Over the years, we lost touch with almost all of our feelings. Our thick skin didn't protect us from life's slings and arrows as much as it deadened our sensitivities. It's not surprising that we were attracted to chemicals that helped us forget and drown out our feelings.

We are learning to avoid scolding or shaming our children when they cry, no matter how old they are. We don't minimize or trivialize their losses. While a misplaced baseball glove may not seem important to us, we respect our child's feelings. We don't scold the child for losing the glove or for crying about losing it.

I am making it as easy as I can for my children to express their tears.

Coping with Self-Doubt

. . . .

*W*e never heard our parents admit to feelings of self-doubt or uncertainties of any kind. No matter how out of control their lives became, they put up false fronts of bravado and self-assurance. Sometimes they demanded that we agree with them and support their phony authority. We see now that they were using us to bolster their sagging egos when they were filled with self-doubt.

We don't want to exploit our children in this way. We want to show them we're big enough to admit when we're fearful and uncertain. We want them to know we are human, that we have feelings, doubts, and uncertainties. We want to show them how to accept their feelings and deal with doubts and uncertainties directly.

We're learning to use the tools of our Twelve-Step program to deal with self-doubt rather than expecting our children to pick up our spirits and bolster our egos. We use the tools of honesty to reach out and ask for support from appropriate sources when we doubt ourselves. Using our children to rescue us from self-doubt and uncertainty is like using a teddy bear for a hammer. It's hard on the teddy bear and doesn't much impact nails.

I use the tools of my program, not my children, to help me cope with self-doubt.

Catastrophizing

. . . .

*O*ur parents lived by the motto, "If things could be worse, they will be worse." They expected the worst regarding our future. When we needed glasses in grade school, they saw us with white canes and seeing eye dogs. When we got caught stealing, they saw us in maximum security prisons. When we failed classes in school, they saw us on welfare unable to get jobs. When we got caught with beer, they saw us on skid row.

In our recovery, we've begun to take responsibility for our thoughts and feelings. We learn how to control the thoughts we dwell on. Our negative thoughts used to play in our minds like a phonograph record that was caught in a groove. We went around and around dwelling on negative thoughts until we felt crazy. We no longer allow certain negative thoughts to fill our minds and destroy our serenity. We can now face an unpleasant reality without exaggerating the negative possible future implications or slipping into denial.

We accept the facts in our children's lives without projecting into their future, the way our parents did. For example, if a child is diagnosed with a learning disability, we control our initial fears and listen to the facts. We don't allow our fears to cast a black cloud over any child's entire future.

I do not allow my fears and negative thoughts to create bleak futures for my children.

Encouragement

· ·

*O*ur parents did not know how to help us when we were frustrated and discouraged with our progress in school, sports, or music. Mostly they scolded us when we were discouraged, saying things like, "What's wrong with you?" or, "You're just not trying. If you would just put out a little effort once in a while." These remarks made us feel worse rather than better. We learned not to expect anything positive from our parents.

By sharing with other parents in our recovery groups we learn how to provide our children with encouragement. We discover the importance of a positive attitude, encouragement, and of building on strengths. We all, including parents, need encouragement from time to time. We need someone to have faith in us when we temporarily lose faith in ourselves. We need someone to tell us we can do it and not to give up.

When our children are frustrated and discouraged, we first listen to their troubles. We encourage them to get their feelings out. We don't criticize them for feeling discouraged or tell them they shouldn't feel this way. After they have thoroughly vented their feelings, we remind them that everyone starts slow and builds their skills through practice. By letting them know that we, too, have felt this way at times, we assure them that their feelings are normal.

I listen to the frustrations of my children and encourage them without discounting their feelings.

Rational Discipline

· ·

*M*any of us grew up with parents whose discipline was anything but rational. They often raged, abusing us both emotionally and physically. They did not instruct, correct, train, or educate us but rather condemned, humiliated, berated, and tormented us. They claimed to be doing this for our own good, in order to teach us a lesson. The lesson we learned was to hate and despise them and/or ourselves. We also learned how to humiliate others.

When we became parents, we used our lessons well, practicing the same kind of discipline with our children—until we got into recovery. Recovery opened our eyes, and we recognized the emotional and physical abuse we suffered as children in dysfunctional families. We're determined to break this destructive pattern in our generation. We remain calm and control our anger before we attempt to discipline our children.

Now we think of our children as people, even when they provoke us with their misbehavior. We consider their feelings as well as our own. We think about what we want to teach them and what behaviors we want them to change before we open our mouths to discipline them. Often, this means we have to count to at least twenty before we begin. We sometimes wait for an hour or more before we talk to them about their misbehavior. This gives us time to reflect on what we want them to learn from this experience.

I am learning to discipline from reason instead of anger.

I Can't Take It

"*I* just can't take it any more!"

We remember hearing our parents say this. We began saying it ourselves to express our frustration when we were at the end of our rope. Whenever we said these words, we checked out. We weren't accountable for what we did after saying these words. They were magical words, like "King's X." After saying them, we could rage at our children or abuse alcohol, drugs, or food.

In recovery, we're learning to give it to God when we can't take it. We still get frustrated, but we no longer feel alone. We are learning that, with God, all things are possible. We may be at our wit's end, but God is not. He has options and possibilities we can't fathom. By turning to our Higher Power when we are exhausted and defeated, we discover new strength and patience.

We look to our Higher Power to help us deal with our frustrations so we don't pass them off to our children. We notice that they seem more relaxed and peaceful when we are relaxed and peaceful. Now when we find ourselves thinking, "I can't take it anymore," we say a prayer asking God to take it for us. We no longer rage at our children when we're exhausted and frustrated.

With God's help, I can take whatever life deals me.

Adversity

· ·

*M*any of us grew up looking at life through pessimistic lenses. Our parents were always down on their luck and complaining of being misunderstood and mistreated by the "system." They considered every disappointment a catastrophe. They looked at things in negative lights, expecting the worst—and usually getting it. We became so accustomed to pessimism that we thought ours was a normal, objective view of life.

Recovery has helped us see there are different ways of looking at the same facts. Not everyone draws the same conclusions. Adversity is a matter of interpretation and not necessarily an incontrovertible fact. We have some control over how we view most situations in life. We can catastrophize by expecting the most disturbing outcome, or we can look at the same set of facts and find some advantage. We look for the positive elements within adversity.

We teach our children to do the same, one day and one incident at a time. When they're upset and disappointed, they're in no mood to look at situations positively. We listen and give them emotional support when they are upset. Later on, we help them reexamine the situations and encourage them to look at them in as many different ways as possible. This is helping them and us break the habit of seeing all disappointments as failures or letdowns.

I can teach myself and my children to look for the positive elements in every situation.

Immediate Needs

. . . .

*W*e used to worry about what others thought of us when we took our children out in public. We compared ourselves with other parents—and were afraid of appearing inadequate in their eyes. We spent our mental energy managing our images rather than paying attention to our children's needs or the needs of the situation. If one of our children fell down and cried, we were more concerned about the reactions of other parents than about our children's discomfort or injury.

In recovery, we've come to understand the extent of our codependency on the opinions of others. We realize how much energy we had used in managing the impressions we made on others, including our children. We were giving other people and our own obsessive thoughts power over our feelings. We were letting others judge our adequacy and determine our worth. We put our self-esteem in the hands of others—our children's and other adults.

We're learning to let go of our concern for image. We have learned to get outside of ourselves and our obsessive thoughts and focus on the world around us. When we take our children shopping, we focus on what we are shopping for and the needs and feelings of our children. We no longer obsess about what others may or may not be thinking about us or our children.

My self-image improves when I focus on the needs of the situation.

Contagious Moods

. . . .

Some of us grew up in families where moods were both unpredictable and violent. We learned to lay low when one of our parents was in a bad mood. We were regularly scolded when they were unhappy or angry, even when we were completely innocent. Bad moods had a way of turning our parents into unreasonable, ugly, and often violent adults, especially when alcohol was involved. Our physical and emotional security depended on our ability to read our parents' moods and adjust our behavior.

In recovery we're learning that moods are often contagious. Those around us are frequently affected by the mood we're in, especially our children. When we wake up tired and irritable, it seems our children are irritable and cranky too. When we wake up happy and refreshed, they are more cooperative and easygoing. And vice versa—those of us who are adult children of dysfunctional families seem especially sensitive to other people's moods.

When we pay closer attention to our own moods, we avoid blaming or scolding our children when we are cranky. We also avoid blaming them for putting us in bad moods. When we are feeling irritable and crabby, we tell our children so and reassure them they are not to blame. This makes everything go more smoothly. They are relieved to know they are innocent and won't be scolded or blamed for our moods.

I am taking responsibility for my moods and telling my children when I'm irritable.

Imperfection

. . . .

*O*ur parents had to be right and never admitted their mistakes to us. They lied to cover up their shortcomings. They tried to make us believe they were perfect. As we grew, we saw through this, and their feeble attempts to hide their imperfections made them seem petty and morally weak, especially when we were teenagers.

Before we came into the program, honesty meant we didn't lie outright to those who deserved the truth or asked the right questions. Like our parents, however, we believed that children did not always need to know the truth. We saw no value in telling them about our mistakes and shortcomings. In recovery, we are learning the importance of being honest. Honesty is essential for our recovery and the quality of our relationships, including those with our children.

We no longer want to be on pedestals in our children's minds. As we begin leveling with our children about our faults and shortcomings, we find our relationships with them becoming relaxed and open. When we tell them about our struggles and the mistakes we make, they seem more open with us. We want them to understand that the goal of life is not to get from the cradle to the grave with the fewest mistakes, but rather to live with honesty, courage, and dignity.

I am learning to be honest with my children about my shortcomings and imperfections.

Forgive and Forget

. . . .

*M*any of us remember our parents scolding and humiliating us with reminders of our mistakes and failures. They never forgot our mistakes, and they used them to humiliate us. They brought up our failures whenever we tried to do something new. We couldn't escape their reminders, which only discouraged us and undermined our tenuous self-confidence. We don't want to do the same thing to our children.

We're regaining self-confidence through our recovery. In our step group, we're surrounded by people who encourage us rather than tear us down. This support and encouragement is something new for most of us, and it feels wonderful. We have discovered that the Twelve-Step program builds people up rather than tears them down.

We want our children to learn from their mistakes so they won't repeat them. When they repeat a mistake, we used to scold them by reminding them of their previous errors. We're learning to support and encourage our children when they mess up. They're the first to realize when they fail or make mistakes, and constantly reminding them does not help them learn or recover. If they fail, we help them put their failure in proper perspective so they are not overly discouraged by it. We enjoy watching them shake it off, get back on their feet, and try again.

I support my children when they make mistakes, rather than tear them down.

Monitoring Expectations

· ·

*W*hen we got married, we expected our partners to know what we needed and supply our needs without being asked. We were prepared neither to ask for what we needed nor to negotiate. The very thought of asking or negotiating seemed humiliating. We believed a loving partner would sense our needs and generously offer to meet them. When this did not happen, we felt angry, unloved, and disappointed.

In recovery, we learn to seek the support we need from more than one person. We learn to expand our support system so we don't depend entirely on any one person for our emotional support. When we expect one person to always be available and willing to meet our needs, we set ourselves up to be disappointed. By learning to manage our emotional needs and expectations, we take charge of our circumstances rather than let our needs control us.

Managing our emotional needs is like watching the fuel gauge on the car and filling up when it falls below a quarter tank. It is more important to fill up before we run out than to insist on returning to our favorite gas station and risk stalling on the highway. By asking many people to help contribute to our emotional well-being, we keep ourselves filled up and we avoid becoming overly dependent on any one person.

I look to many people for emotional support.

Authority Figures

· ·

 S ome of us never questioned anyone in authority. Others of us challenged any authority figure who tried to tell us what to do. Growing up in a dysfunctional family created conflicts and ambivalence regarding authority. When the adults we depended on to protect us caused us emotional and physical harm, we felt confused and betrayed. This confusion made it difficult for us to accept legitimate authority roles in our own lives. We didn't know how to act as parents.

In recovery, we're learning to respect ourselves and others, including those in authority. Some of us have begun to let go of the anger and resentment we feel toward anyone in authority. Others, who were used to putting everyone else's head higher than our own, have learned to treat ourselves with respect. Although we don't automatically defer to those in authority, we do understand the proper balance between self-respect and respect for authority.

We want our children to develop proper respect for authority without putting themselves down or assuming they are less worthy than parents, teachers, coaches, employers, or other authority figures. We are doing our best to provide our children with healthy models of parental authority. We strive to earn their respect by showing respect for their needs, feelings, and self-esteem. This is making it easier for them to respect both themselves and authority figures.

I am teaching my children the proper respect for
authority by being a trustworthy parent.

Single Parent

. . . .

*S*ome of us were raised by single parents. Some of us lived with moms who depended on us, and we became self-reliant and ostensibly independent at too early an age. Others of us were forced to become "moms" because we lived with our dads. Not only did we clean house, shop for groceries, and cook meals, but we also had to act as confidant when our single parents were discouraged and lonely. We were robbed of our childhood.

Those of us who are single parents now want to spare our children the burden of taking care of us. So we're learning to depend on other adults for our support. Our Twelve-Step group has become a place where we share our struggles, let off steam, and get support. By talking with other adults who are going through the same struggles we don't feel so alone. Our weekly meetings help keep us from becoming lonely and depressed.

We are learning to manage as single parents without leaning on our children for our emotional support. We no longer burden them with our problems and frustrations. As we become stronger and more self-confident, we no longer feel sorry for our children or compensate them for having to live with us instead of with both of their parents. We teach them to share in the household responsibilities, but we no longer expect them to be little adults.

I am confident I can live day by day without using my children as a confidant.

Opposite Sex

. . . .

*M*ost of us hid our sexual curiosity and feelings when we were growing up. We didn't let anyone know we were interested in members of the opposite sex when we were in high school. Our siblings teased us and our parents condemned us, so we learned to keep our sexual thoughts and feelings very private. Being condemned and ridiculed for something natural was so confusing that we sometimes had doubts about whether we were normal.

We want our children to feel free to share their questions, thoughts, concerns, and feelings about sexuality with us. In order to create this open and trusting atmosphere, we are working on becoming more comfortable with these topics ourselves. We are learning to get more comfortable with these issues by talking with our partners and close friends about sexual topics. At first, we felt anxious and our conversations felt awkward. With practice, however, we are becoming more comfortable discussing sexual attitudes and feelings.

The acceptance and honesty that is a part of our Twelve-Step meetings has inspired and encouraged us to risk speaking more openly about issues that, at one time, we avoided at all costs. Our children may not be immediately at ease with our new approach, but, over time, we experience more openness in our communications with them. Our most modest efforts are light years ahead of the cold hostility that many of us experienced as children.

I am doing everything I can to create an accepting atmosphere for my children.

Peace of Mind

. . . .

*M*any of us grew up in blaming, faultfinding families in which every disappointment was someone else's fault.
No one took responsibility for their feelings. When we felt
mad, sad, or any other form of distress, we looked for the
other person who "caused" our feelings. We insisted we were
innocent victims of the emotional manipulations of others.
This belief was also used to excuse all of our irresponsible behavior. "She made me so mad I had to hit her" was a common
defense.

In recovery, we are learning that we are each responsible for
our own feelings, behavior, and recovery. We were so steeped
in the tradition of blaming and scapegoating that it was
difficult for us to see our own role in these things. We were
convinced that we could not change until others changed.
After all, we were simply reacting to their crazy behavior.

Now that we have found the key to serenity and inner peace,
we are eager to share this with our children. We are teaching
them that they control their feelings and behavior more than
they imagined. We show them that by paying attention to their
self-talk and changing it, they can change the way they feel
inside. We share the secrets of recovery with them so they will
be able to influence their inner peace and serenity.

I enjoy sharing the fruits of recovery with my children.

Why?

. . . .

When we did something wrong as children, our parents grilled us. They believed in using shame and humiliation as deterrents. They didn't simply ask us to explain our actions, they rebuked us with shaming questions like, "Who do you think you are? What in the world is wrong with you? What were you thinking? Don't you have any brains in your head?" Although there was nothing we could possibly say that would satisfy them, we nonetheless became experts at creating interesting alibis.

We want our children to be accountable for their behavior, but we don't want them to feel humiliated. We are learning in our recovery that shame and humiliation cripple self-esteem and are not corrective. When we are shamed and humiliated, we do not think clearly, make sound decisions, or examine our behavior objectively. We become preoccupied with defending ourselves and are unable to step outside ourselves to see the world around us objectively.

We are learning not to ask our children why they did something wrong. This only tempts them to lie to us and make excuses. Instead, we explain our disappointment in their behavior and ask them to apologize and make amends if they have hurt someone. When appropriate, we give them a consequence that is related to their misbehavior. We make a point of helping them get back in our good graces.

I am holding my children accountable without deliberately injuring their self-esteem.

Family History

O C T O B E R   2 3

*M*any of us know little or nothing about our parents' lives as children. It is as if they were ashamed of their pasts or perhaps couldn't bear to re-experience childhood feelings. When we asked questions about our grandparents or other relatives, they either refused to talk or said very little. Consequently, we were cut off from our family roots.

We want this to be different for our children. We want them to know who they are and where they came from. At first, it was difficult for us to openly share details about our childhood with them. It felt as if we were violating some unspoken rule, telling secrets we had sworn never to reveal. There were many childhood memories that were unpleasant for us to recall, let alone share with our children. Our children, however, were eager to learn all they could about us when we were their ages. They neither judged us nor reacted the way we feared they might to some of our unpleasant stories.

We realize that in sharing the stories of our childhoods, we pass on sacred, oral tradition. These stories help our children understand us and know themselves. Sharing these stories brings us together in a deep, intimate way. It forges us together like links in a chain that extends backward in time. We enjoy the warmth and closeness we feel as we share ourselves honestly with our children.

I enjoy connecting with my children by sharing the stories of our common past.

Slights

. . . .

*M*any of us have kept careful records of all the slights, indignities, and sarcastic remarks others have made toward us. When we felt that someone had slighted us, we clung to the experience, nursing our hurt feelings until we were miserable. We would carefully review the scene over and over in our minds until it was deeply ingrained in our memory. Sometimes we plotted revenge or thought of all the snappy comebacks we should have said.

We used to feel powerless over our thoughts and moods. Many of us became dependent on chemicals to alter our moods. In recovery, for the first time, we figured out that we can influence what we dwell on. We have more conscious control over our thoughts and moods than we once believed. We are determined to fill our minds with positive thoughts and images, rather than those that disturb our thinking and cause us to become emotionally upset.

When others make unkind remarks, we don't dwell on their words but focus on positive thoughts. We no longer nurse our hurt feelings. If someone slights us or makes a snide remark about us we let it go. We have confidence in ourselves and our recovery, and we no longer waste our time rehearsing snappy comebacks or plotting revenge. We're learning to take charge of the things we dwell on.

I'm letting go of hurtful remarks and filling my mind with positive thoughts.

Nobody Cares

· ·

*B*efore we came into the program, we felt totally alone. We were convinced that no one could really understand our despair. We felt unique and separate from the rest of humanity and believed no one cared about our problems or even whether we lived or died. We felt completely isolated from the people around us. Being in a room full of people did nothing to relieve our despair and loneliness.

In recovery, we're never alone. When we began attending Twelve-Step meetings, we discovered others like ourselves. We soon felt less isolated and alone. Then we were introduced to the concept of a Higher Power. While this was often not easy for us to grasp, we have come to accept that there is a power higher than us that understands everything we feel and think and every temptation we struggle with. Developing a personal relationship with our Higher Power gives us the ultimate shield against isolation and loneliness.

Turning to our Higher Power when we feel isolated and alone gives us a sense of inner peace we never knew before. The combination of a fellowship with others in recovery and knowing that our Higher Power understands us totally, and accepts unconditionally, even in our brokenness, has helped us overcome our tremendous isolation. Now we can enjoy being surrounded by family and friends without feeling lonely in their midst.

I am no longer isolated from myself and others, thanks to my Higher Power.

Accepting Limits

· ·

When we divorced, most of us felt terribly guilty about hurting our children. Those of us who had grown up with single parents immediately projected all our heartaches and childhood disappointments on our children. We were determined to compensate our children for their suffering by giving them everything we possibly could. Sometimes we defended ourselves when they complained about the changes in their lives by blaming our ex-spouses for our divorces.

In recovery we're training ourselves to see the good in every situation, including divorce. We're not blind to the many adjustments we're facing in our divorce, but we choose to set our sights on the opportunities for growth and healing. We are learning to accept reality without making excuses or blaming others. As we come to understand the dynamics of our shame, we no longer feel the need to defend ourselves when our children express disappointment about any aspect of their lives.

At the same time, we are listening to our children's disappointments without feeling guilty or compelled to compensate them for their losses. We help them accept limits in their lives. We no longer blame ourselves or our ex-spouses. Instead, we acknowledge our children's feelings and help them make the best of situations by focusing on what is present in their lives instead of what is missing.

As I accept my limits as a single parent, both my children and I can focus on what is present.

Feeling Overwhelmed

· ·

*B*ecoming a parent for the first time is like learning to share our best friends. Going from a two-person adult relationship to a three-person relationship involving a demanding baby is a difficult transition. Husbands often feel jealous and wives may feel as though they are doing a tricky balancing act. Adding another child to the family makes this balancing act even more tricky.

It's easy to feel overwhelmed by the demands of our children. Babies need constant attention. Preschool children need supervision. Schoolchildren need different kinds of attention than babies do. Teenagers need us to be available when they are hurting, stressed out, or when they just want to talk. Our children's needs cannot wait until we are in the mood to deal with them.

Parenting is not a set of chores or responsibilities to be wedged into already busy lives for our own convenience and gratification. Parenting requires a wholehearted commitment of time, attention, and energy to the care and development of another human being—who is as worthy of consideration as we are. To avoid feeling overwhelmed by this lofty commitment, we take one day at a time. By focusing on the joys and demands of each day, we learn to live in day-tight compartments, prizing nothing more highly than the value of each day.

Focusing on the needs and joys of the moment, I delight in my children.

Healthy Dependency

. . . .

*M*ost of us have spent our lives hiding our faults, blemishes, and weaknesses from others. We may have covered our weaknesses with distractions, withdrawal, bravado. Many of us overdeveloped whatever assets we felt we had. As adults, we carefully avoided situations that would expose our weaknesses. Our sense of personal inadequacy led to our unhealthy dependencies on substances and/or compulsive behaviors.

When we began to recover from these dependencies, we were determined never to be dependent on anything or anyone again. We came to regard all signs of dependency as damning evidence of a personal weakness or mental sickness. Our stubborn resolve to be totally self-reliant and independent was misdirected. It was a reaction against our neediness rather than movement toward fulfillment. We threw out the baby with the bath.

We are learning that dependency is not necessarily a sign of mental illness, but is, in fact, essential to our humanity. If it were possible to be totally independent and self-reliant, we would have no need of love, companionship, community, family, bonding, intimacy, or God in our lives. Our dependency needs didn't lead to our addictions. Our inability to accept our needs and find healthy ways to get them met did. Creative dependency is recognizing that the holes in our lives are not sources of shame. They are like the holes in Tinker Toys® that make it possible to link up with others.

My dependency needs provide opportunities to connect with God and others.

Order

. . . .

*O*nce we took an honest look, it was easy for most of us to admit that our lives were unmanageable. All we had to do was look at our bedrooms! Our bedrooms had become disheveled hovels, cluttered with piles of clothes, magazines, books, dishes, and junk—all of which we were going to organize and put away soon. Occasionally, we resolved to straighten out our houses—and our lives—all at once. However, the task so overwhelmed us that we avoided it by slipping back into our denial.

The task of restoring order to our lives felt overwhelming. Everything was a mess—our living space, our family lives, our relationships, our finances, our health, and most of all, our spiritual lives. We had denied this reality for so many years that it was difficult for us to face.

The most important tool in learning to restore order to our lives is the principle of a day at a time. By starting with tiny steps, and celebrating small victories, we begin restoring order to our lives. We're learning the importance of focusing on the task at hand and not allowing ourselves to get overwhelmed by everything that needs to be done. As we live in the present, it's encouraging to see little corners of our lives emerge from disorder and chaos. We feel so much better as parents and as people.

I can use the principles of the program to maintain order in my life—one day at a time.

"**W**e'll make it up to you." Many of us heard this or similar messages whenever our parents realized they had forgotten promises made to us. Their promises to make things up to us later were no more reliable than their original ones. These promises were supposed to appease us. As parents, we have done the same thing. We've felt so guilty about all the times we ignored our children that we wanted to compensate them for their losses.

In recovery, we're learning to accept our humanness without undue guilt. We've stopped trying to cover our mistakes with gifts, bribes, or denials. We admit our wrongs, make appropriate amends, and go on with our lives. We are learning how to let go of the painful and tragic aspects of our past lives without wallowing in them. When we are reminded of our previous neglect of our children, we do not beat ourselves up with guilt.

When we see signs of poor self-esteem, self-doubt, or shyness in our children, we hurt inside. We imagine these are the result of our past neglect. Although we want to fix everything by making it up to them with gifts, privileges, or special opportunities, we resist. We recognize the temptations to compensate our children for their losses. Instead, we live each new day, one at a time.

I accept my humanness, and raise my children, one day at a time without dwelling on the past.

Halloween

. . . .

*W*e used to view Halloween as a good excuse for overindulging in sweets, alcohol, and risqué behavior. We were more involved in planning adult parties than sharing in our children's excitement and anticipation. We spent little time or attention on their costumes, perhaps left them for the evening in the care of a babysitter. We were too self-indulgent to concern ourselves with our children's wishes.

In recovery, we discovered that our self-indulgence was the result of our unmet emotional needs. By learning to identify these emotional needs, and finding responsible ways to meet them, we are becoming less self-indulgent. As we learn to talk about our feelings of isolation and loneliness, for example, we feel more emotionally connected and not so alone. By talking about our hurt and fear, we no longer feel angry all of the time. As our self-indulgence diminishes, we are more open to the needs and feelings of our children.

We share in our children's excitement as they anticipate dressing up in costumes and participating in Halloween. After all, this is an annual event for children. Sharing in the anticipation and excitement of our children is one of the blessings of being a sober parent. This is better than any chemically induced high because no one suffers and all of our memories are happy ones.

Sharing in anticipation and excitement at Halloween meets my children's needs and mine.

Progress, Not Perfection
. . . .

*W*e're learning each day to be better parents. At one time we believed raising children would be as natural as breathing, but we've learned that it requires conscious thought, effort, and skill. While we try to acknowledge our growth, we keep getting tangled up in our perfectionism. It's hard for us to accept our mistakes and imperfections. We keep reminding ourselves that our goal is improvement, not perfection.

As children, many of us seemed to be in trouble all the time. We believed if we could only be perfect, things would be different. If only we were perfect, we thought, then we wouldn't get yelled at, hit, ignored, belittled, laughed at, or constantly criticized. In our recovery, we learned that our parents' treatment of us was not our fault. We were just kids, doing the best we could. They scolded us so much that, naturally, we thought if we were perfect, their scolding would stop.

We now realize that parents yell for their own reasons, usually having nothing to do with their kids. If we had only known that at the time! If only we could have detached from their abusive behavior and remained unscathed. We didn't have the necessary insight to recognize we were innocent. We're working on letting go of our perfectionism, and accepting ourselves as good enough for today.

I am focusing my attention on my improvements instead of my imperfections.

Self-Respect

. . . .

Some of us were so codependent with our children that we enabled them to remain irresponsible and totally dependent on us. When, for example, they failed to do their chores, we did them ourselves rather than hassle them about their responsibilities. Although we harbored resentments and were often irritable and crabby with our children, we told ourselves we were being kind and generous toward our children.

In our codependents support group we learn that this kind of generosity is unhealthy, both for ourselves and our children. We've come to understand that we were enabling our children to be irresponsible. By providing no consequences when they ignored their obligations, we reinforced their irresponsibility. By providing no structure for accountability, we taught them not to be accountable. We were, in effect, rewarding them for their irresponsible, self-centered behavior. We were also setting ourselves up to feel unappreciated, victimized, and abused.

We now make a point to treat ourselves at least as well as we treat our children. Because we do not expect our children to do our chores, we won't do theirs. Because we would not force one of our children to pick up the slack for an irresponsible sibling, neither do we expect this of ourselves. We are modeling self-respect by using the same measure in our treatment of ourselves as we use in our treatment of our children.

I respect myself as I respect my children.

Boundaries

. . . .

*M*any of us had no privacy as children. Some of us were physically and sexually abused by family members or other adults who treated us as objects for their pleasure. We did not know we were entitled to control our own bodies and set boundaries on who could touch us. We believed that adults could do whatever they wanted to us because we were only children. When we became teenagers, we let others touch us, even when we didn't like it, because we were afraid to resist.

We're learning in recovery that dignity and self-respect mean setting and maintaining personal boundaries, including physical ones. We no longer allow people to touch us unless we want them to. We're learning to set these limits without feeling guilty or unnecessarily anxious. This has been enormously important in regaining our self-respect. We've also learned to respect the physical boundaries of others, including our children.

Now we are teaching our children to own their physical boundaries and to respect the boundaries of others. Some of our children have expressed displeasure over being kissed by their relatives at family gatherings. We have assured them it is their right to control who touches them. Together we've planned how they will let their relatives know how they feel. We assure them that we support their positions.

I support my children's rights to set their own physical boundaries.

Attitudes

. . . .

*M*ost of us grew up with little or no emotional stability in our lives. Moods and emotions ruled, and we felt out of control most of the time. When one of our parents was in a bad mood, the whole house was in an uproar. When we were in a bad mood, we tried to avoid others so we wouldn't bring them down too. Some of us tried to gain control of our moods with alcohol and drugs. Disaster followed.

In recovery, we're learning that we don't have to be controlled by the attitudes of others. We're learning how to directly influence our own attitudes and no longer feel controlled by the moods or attitudes of those around. We have discovered that attitudes are governed by thoughts. This radical discovery challenges the notion that we have no control over our moods and attitudes. By concentrating on our own thinking, and especially our inner conversations, we've learned to take charge of our attitudes.

We're teaching our children how to influence their own attitudes. When they complain that their friends or siblings are making them angry or depressed, we explain that no one can control their thoughts and feelings but themselves. We have them practice different kinds of self-talk, posture, and body language to show them how to influence their moods and attitudes. Once they have experienced an immediate change in their attitudes, they believe in themselves.

When I take charge of my own attitudes, I can help my children take charge of theirs.

Forgive Mistakes

. . . .

*M*any of us did not experience the healing power of forgiveness as children. We lived in guilt and shame, carrying the baggage of our past offenses and mistakes with us wherever we went. Whenever our parents were angry with us, they would recite to us from the list of our offenses. We felt helpless and hopeless. We could never escape from our past.

The Twelve-Step program has shown us a way to free ourselves from our negative pasts without denying or running away from them. We're learning to accept ourselves, warts and all. We now know we can let go of past mistakes—our own and others. We are grateful for this liberating approach with its promise of a new way to live. We are no longer afraid of our humanness or wasting time hiding our selves from others.

We practice the healing power of forgiveness with our children. We want them to grow up without being afraid to take risks because they might make mistakes. We enjoy watching them take risks, try new activities, attempt difficult tasks without fear of embarrassment or humiliation. We are doing everything we can to maintain good relationships with them when they break our confidence or get into trouble. They are benefiting from the changes we have made in our lives.

I am practicing the healing power of forgiveness with my children.

New Problems

· ·

*B*efore we began our recovery, we were totally absorbed in our problems and addictions. We went from one high to the next, ignoring everything in between. We tolerated our miserable existence by rewarding ourselves with booze, drugs, food, sex, shopping, gambling, and other compulsions. We had no time for the feelings or needs of others. Our only concern was getting through the day so we could get our little reward.

We thank God daily that our recovery has changed all this. We are learning to care about others' feelings and needs. We genuinely care about ourselves as well. We no longer obsess over the petty details of our lives. We experience the serenity that makes it possible to get outside of ourselves and truly notice the world around us. We're beginning to care about our community.

Early on, we thought recovery would eliminate all the problems in our lives. As we experience deeper recovery, for the first time in our lives we are focusing on God's will. We discover that being in recovery doesn't mean we won't have problems, but that God will grant us the courage, wisdom, and serenity to deal with them. God is putting us on a new, more challenging path, calling us to share our recovery by loving others—those closest to us and those in our community who suffer as we once did.

I gratefully accept the new challenges that God places before me.

Balance

. . . .

We want our children to be kind, generous, and sensitive to the needs and feelings of others. But we don't want them to become codependent, to live only for others, as many of us did. We weren't allowed to express any concern for ourselves. We were expected to adapt ourselves to the needs of others and ignore our own needs. When we expressed our needs or desires, we were scolded for being selfish. Consequently, we became people pleasers who did not deal with our own needs.

In recovery, we learn to balance concern for others with concern for ourselves. At first we may feel guilty for even talking about ourselves and our needs. Gradually we learn to recognize our needs and talk to others about them without whining or being manipulative. We learn to assert ourselves when our needs are urgent without feeling ashamed or guilty. We can also reach out to help others without feeling resentful that they are getting the attention we secretly desire.

We're teaching our children to think about others as well as themselves. When our children act stingy and are unwilling to share their things, we gently urge them to be more considerate of others. When they show signs of letting others take advantage of them, we encourage them to speak up and assert their needs in the relationship. We encourage them to talk about their needs and feelings with us.

I am teaching my children to balance their concern for others with concern for themselves.

Sniping

. . . .

We hated it when our parents berated and belittled one another in front of us. They took sarcastic jabs at one another until it became unbearable to listen to. At first, we responded as if it were humorous, but it was too painful to laugh about. We gradually tuned it out until our spouses brought it to our attention again, saying how uncomfortable they were with our parents' bickering. Once we tuned in to their sarcastic banter again, we felt both sad and angry.

In our recovery group, we're learning that sarcasm is indirect anger. We now see that our parents belittle one another because they've never learned to express their anger directly. We recognize the same tendency in ourselves, and we are working to change it. We begin to recognize when we are harboring resentments toward our partners. We make a point to deal with these resentments by talking them out with our partners instead of sniping at them.

We're learning to deal with our resentments directly. Sometimes it helps to commiserate with a close friend just to get things off our chest. After we have unloaded our frustrations with our partners, we feel more peaceful and relaxed. Before we share our frustrations with our spouses, we ask for their agreement to listen without becoming defensive. We can then talk more calmly with them about our frustrations or resentments.

Airing my resentments openly makes both my partner and me breathe more easily.

Daughters

· ·

*T*hose mothers among us who grew up in dysfunctional families were especially susceptible to becoming dependent on the men in our lives. We were taught not to live or ourselves, but for others, especially men. Our mothers were caretakers and taught us to be caretakers. Our brothers always got first dibs on food, cars, educational opportunities, and anything else they wanted. We were expected to defer to men on everything. We saw our mothers look up to our fathers, even when they were wrong, abusive, or out of line. We came to believe that we were inherently inferior to even the worst men.

Recovery opened our eyes. We no longer regard ourselves as second-class citizens or members of the servant class. We no longer look up to men but look eye-to-eye with them as our peers. We're gradually changing our responses to men from automatic deference to thoughtful evaluation. We're learning to trust ourselves and our ability to discern between trustworthy men and those who are not. And we're learning to believe in ourselves and our ability to manage our lives through our own efforts.

We encourage our daughters to develop self-confidence in themselves as women and to see themselves as complete persons in their own right. We want them to feel comfortable around men without feeling they should look up to them in any special way.

I am preparing my daughters to be first-class citizens.

Protection

· ·

*S*ome of us were severely beaten as children. Our fathers raged at us, especially when they had been drinking. Some of us were punished with straps, brushes, or paddles. Others were slapped, knocked down, or kicked. Our mothers looked the other way because they were too fearful and dependent to intervene and protect us. We resented our fathers for beating us and our mothers for failing to protect us. Or, in some families, vice versa.

Although we vowed that we would never let anyone abuse our children when we became parents, we gradually slipped into denial when our partners started getting rough with our children. We kept telling ourselves it was not as bad as what we had experienced as children. We rationalized the situation as long as we could. When we could no longer ignore the abuse, we took action to protect our children.

We're learning to stand up for our children, even when it means confronting our partners and jeopardizing our relationship with them. We asked them to get help for their rage. When they refused, we asked them to leave the house. Some of us went so far as to get restraining orders to have them removed until they got professional help. We were determined to protect our children first and deal with the consequences in our relationships second.

I am proud of protecting my children and promoting healing for my partner.

Self-Trust

. . . .

We did not receive support for our reality as children. If we told our parents we had a headache or a stomachache, they either ignored us or accused us of making it up just to get out of going to school or doing our chores. When we shared something we learned in school, they accused us of lying or making it up. When we were afraid of the dark, we were scolded and shamed. We learned to keep our thoughts and feelings to ourselves.

In recovery, we're learning to share our thoughts and feelings with others. At first, this was difficult because we expected others to ignore or challenge us. We're breaking from our codependent patterns in which we needed the approval of others in order to feel secure. We no longer need to persuade others to our view in order to feel secure. We have confidence in ourselves and in our reality.

When someone challenges us, we no longer automatically assume others are right and we are wrong. We trust ourselves enough to listen to the views of others and consider them thoughtfully, without attacking them or abandoning our own. This has greatly improved our self-confidence. We are calmer and far less abrasive in our discussions with others, especially when discussing personal or controversial topics.

I can trust my reality, express myself with quiet confidence, and pass that on to my children.

Shame

. . . .

*O*ur parents were quick to shame us when we made mistakes. They were more concerned with punishing us than with helping us learn from our mistakes. They took our mistakes and accidents personally. If we had an accident with the family car, they yelled and screamed at us as if they believed we'd planned the accident in order to inconvenience them. They asked us rhetorical questions like, "What were you thinking? When are you going to learn? What makes you think you can go around smashing up cars?" These shaming and humiliating questions were, of course, impossible to answer.

In recovery, we've discovered the ongoing crippling effects of shame in our lives. Most of us in recovery are unusually sensitive to shame. We feel personally defective and worthless when we make mistakes. We feel exposed, helpless, and beyond repair when our shame is triggered. This is so excruciatingly painful that we do not want to do anything to cause our children to experience it.

We're learning how to correct our children's mistakes and hold them accountable without giving them the message that they're incompetent. When they have an accident or make a mistake, we calmly talk to them about what happened. We express our disappointment, but we don't rage at them. We want them to learn from their mistakes without feeling ashamed or humiliated.

I can help my children learn from their mistakes without humiliating them.

Prejudice

. . . .

Some of us learned to look down on those who were less fortunate than us. Our parents were condescending, and we learned that same attitude. We delighted in seeing poor people because it reminded us of how much more ambitious and intelligent we were. The more unmanageable our lives became, the more we needed to look down on others in order to prop up our sagging self-esteem. By the time we got into recovery, we were becoming snobbish boors.

In recovery, we've learned that addictions are great equalizers and no respecter of class. In our recovery groups, we were cast in with people we might never have associated with. We soon discovered, however, that we have more in common than we imagined. The moment we allowed ourselves to receive help from those we once looked down on, our attitudes began changing. As we grow in our recovery, we shed our old prejudices and arrogant attitudes.

When we overhear our children talking about someone in a condescending manner, we call them on it. When we are with our children in public, we never make disparaging remarks about those who are different because of race, poverty, or physical handicaps. We remind our children that everyone is a beautiful child of God. We encourage our children to become involved in charitable groups at school and church that serve less fortunate people.

I am teaching my children sensitivity and respect for all people, especially those who are different.

Broken Promises

. . . .

*M*any of us grew up with parents who broke more promises than they kept. We gradually stopped expecting anything they promised us. And we learned to mistrust everyone, just to be on the safe side. In our recovery, we're gradually learning to trust people once again. But it may take us a long time to believe that people honor their word. We may still be suspicious of most promises that people make to us. Or we may be reluctant to make promises. We are working hard to mean what we say and say what we mean.

We also fear we'll damage our children if we can't keep a promise we've made to them. If we tell one of our children that we will pick them up at 3:00 at a friend's house, and we are unable to get there until 3:30, we worry about having broken our promise. How can we keep from destroying their trust?

We can explain that there are times when we simply can't keep our promises because of things beyond our control. We can make amends when needed without driving ourselves crazy every time something comes up that we can't control. Our Higher Power knows we would keep these promises if we could. We can trust ourselves to know that too.

I am learning to be gentle with myself when there are things beyond my control that cause broken promises.

Don't React

. . . .

*W*e used to react very badly when our children were angry at us. We were yelled at so often as children that, although adults, we reacted automatically when our children yelled at us. We felt like scolded children when our children were irritable and angry toward us. We became defensive, angry, and hostile toward them. We felt indignant that our own children were scolding us. How dare they!

In our recovery group, we're learning to understand our reactions toward our children's anger and to control our responses. We have come to recognize that we are emotionally sensitive to anyone who raises their voice. We hate being yelled at by anyone, our children included. A loud, angry voice causes us to feel shamed, whether or not we are doing anything to be ashamed of.

Now that we recognize our sensitivity to shame and loud voices, we no longer get hooked. We do not react automatically with anger and defensiveness when our children express their frustration by raising their voices. Even when our partners show irritation in their voices, we are able to detach enough to keep calm. We still won't tolerate verbal abuse from anyone, but we are less tense and defensive when anyone expresses anger and irritation with a raised voice.

I can respond as a secure adult when my children show irritation by raising their voices.

Depending on God

· ·

At first, we were afraid of becoming dependent on A.A. and God, as we had been dependent on alcohol. Some of our friends warned us that people in A.A. simply traded one addiction for another. Instead of going to bars every night, they went to A.A. meetings, which wasn't much different. Some of us skipped A.A. meetings now and then just to prove to ourselves we weren't addicted to them. We learned, however, that skipping meetings did nothing for our sobriety and actually disturbed our serenity.

When we began recovery, our treatment goal was to totally eliminate all signs of dependency. We thought all forms of dependency were pathological. Now we are learning that harmful dependency is life threatening, while healthy dependency is life sustaining and life enhancing. Harmful dependency results in the neglect of occupational, social, recreational, and spiritual activities. Healthy dependency enhances these areas of our lives.

When we were addicted to substances, we denied our dependent nature and denied we were addicted. We now accept our dependent nature and neither deny it nor fight it. Instead, we turn to our Higher Power for our dependency needs. By admitting our basic spiritual neediness, and depending on God to meet this basic need, we no longer live in a state of denial that keeps us out of touch with reality.

I accept my dependent nature, rejoice in my spiritual source, and enjoy the fruits of my recovery with my family.

Positive Experiences

*W*e have few positive memories from childhood. We were surrounded by negative events, negative thoughts, and negative feelings. The closest we came to anything positive was in distracting ourselves from reality with our imaginations or, later on, with booze. We regarded ourselves as realists and viewed positive thinkers as mental sissies who couldn't cope with reality. We prided ourselves in being tough-minded enough to deal with the negative aspects of the real world.

In recovery, we began associating with people who practiced positive thinking. At first we didn't trust them. They didn't preach or try to convert us, they simply shared how they influenced their thoughts and attitudes. We couldn't avoid seeing the unusual peace and serenity they experienced, even when events were unfavorable. We have come to see that what we believed was a realistic outlook was biased by the negative worldview of our childhood.

We are teaching our children to look at the positive things in life rather than dwell on the negatives. We invite them to share their positive experiences with us. When they do so, it causes them to think about their lives in positive ways. This was something we never experienced as children. Sharing positive experiences with another is like getting extra credit in class. When we share them, we reexperience them and reinforce our self-confidence.

I encourage my children and myself to share positive experiences.

Friendship Without Domination

. . . .

*N*o one likes to have bossy friends. When we see another child bossing one of our children around, we feel angry. We don't want our children acting bossy toward their friends either. Many of us have felt dominated by others for most of our lives. We were dominated by our parents and our friends when we were children and by our partners when we got married. Some of us reacted by becoming bossy and dominating ourselves. We don't want this to happen to our children.

In recovery, we're learning about the many forms of codependency, including domination of others. We learn that neither domination nor submission is a healthy way to relate to family and friends. More important, we learn to have healthy relationships in which both persons respect each other and share in the decision making. We want to share this new discovery with our children.

We teach our children to cooperate with their friends. When we notice our children dominating their playmates, we make a point to tell them in private that they will probably get along better if they allow their friends to choose some of the activities. We talk to them about sharing decision making as well as sharing their toys. We use the Golden Rule to help them understand the importance of sharing.

I teach my children to cooperate with their friends so that no one dominates or submits.

Friends

· ·

*T*hose of us who grew up in dysfunctional families tended to overreact to the anger or disappointment of those close to us. We wanted everyone to like us. When our friends were upset with us, we automatically felt guilty and assumed total responsibility for the misunderstanding. Sometimes we defiantly defended ourselves in vain attempts to avoid feeling bad. At other times, we obsessed over their criticism until we became depressed and despondent. We do not want our children to suffer from this type of codependence.

Of course, it's normal to feel bad when someone we care about is upset with us. It is unhealthy, however, to become overwhelmed with guilt. In our recovery, we dismantle our automatic guilt routine. In its place we put healthy regret. We've come to realize that most of our guilt feelings are the result of our own unrealistic expectations. Now that we've stopped trying to please everyone all the time, we're experiencing much less guilt.

We talk to our children about being sensitive and considerate of others and about not becoming overly anxious when friends are angry and upset. We help our kids live comfortably with the reality that their close friends will, at times, be upset or angry with them. When this happens, we help them deal with their feelings. They are better able to handle the disappointment of others when they feel secure.

I am teaching my children to deal with their friends' disappointments without undue guilt.

Most Loving

. . . .

*O*ur egos used to be involved in all of our decision making. We could not make decisions regarding our children without considering their effects on us. We wanted to look good in every situation. It was far more important to us to look good than to do good. When we knew that doing the right thing might not make us look good in our children's eyes or the eyes of other adults, we felt stuck. It was hard, for example, for us to urge our children to report their friends for violating the high school athletic alcohol code.

Recovery has helped us get a better perspective by considering our Higher Power, rather than our image or ego, when we make decisions. Because of our self-centeredness and preoccupation with image, this is a radical approach for us. Now, we're actually considering our decisions in a context of moral and spiritual values, instead of personal interest.

Asking ourselves, "What is the most loving thing to do in this situation?" has radically changed our approach to parenting, especially in disciplining our kids. When one of our children gets in trouble at school or in the neighborhood, we first ask God to show us a loving response. We use discipline to express our moral and spiritual values, not just to flaunt our authority and protect our ego.

Striving to do the most loving thing affirms my children and keeps me from self-preoccupation.

Understand

. . . .

*M*any of our parents never seemed to know where we were coming from. If we were accused by anyone of doing anything wrong, they refused to listen to our side of the story. They chose to believe negative reports about us without talking to us. We felt discounted and humiliated. When our children were accused of mischief, we used to do the same thing. We assumed they were guilty until they could prove to us they weren't.

In recovery, we're learning to treat ourselves and our children with respect. Now we treat them as innocent until proven guilty and give them the benefit of the doubt. We put ourselves in our children's shoes in order to better understand their feelings and their perspective. This requires us to see our children as separate people, rather than as extensions of our egos. We no longer assume that our children make mischief just to get back at us.

Once we're able to restore a sense of calm, we can look at problems more objectively. We can properly handle a disciplinary situation only if we find the facts and review them with an open mind. When we take the time to understand where our children are coming from, they open up to us. Now we are able to resolve most situations without undo tears, misunderstanding, and resentments.

Listening to my children's side of the story demonstrates that I understand them and assume their innocence.

Safe Haven

· ·

*M*ost of us stayed away from home as much as we could as soon as we were old enough to get a job and drive a car. We were eager to avoid the constant turmoil and chaos in our families. We joined clubs, teams, and organizations in order to have legitimate reasons to avoid being home. We never invited friends to our home because we were too embarrassed to have our friends see our parents fighting with each other or yelling at us.

In our recovery, we're practicing communicating our feelings without fighting, pouting, or taking them out on others. We are creating an environment of mutual respect and emotional safety in our homes. When a discussion turns into a heated argument, we agree to take time out to cool off before we continue. Violence and the threat of violence have been eliminated from our homes.

We are encouraging our children to see home as a safe haven and to extend their hospitality. We want them to feel comfortable inviting friends home. We only ask that they give us sufficient notice if they want to have a group over. And, when their feelings are hurt, or their pride is wounded, we want home to be a haven from the storm, and a safe place of retreat.

Keeping the lines of communication open with my children makes our home a safe haven for all of us.

Reminiscing

. . . .

As adult children of dysfunctional families, many of us have few childhood memories. Our memories are apparently blocked from consciousness in order to protect us from reexperiencing the painful things we lived through as children. We often feel left out when others share fond memories from their childhoods. We may have even made up stories in order not to feel left out when others reminisce.

In recovery, we're learned to savor our positive experiences and share them with others in the group. We experience a warm glow whenever we share a recent experience that was meaningful for us. Reminiscing is like going back over the week with a highlighter pen and emphasizing all the good that we accomplished or experienced. This is a new and wonderful experience for us. We were never encouraged to do this as children, at least as far as we can remember.

When we set aside time to reminisce with our children about events of the past week, we're both living in the present and building for the future. We encourage each of them to share the best moments of the previous week. Doing this together is creating memories we all can savor. We feel surrounded by warmth and happiness, and everyone gets to highlight good feelings, whether from accomplishments or from pleasant experiences. This enhances the joy we are experiencing with our families.

I enjoy reminiscing with my family each week.

Taking Our Kids for Granted

. . . .

*S*ometimes we take our children for granted. We get so busy with our lives and the details of the household that we forget how lucky we are to have been blessed with children.

We can easily forget how wonderful they are when they ignore our repeated requests to pick up their rooms. As we travel hundreds of miles together in the family car, listening to their arguing and bickering, it is easy to forget how lucky we are. At times like these, we imagine how peaceful it will be when they're grown and gone.

Yet when we dare to think about what our lives would be without our kids, we can hardly imagine it. The loss of our children would bring our heads down to the grave in sorrow. The house would be quiet . . . too quiet. Their rooms would stay clean forever . . . but who would notice or appreciate it? There would be less laundry to do . . . fewer hugs and kisses, less laughter, less excitement . . . and fewer annoyances. Our busy lives would lose much of their meaning without our children.

My kids get the message that I don't take them for granted when I tell them how much I appreciate them— even when I feel annoyed by their behavior.

Higher Power

. . . .

As many of us began our journey of recovery, we were uncertain about the practice of daily meditation. Although most members of our step groups practiced a time of daily reflection and renewal by reading meditation books, we resisted. We were suspicious of any religious practice that was not sponsored by our denomination. Or we were afraid our parents would condemn us for adopting a new religion. (In fact, we used to hide our meditation materials when our parents came to visit.) Or we resisted any sort of religious practices at all.

In recovery, we find God within ourselves, rather than depending on rabbis, priests, ministers, or other religious authorities for spiritual guidance. Even though Jesus said, "The kingdom of God is within you," most of us had been conditioned to look to others for spiritual direction. We were not taught to recognize spiritual needs or to trust our spiritual nature. Consequently, we ignored our spirituality, confusing it with religious practices.

By taking time each day for prayerful reflection and reading from Twelve-Step meditation books, we discovered that spirituality is not the same as religious belief and practice. Spirituality is essential, both to our serenity and to the quality of our recovery. For us, spirituality isn't a Sunday morning thing, or a correct belief thing, it's personal, daily contact with a power greater than ourselves that's restoring our lives to sanity.

I rejoice in my spirituality, without feeling defensive about it.

Normal or Perfect?

. . . .

We all want to have normal families, but many of us realize that we don't know what normal family life is. Many of us had so many emotional traumas in our dysfunctional families that we don't trust our own judgment, instincts, or even our memories. When we talk with friends in our recovery program about the things we do with our kids, they may tell us we're trying too hard to be perfect. We thought we were just trying to be normal. Perhaps we have set standards for ourselves that are impossible to meet.

In an effort to create normal families, some of us have become perfectionists. Addiction is a disease of extremes. Just ask anybody in recovery—we tend to do everything in extremes. Maybe we are trying too hard to raise normal children. We don't want them to have the emotional wounds and hang-ups we've had to struggle with. We want them to have wonderful childhood memories—memories of family picnics, holiday traditions, and special moments with their parents.

It's hard for us to settle for anything less than the best for our children. We're learning to have the courage to be imperfect and to moderate our expectations and demands so we won't drive our kids crazy. As we grow in self-acceptance, we're accepting our children as children.

I pray for the courage and humility to be imperfect.

Smart Aleck

. . . .

We get upset when our children act like smart alecks. Their cocky attitude may get them a few laughs at school, but it does not make them popular. Those of us who used cocky arrogance to cover our painful loneliness know exactly how deceiving this mask can be. While smart alecks seem confident and self-assured, underneath their false fronts they are insecure and lonely.

Our recovery teaches us that everything is not always as it seems with people. Those who seem the most confident and self-assured are sometimes the most needy and insecure. Each of us in our Twelve-Step group had a way of fooling the outside world by covering our pain. As we got honest with ourselves and shared our stories in group, we began to understand many of these clever cover-ups.

Now we can begin to see through the smart aleck masks of our children and reach out to their emotional insecurity. We no longer feel provoked when they act cocky and arrogant. Instead, we feel concern for the deeper feelings they are masking. Without reacting to their provocation, we quietly tell them we love them. We make it a point to show interest in their lives and engage them in conversation about the things they do well. We reassure them of their place in the family.

I'm learning not to be provoked by smart aleck behavior and to provide emotional support to my children.

Taking Over

. . . .

We used to step in to rescue our children whenever they dropped the ball. If they went off to school without their lunch, we'd drop it off on our way to work. If they forgot to clear the dinner dishes before running off to play with their friends, we'd clear them ourselves, rather than hassle with our kids. We were more interested in keeping peace in the family and avoiding scenes than in holding them accountable.

When our children got involved with alcohol and drugs, we were forced to look at all aspects of our family life, including our accountability system. We began to see that our preference for peace and harmony over responsibility and follow-through conveyed the wrong message. Our children believed we would always cover for them. They had no incentive to keep their commitments, fulfill their obligations, or remember where they left their things.

We no longer rescue our children from themselves. We respect ourselves and our children by letting them experience the consequences of their actions. This was difficult for us to do at first, and they were angry at us for holding them accountable. Within a short time, however, our relationships became open and honest. We no longer felt resentful toward them for taking advantage of us, and they no longer felt we were treating them like little children.

I treat myself and my children with respect by holding them accountable.

Emotional Reality

· ·

*M*any of our parents tried to protect us from feeling certain feelings that they believed would hurt us. When we were frightened, for example, they tried to talk us out of feeling fear. Sometimes they criticized us by saying, "Don't be scared. There's nothing to be scared about." At other times they contradicted our experience, "You don't really feel that." When we felt angry and bitter, they said, "You shouldn't feel that way." These efforts to protect us from hurtful feelings, however well intended, undermined our self-confidence. We became insecure, trusting neither our inner experience nor our grasp of reality.

Before we started in recovery, we were so out of touch with our inner experience that we were often unable to identify why we were agitated, depressed, or angry. In recovery, we're learning the importance of recognizing our feelings. We get in touch with our feelings about ourselves, others, and events around us. Knowing how we feel has become essential to our honesty and the integrity of our relationships with others. As we've rediscovered how to connect with our inner feelings, we no longer experience as much confusion in our lives.

We show respect for our children's feelings so they will be able to trust their inner experience of reality. We don't want them to experience years of denial and emotionally barren relationships like we did. We're enjoying their growing sense of self-confidence.

I encourage my children to experience their emotions.

Practice Letting Go

. . . .

*M*any of our parents did not handle our leave-taking well. Some of us left home after huge fights in which we were thrown out of the house. We felt as if we'd been thrown out of our families as well. Others of us were fearful of moving out because we were overly dependent on our parents. It was difficult for us to take our leave with joy and celebration when our parents were suffering.

In recovery, we let go of many things we once could not live without. In our addictions, we believed we could not live without alcohol, drugs, sex, gambling, or overworking. We surrender our lives to our Higher Power so we can live free of these obsessions and addictions. We've come to recognize we must also let go of our children. We depend on our recovery group for support as we learn this difficult lesson.

We're practicing letting go of our children in little ways during the daily dance in which they go away and come back. We are always here when they return, and they feel more confident each time they venture out into the world. We're learning to develop other interests in our lives so we will be able to send them off joyfully, knowing we will both manage well without the other.

I prepare my children and myself for their eventual leave-taking by letting go of them in little ways each day.

Privacy

. . . .

*M*any of us grew up where there was little privacy. All space in the home was shared space. According to our parents, closed doors meant we were keeping secrets or getting into mischief. Some of us had no emotional privacy either. Our parents badgered us until we told them everything we were thinking and feeling. They pried into our lives with no respect for our wishes to be left alone. We had to leave the house if we wanted solitude. So we grew up with little awareness of our personal boundaries.

In recovery, we've begun to be able to tell the difference between privacy and keeping secrets. Secrets cause dissension and mistrust; privacy teaches children about their boundaries. We're learning to respect our children's rights to keep certain thoughts and feelings to themselves. Because we didn't like it when our parents forced us to talk when we wanted to be left alone, we don't force our children to talk.

We respect our children's right to have private time, private space, private thoughts, and private feelings. We encourage them to share their lives with us, and we make this a pleasant experience. We don't force them to share. We always knock before entering when a door is closed. We don't go through their drawers while they are away from the house. We respect their right to decide if they want to be touched as well.

Respecting my children's boundaries and privacy helps me maintain and respect my own boundaries.

Don't Interfere

. . . .

*M*any of our parents disagreed on how to raise us. They argued about discipline—who was too strict and who was too permissive. They accused each other of ruining us by using the wrong approach. One argued that we were being punished too severely, causing us to become bitter. The other countered that we were being overindulged and mollycoddled. We hated hearing them fight over us, but we had similar arguments in front of our children because we didn't know any other way.

In our parents support group, we discuss our differences over approaches to discipline when our children are not present. We're discovering that when a parent criticizes, belittles, or berates the other parent in front of the children, the children lose respect for the belittled parent's authority and begin defying him or her. Over time, belittled parents lose credibility in the eyes of their children. And children come to believe that those of the gender of their discredited parents are inferior.

We're learning to respect our partners' right to relate to our children differently than we do. We no longer believe there is one proper way to raise children. We also respect our partners' right to discipline differently than we do. When we are uncomfortable with their approach, we no longer interfere, and we talk about our differences in private. This new level of mutual respect between us has greatly improved the peace and harmony in our household.

I respect my partner's right to parent differently than I do.

Objectivity

. . . .

DECEMBER 3

*W*e remember feeling abandoned by our parents whenever they heard anything negative about us from other adults. We do not want to abandon our children emotionally in the same way. On the other hand, we don't want to act naive, like parents who cannot accept any information that disturbs their "My child is perfect" illusion. We want to be both objective and loyal.

We often see things differently from the outside than from the inside. As an outsider, we see things in others' children that they miss, either because they are too close to notice or because they don't want to see certain things. We're learning to accept that it is normal to have a positive bias on behalf of our children. We do not apologize for feeling loyalty toward our children when outsiders offer advice or concern.

Although we often feel uncomfortable when adults who work with our children in school, church, or other activities share concerns about one of them, we listen openly and objectively. After we have heard what these adults have to say about our children, we consider it carefully before responding. We refuse to immediately condemn or defend our children. We always talk to them first and give them the benefit of the doubt. We put our relationships with our children ahead of our concern for our image in the community.

Listening objectively to information from others about my children helps me support my children.

Healthy Self-Care

· ·

We used to work long hours, eat poorly, never take breaks, and never take time to relax. In our recovery we've learned to take much better care of ourselves. We used to think that self-care was a wimpy thing for those who weren't tough enough to stay in the game. We now realize that these attitudes reflected self-disgust, and, in some cases, self-hate. Many of us had internalized the rigid, unrealistic demands that our parents once placed on us. We took over their roles and pushed ourselves like slave drivers. We have gradually learned to treat ourselves with compassion instead of self-disgust.

We're learning to take time out of our busy schedules to do things just for ourselves. As we have gradually become more like compassionate friends with ourselves, we've noticed that we're more sensitive, tender, and compassionate toward our children as well. We no longer expect them to "play hurt" or to push themselves to be perfect.

We are learning to re-parent ourselves by giving ourselves more loving, compassionate messages in our inner dialogue or self-talk. As we practice this re-parenting, our parenting is also taking on a friendlier tone. We used to act stern toward our children most of the time, as if they would take advantage of us if we were gentle with them.

I'm learning to be my own best friend and to model compassionate self-care for my children.

Never Do What Was Done to Me

. . . .

When we look at our children we often remember ourselves at their ages. Unfortunately, our childhood memories are not always happy ones. In fact, many of us long ago promised ourselves we would never do to our children some of the things that were done to us. This was an easy promise to make at the time.

Now that we are parents, however, it's not necessarily an easy promise to keep. Most of us raise our children the same way our parents raised us. We hear ourselves saying the same things to our children that our parents said to us, especially when we're angry. This alarms us because some of us remember terrible things happening when our parents were angry.

As we learn to accept our anger and take responsibility for our feelings, we are less apt to blame our children or to take our anger out on them. When we are upset, we tell them so. When the reason we are upset has nothing to do with them, we make a point of telling them it has nothing to do with them. When we are upset with them, we tell them exactly what behavior upset us and describe the behavior we expect next time. Learning to deal honestly and openly with our feelings makes it easier to deal with the feelings and actions of our children.

I am thankful for my program because it helps me accept my own feelings.

Besting Us

· ·

As teenagers, many of us avoided competing with our parents in games of skill or knowledge. We were afraid to beat them in fair competition for fear of embarrassing them because we believed they would punish us for shaming them. If we beat them in chess, checkers, tennis, or some other game of skill, they became visibly angry. Sometimes they got so defensive they insisted they had deliberately let us win, thereby cheating us out of the joy of besting them fair and square.

In our parents support group, we're learning to treat our children as equals. This was very difficult for some of us to do. Most of us were raised in families where parents were to be feared and revered. There was a defined hierarchy: father on top, then mother, then older children, younger children, then, maybe, the family dog. Father was not to be bested . . . in anything. His ego was to be accommodated.

Working with other parents and sharing stories, we begin to see how children can be treated as equal human beings. We celebrate their new skills and abilities, even if it means losing games to them. We encourage their growing competencies, even when they pass us by in some area of skill or knowledge. We don't avoid competing with them for fear they will best us, and we don't shame them if they do. Instead, we rejoice with them in their success.

Supporting my children's growing competencies demonstrates my respect for them.

Our Future

. . . .

DECEMBER 7

At one time, we were afraid of almost everything. We were afraid of our feelings, other people, and, especially, the future. We worried all the time and expected the worst in all situations. We medicated this constant anxiety by abusing substances and hiding behind compulsive behaviors. We felt so overwhelmed by the future that we avoided thinking about it by using massive doses of denial. We were always on the run—especially from ourselves.

In recovery, we were introduced to the concept that a power greater than ourselves could change all of this. By then we were willing to try anything. Little by little, we began developing a personal relationship with this Higher Power, and eventually recognized that our Higher Power was God. Having a personal relationship with God has changed everything. Our anxiety is miraculously transformed into peace and serenity, which goes infinitely beyond our understanding.

We're realizing that our limits are not God's limits. Although we don't know what our future holds, we no longer use denial to avoid thinking about it. We can neither stray into a future where God can't find us or charge into a future where God hasn't already been. God will meet us there and give us the red carpet treatment and the VIP tour when we arrive. Consequently, the future no longer overwhelms us, and we expect good things for our lives.

I no longer fear my future because it is in God's hands.

Teasing

. . . .

D E C E M B E R   8

As children, many of us were teased unmercifully. If we objected or, heaven forbid, cried when we were teased, we were told that we were crybabies or too sensitive. Teasing was a game in which the object was to dish out as much sarcasm and as many put-downs as possible before the other person tagged you back with the same. It was often cruel. There were no rules and no referees. If we cried, we automatically forfeited the game.

In recovery, we're learning to respect everyone's feelings. While teasing can sometimes be affectionate and playful, we're learning to tell the difference between affectionate teasing and abusive teasing. In our abusing days, we cared nothing about other people's feelings and assumed that no one cared about ours. Teasing was a competitive sport in which we were expected to fend for ourselves.

As parents in recovery, we now intervene if one of our children teases another child who is feeling vulnerable. We are teaching our children to let others know when they don't want to be teased. This request must be honored by everyone. We set the tone in our household. We're careful to respect everyone's feelings, and we don't tolerate emotional abuse in any form, including unwanted teasing.

I discourage abusive teasing by modeling respect and intervening if my children tease in hurtful ways.

Problem Solving

. . . .

When, as children, we were frustrated and struggled with problems, our parents often responded by either refusing to help us at all or by taking over and solving the problem for us. Either way, we felt stupid and inadequate. We felt discounted by both responses. They didn't know how to help, assist, or guide us. They were more worried about being inconvenienced than about helping us. We felt we were in their way when we asked for help.

With other parents in recovery, we can explore ways to allow our children to experience and express frustration without jumping in to rescue them immediately. By automatically rescuing them when they show any sign of frustration, we keep them helpless and dependent on us. We interfere with their development, and we undermine their self-confidence. We want to show our children that we're supportive and willing to help without denying them the opportunity to figure things out for themselves.

We carefully resist the temptation to solve our children's problems before they have a chance to find their own solutions. When they ask us for help with problems, we first inquire about what they have tried so far. In explaining, they often see the answers themselves. When we offer suggestions on how they might solve their own problems, they learn without any loss of self-confidence. In fact, their self-confidence increases because they discover their own solutions.

I enjoy empowering my children to solve their own problems.

Unmet Needs

. . . .

We used to think our children were deliberately trying to get to us with their irritating behavior. They seemed to know just what to do to annoy us. Our toddler waited until we were on the phone to pull all the pots and pans from the kitchen cupboard. When we were tired and hung over on Saturday morning, they turned the television on louder. We were convinced they were deliberately being mean, just to get back at us.

In our parents support group, we're learning that all behavior is communication. When our children act out, they are trying to tell us something. They're usually trying to communicate their needs, especially their emotional needs. Perhaps they need our time or undivided attention. Perhaps our toddler does not want to share us with the telephone. Once we began to see their behavior as communication, we were less annoyed with them.

We're learning to listen as closely to our children's behavior as we do their words. We help them put their feelings and needs into words by encouraging them to tell us what they need when they are acting out. We no longer get angry the moment they get into some mischief. As we practice this two-way communication, it becomes easier for us and our children to express our needs in words, instead of mischievous behavior.

Learning to understand the purpose of my children's behavior means I'm less easily provoked by it.

Explaining

. . . .

Some of us had parents who were poor teachers, and yet they expected us to know things we'd never been taught. We were blamed and scolded for not knowing the social rules when no one had taken the time to teach us. We may not have been taught proper manners or personal hygiene, for example. When we made mistakes or showed our ignorance, especially in public, they shamed us instead of explaining the rules. They said things like, "You should know better than that."

In recovery, we're learning about the damaging effect of shame in our lives. We see how shame was used to control our behavior, thoughts, and feelings. Because we were shamed by our parents, we believed shaming was normal. We shamed our children when they disappointed us. We echoed our parents' shaming questions, saying to our children, "Who do you think you are?" "What gives you the right to . . . ?" "What makes you think you're so special?" "When will you ever learn?"

We are determined to stop shaming our children. We're learning to avoid the use of shaming rhetorical questions when we discipline them. We now realize that scolding them with impossible questions does not teach them how to act or what we expect. We are learning to explain rather than shame. We're learning to calm down before we correct them.

Both my children and I learn more when I explain rather than shame.

Fifth Step

· ·

*O*ur relationships with our children were contaminated with guilt and shame. We had systematically abused them. Whenever we were irritated, angry, or frustrated, we took it out on them. Even when they needed discipline, they never deserved to be slapped, kicked, beaten, called names, or screamed at. Although we told ourselves we were teaching them a lesson, we did not recognize that the lesson we were teaching was one of family violence and not responsibility and good conduct.

In our Twelve-Step recovery process, we did fourth and fifth steps around our abusive parenting. For the very first time, we honestly admitted the exact nature of our abuse. It took us days to make this list because we were unable to write down the details of our behavior without crying. We wept over our detailed inventory as we felt all the unnecessary pain we had caused our children. We vowed never again to strike them in anger.

Telling another person about our conduct set us free. For the first time in our lives, we are able to experience the joy of being parents. We're now freely able to hold our children, kiss them, and play with them because we no longer repress feelings of shame and guilt. The peace in our hearts is like nothing we have ever known. We have been given a second chance to love and nurture our children.

Admitting my abusive behavior to another person lifts my shame.

Compulsions

. . . .

*M*any of us struggled with compulsive behaviors such as overeating, drinking, gambling, or sexual obsessions. We want to safeguard our children from getting hooked on these destructive habits. We have come to understand that our compulsive behaviors were short-term remedies for dealing with pressures, worries, and the stress of life. Unfortunately, these remedies quickly got out of hand and began consuming our lives, taking up more and more of our time and attention, while producing diminishing benefits to our troubled souls.

In recovery, we learn to face life head-on without the crutch of our old compulsions. We learn that life has a certain amount of frustration and pressure that cannot be avoided. We're sharing our worries and talking to others about the problems and pressures we experience. Much to our surprise, talking works better than our past compulsive behavior did. And talking has none of the negative side effects.

We encourage our children to share their feelings with us, especially their troubles and worries. Because we're learning to listen without being judgmental or giving unsolicited advice, they now share many of their feelings with us. We encourage them to talk with their friends as well. We watch for signs of compulsive behavior, irritability, or acting out. When our children seem especially anxious, irritable, or worried, we help them put their feelings into words.

Helping my children put their worries into words helps them cope.

Transform Worries

. . . .

We used to worry about everything—things we could change as well as things we couldn't. We managed to pollute every day of our lives with worry. When things were going well, we worried about how long it would be before they turned sour. When things were sour, we worried that our lives would never be pleasant again. Worrying about everything ensured we never enjoyed the present moment.

In recovery, living one day at a time helps us let go of self-defeating worry. By living in day-tight compartments we no longer beat ourselves up over the mistakes of yesterday or worry ourselves sick about what might arise tomorrow. We focus our attention on the needs of the situations at hand and the joys of meeting these needs with courage and integrity. By practicing the principles of the serenity prayer, we do what we can each day, and let God handle the rest.

We are teaching our children to separate useless worrying from productive worrying. When they tell us they are worried, we first listen to their concerns. Then we encourage them to ask themselves these questions: "Am I worrying about the past or the future? Is there some action I can take today that will improve the situation? Am I using worry to distract myself from some decision, responsibility, or challenge?"

I am helping my children to avoid useless worrying.

Competition

. . . .

*W*hen our daughter entered her first dance competition, we didn't realize how it would change her. She's become totally preoccupied with winning. Now she's nervous, insecure, and self-conscious about her dancing. What used to be a source of joy and pleasure has become the cause of stress and anxiety. She has become so obsessed with competing that she is crushed when she doesn't win first place. She no longer enjoys dancing for its own sake.

We encourage her to think more about her own dancing and less about the other girls and their performances. This advice doesn't seem to help, however. Winning over others has become her only goal, an attitude that has alienated her from many of her friends. We've always encouraged her to try hard and to do her best, but we didn't expect this advice to lead to intense worry and alienation.

Did we teach her that winning is everything? Perhaps our competitive behavior contradicted our words. We may have competed aggressively while telling her it's not okay for her to do so. Yet, we don't want her to put winning ahead of her friendships when she competes. We encourage her to talk to us about why winning is so important. We applaud her when she doesn't win and talk with her about what it feels like to do something just for the fun of it.

I review my own attitudes about competition, friendship, and the importance of winning.

Loving Myself

. . . .

*O*ne of the most important blessings of our recovery has been the gift of self-acceptance. As we have grown in our capacity to accept ourselves as good, albeit fallible, human beings, we have become more compassionate with ourselves. We're learning to be gentle with ourselves when we make mistakes.

We used to be critical and harsh, at least on the inside. To the world, however, we presented an invulnerable and flawless facade. We were so filled with shame and guilt that we hid our true selves from anyone and everyone. We hated feeling so inadequate that we pretended to be super adequate, defending ourselves from every hint of wrongdoing. Our growing self-acceptance has made it much easier for us to accept others, especially our families. If God is loving toward us, we can be loving toward others.

We're not as harsh, critical, and faultfinding with our children as we were before we got into recovery. Our self-nurturing attitude flows over to them, and we're becoming softer and gentler, even when they make mistakes. We no longer focus all our attention on control and punishment. Rather, we look for ways to nurture good feelings in ourselves and our children. Getting our way has become less important than maintaining positive feelings and relationships in the family.

I am becoming more loving and accepting toward myself and others.

False Praise

. . . .

*O*ur parents wanted us to be winners so badly that they bragged about our performance, even when we did poorly. We were often embarrassed by their false praise. They were totally out of touch with our lives and had no real understanding of how we saw things. When they came to our games, they embarrassed us with loud cheering and bragging about our plays. We don't want to embarrass our children this way.

In our parents support group, we explore the importance of listening to our children and recognizing them as the real experts on their own experience. We were so used to thinking we knew more than they did that we failed to appreciate their expertise on their own lives, especially their thoughts, feelings, and self-appraisal. We respect their opinions, especially about the things they are deeply involved with.

We listen to our children's feelings and do not contradict their self-assessment. When they say they performed poorly, we accept their feelings. Even when we disagree with their appraisal, we don't argue with their feelings. Instead, we let them vent their disappointments to us. We used to want to cheer them up so badly that we sometimes denied the obvious truth of their poor performance. Now we accept their opinions and feelings and assure them we love them even when they perform poorly.

I respect my children's feelings about themselves, even when I disagree with their self-assessment.

Win/Win Parenting

· ·

DECEMBER 18

When we were children, some of us felt like we were at war with our parents. We lived with animosity and hostility most of the time. When they told us to do something, we assumed it would be drudgery and not something fun. They didn't take time or make the effort to hear us or know us—so how could they know if we'd like something? Much of the time we felt engaged in an unspoken cold war, always trying to outsmart them without admitting we were at war.

We don't want this kind of relationship with our children. We want to be their friends, allies, and companions. We want them to know we are genuinely interested in their lives. We want them to see us as their friends, not their enemies. And we want to work well together so we all feel like winners. We don't want to depend on our authority or lord it over them to get them to do what we want.

We realize we can't always be on their side on every issue. There will be times when we have to take a stand they won't like. We want this to be the exception and not the rule, however. And we want our disagreements to be out in the open where we can talk about them. We want to have a win/win relationship with our kids.

I am working to develop a friendly atmosphere with my children.

Illusions

. . . .

Some of us were so fearful of abandonment we became addicted to relationships that were harmful to us. We believed if we did not have a man or woman in our lives we were defective. Because we were willing to do anything to keep partners in our lives, we were easily exploited by the people we chose. Although we tried to do everything they expected of us, it was never enough. When we eventually got out of destructive relationships, we again felt our lives were deficient or defective. We soon found ourselves in other toxic relationships.

When we sought help through a Twelve-Step recovery group, we began to deal with our deep fear of abandonment. As we accepted our feelings and talked about them, we stopped acting out by chasing romantic involvement. Once we owned our fears and faced them honestly, they gradually lost the power to drive us to unhealthy relationships and compromises. Now we are learning to establish boundaries in our relationships. We're learning to say no to people without feeling ashamed and guilty.

We enjoy this wonderful new sense of freedom and self-respect. We realize that we can live our lives without leaning on someone or expecting them to make us whole. We trust ourselves and our ability to function as adults as we gradually wean ourselves from our dependence on the approval of others.

My independence and self-respect are gifts I give myself.

Friendship Without Dependency

. . . .

We don't want our children to give themselves up in order to have friends. Many of us have done this in our lives. Because of our low self-esteem, we would do anything to have friends, including betray our values and beliefs. We did many things as teenagers that we would later regret, only because we wanted to be cool and fit in with our friends. We could not say no to our friends for fear we would be ridiculed or excluded by them.

As we grow in our recovery, we learn we can have good friendships without giving up our ideals, values, or personal interests. We can say no to friends, and they do not turn against us. The friends we have made in recovery are especially respectful of our boundaries. There are exceptions, however. Some friends we had before we began our recovery cannot handle our new way of relating to them. Some family members also dislike it when we stand up to them by setting limits for ourselves.

We teach our children to remain true to themselves in their friendships. We help them by letting them talk out their fears of what might happen if they don't go along with their friends. Sometimes we role play with them to rehearse how they will say no when they face invitations to do things they don't want to do.

I am encouraging my children to stand up for their beliefs with their friends.

Mutual Respect

. . . .

*B*efore we began our recovery, we gave little thought to the way we spoke to our children. When they got into trouble, we reacted automatically. In our frustration and impatience, we gave little consideration to their feelings and needs. Our main concern was to take control of the situation and minimize our inconvenience and distress. Showing respect for our children was the farthest thing from our minds.

We had always insisted that our children respect us and show us proper deference. But it never occurred to us that we should show respect for them as well. Respecting children as persons of equal worth is a radical concept for us. Our parents did not respect us; instead, they reminded us that we were mere children, and they were the adults.

We're learning about mutual respect in our parents support group. Now, when faced with difficult situations with our children, we ask ourselves, "How can we respect ourselves and our children in this situation?" For example, when one of our children asks permission to go on an overnight with friends instead of attending a family reunion that has been planned for months, we consider the request in light of respecting ourselves and our child. This may not make the decision easier, but it does make our relationships more respectful and harmonious.

Showing respect for myself and my children increases our self-esteem.

Overdirecting

. . . .

*A*lthough many of us resented our parents' interfering in our lives, we often found ourselves overinvolved in our children's lives. All they had to do was whine or complain about a problem, and we became a talking suggestion box. "Why don't you do this . . . ? Have you thought about that . . . ? You shouldn't get so upset. Don't let them bother you. . . ." We went on and on. We were so wrapped up in our advice that we got angry when they didn't listen to us.

Now, we're applying the things we're learning about co-dependency to our relationships with our children. We've learned, for example, that an overresponsible parent creates an irresponsible child. We've noticed that when we're too involved with our children's lives, we may be avoiding something in our own lives. This happens often enough that we're learning to take a close look at ourselves when we start to micro-manage our children.

We want our children to be self-reliant and responsible for themselves. Our biggest challenge is to let them figure things out for themselves and learn from their mistakes. Now, when we want to tell them what to do and what to watch out for so they won't get hurt or learn everything the hard way, we resist the urge to butt in. We wait for them to come to us, and we ask them questions that help them solve their own problems.

When I'm tempted to solve problems or give advice to my children, I look at my own life instead.

One-Upmanship

*W*e could never impress our parents. Whenever we told them about something unusual we had experienced, witnessed, or accomplished, they topped our story with one from their own lives. They never let us have a moment of glory. They competed with us for attention and recognition at every turn. Now that we are parents, we have found ourselves, to our dismay, doing the same thing with our children, without realizing it.

With other parents in recovery, we're discovering that our one-upmanship alienates our children by undermining their self-esteem at critical moments in the parent-child relationship. When they seek positive responses from us for their stories, we overshadow their tales with our own. We're resisting the temptation to top their stories. We're learning to compete with our children only in games and only when they are old enough to offer fair competition.

We know that we can get attention in more appropriate places than from our children. So instead of competing, we listen and draw them out with our questions. When one of our children tells us about an encounter with a rude customer at work, we save all of our rude customer stories for another day. When they tell us of their latest achievements in sports, we save our hero stories for another time.

Listening carefully to my children's stories leads to mutual respect and shared self-esteem.

Follow the Crowd

. . . .

We want our children to be able to withstand negative peer pressure. We want them to be able to withstand the pressure to use drugs and alcohol and to be able to say no to sex until they are completely ready. Most of us were unable to withstand peer pressure because we felt like outsiders and wanted desperately to belong and be part of the crowd. Because we were very angry, we did not hesitate to rebel against our parents' rules and expectations.

In recovery we learn the importance of self-determination, for ourselves and for our children. Because we had no say in the things our parents expected of us, we felt no loyalty to their values. Now we replace our rebelliousness with self-determination. We've come to understand why our children need to be included in discussions about morals and values.

We can guide our children's moral development through friendly discussions rather than by preaching at them and demanding total obedience to our values. We help our children prepare for difficult peer pressure situations by role playing with them; we help them rehearse different ways of dealing with difficult peer pressure situations. We encourage them to think through their values by projecting the consequences of different options. We hope they will not be motivated by defiance of our values.

Because I help my children develop their own moral values, they can take ownership of them.

Christmas

. . . .

When we were abusing chemicals and running from ourselves and God, Christmas was a nightmare. We avoided the Christmas season as long as possible because of the painful memories we carried from childhood. We tried to stay busy to distract ourselves from memories of excessive drinking, arguments, and terrible disappointments. We abused chemicals ourselves in an effort to cope with our painful memories.

With our recovery has come a spiritual awakening. This has transformed the Christmas season for us. We still struggle with painful memories at times, but we are busy building a rich new album of family memories with each sober Christmas we share with our children. Although we are grateful to God for each and every day of our sobriety, we are especially thankful at Christmas time. The holiday season was the time we abused chemicals, ourselves, and our children, more than any other.

Now we spend time with our children creating traditions in our family and emphasizing the spiritual meaning of Christmas. We strive to keep things calm and peaceful by attending worship services, special concerts, and family gatherings instead of holiday parties where alcohol is the central attraction. We make a point to reach out to others in acts of charity in our Christmas expressions. This is a reminder that God came into our lives when we were unable to save ourselves.

I thank God this Christmas for saving me from the pain and loneliness of my addictions.

Crisis Living

· ·

*M*any of us were procrastinators. We avoided tasks until our hearts pounded and adrenaline rushed through our veins from the pressure of an impending deadline. Then, like a white tornado, we tore through the tasks before us. We bragged about the amount of work we accomplished under pressure, although we never bragged about its quality. We developed this crisis-driven lifestyle while growing up in dysfunctional families. Chaos, crises, and emergencies made planning useless.

In recovery, we transform our crisis-driven lifestyle into a lifestyle based on serenity. We make plans and trust that our plans will work out. Although we experience disappointments, these disappointments are easier to live with than the despair we used to feel when our lives had no meaning beyond the next crisis. We are no longer afraid to look beyond today. And we are willing to act on behalf of our own future.

We are teaching our children how to pace themselves and avoid living by crisis. When they have deadlines on school projects, for instance, we help them use the deadlines to set up a structure for completing the projects in stages. We remind them that doing a small part of the project each week is like putting money in a savings account. It brings a sense of accomplishment without trauma at the deadline.

I am teaching my children to plan ahead and structure their time.

Overextended

· ·

As single parents, we wanted our children to have exactly the same opportunities they would have had if we had remained married. Consequently, we worked full-time, volunteered at school, and got our children involved in several sports. We went without ourselves so we could buy them hockey skates, private music lessons, and the latest fashionable clothes. We prided ourselves in giving our kids everything they wanted. And then we burned out and crashed into the wall.

In our single parents support group, we're learning to set limits for our children without feeling guilty. We deal with our guilt in healthy ways so it no longer drives us to exhaustion. We are beginning to recognize the subtle ways that kids exploit their guilty parents, shaming them into doing the impossible. Because many of us have come from single parent families ourselves, we don't know what's normal to provide for our kids.

We're setting reasonable limits, based on the reality of our resources of time and money. We no longer drive ourselves to provide everything our children want or demand. We are developing quality relationships with our children by helping them make choices within the limits of our resources. By working through our guilt in our support group, we are able to resist caving in when they express disappointment.

I respect myself and my children by setting reasonable limits on their activities and material demands.

Positives

We used to be cynical and depressed, always looking at the gloomy side of life. We obsessed about all the things that were wrong in the world. Although we wallowed in despair, we convinced ourselves that we were simply being realistic. We believed that keeping our hopes and expectations low safeguarded us from the pain of disappointments. We never rejoiced in good fortune or celebrated victories, for fear we would come crashing back to earth. Our motto was, "Pride goes before a fall."

Recovery has restored our faith in God, one another, and ourselves. The power and love of God, which restored our sanity, has opened our eyes to all that is good and beautiful. We are learning to look for the positives in life instead of the negatives. We are training ourselves to notice what is right with our children instead of obsessing over their shortcomings. And we gracefully accept the things we cannot change.

We are paying attention to what is good and beautiful in each of our children. We no longer criticize them unmercifully in an attempt to eliminate their faults and shortcomings. We watch them blossom and grow in the bright sunlight of our positive and affirming attitude toward them. Although we are still aware of their shortcomings, we are deliberately focusing our attention on their gifts and positive attributes.

My children and I both blossom in the light of my positive attitude toward them.

Lost

. . . .

Some of us remember being scolded and ridiculed for getting separated from our parents as children. By the time they found us, we were terrified and in tears. Instead of comforting us, they scolded and humiliated us for getting lost. They minimized our feelings, and ridiculed us for being scared. To this day, being temporarily lost causes acute anxiety for many of us. We feel as though we are again four years old, lost in the maze of aisles in a large department store.

As recovering parents, we comfort our frightened children, rather than scold, shame, or ridicule them. Even though we may be scared and angry that one of our children has wandered away and is now causing a public scene with tears, we are willing to put his or her need for comfort ahead of our self-consciousness. We're learning to treat our children's feelings with sensitivity and respect, and we make it a point to never scold a frightened child.

We don't want our children to suffer acute anxiety, shame, or humiliation when they are temporarily lost, literally or figuratively. We all get lost sometimes in life, and it's nothing to feel ashamed of. We need to be able to think clearly when we are lost. Shame interferes with clear thinking and problem solving, making us feel helpless, weak, and generally miserable.

I comfort my children when they are scared and upset.

Teaching Us

. . . .

*M*any of our parents always had to be right, even when they were wrong. They refused to admit that we knew anything worthwhile that they did not know. They never allowed us to teach them things we were learning. If they did not know it, it wasn't worth knowing. If, by some slim chance, they admitted to needing to learn something we knew, they would go to another adult for instruction. Or they would learn from us without crediting our efforts, acting as if what they had learned from us they had always known.

In talking with others in our parents support group, we begin to recognize that our children have special gifts, many of which we ourselves do not have. We treasure their gifts and, more important, let them know we treasure them. We all like to be acknowledged for our gifts and talents, and we love to share them with others. Children are no different. They love to impress their parents with their talents, discoveries, and newly acquired skills.

Even our youngest children can teach us. They show us the simplicity of life we too often overlook, teach us how to laugh and play, and inspire us with their innocence and trusting faith. Our children teach us to pay more attention to the basics of life, including love, family, trust, simplicity, and the majesty of nature.

I enjoy learning about the true meaning of life from my children.

New Year

. . . .

We used to look forward to New Year's Eve as another excuse to get high, party all night, and sleep in. Consequently, we have almost no memories of New Year's Day. Because we were running from ourselves in those days, we avoided personal reflection as much as possible. Occasionally, we bared our souls when we were high, but we neither remembered our words the next day, nor followed through on any resolutions we made.

In recovery, we discovered the healing and renewing power of taking our personal inventory on a regular basis. This cleansing and renewing act rejuvenates us by healing relationships that may have suffered from neglect or misunderstanding. It also cleanses our souls and refreshes our contact with God. We look forward to times of personal reflection because we're no longer running from God, or from ourselves.

We look forward to New Year's Day as an opportunity to thank God for grace and guidance in our lives in the past year. After we review the past year, we renew our commitment to carry out God's will in our lives in the coming year. By taking time once a year to review and renew our lives, we recharge our spiritual batteries. When we focus our thoughts on what is good in our lives, we feel empowered.

As I look back, I rejoice in God's grace. As I look forward, I recommit myself to doing God's will.

The Twelve Steps of Alcoholics Anonymous

. . . .

1. We admitted we were powerless over alcohol—that our lives had become unmanageable.

2. Came to believe that a Power greater than ourselves could restore us to sanity.

3. Made a decision to turn our will and our lives over to the care of God *as we understood Him.*

4. Made a searching and fearless moral inventory of ourselves.

5. Admitted to God, to ourselves and to another human being the exact nature of our wrongs.

6. Were entirely ready to have God remove all these defects of character.

7. Humbly asked Him to remove our shortcomings.

8. Made a list of all persons we had harmed, and became willing to make amends to them all.

9. Made direct amends to such people wherever possible, except when to do so would injure them or others.

10. Continued to take personal inventory and when we were wrong promptly admitted it.

11. Sought through prayer and meditation to improve our conscious contact with God, *as we understood Him,* praying only for knowledge of His will for us and the power to carry that out.

12. Having had a spiritual awakening as the result of these steps, we tried to carry this message to alcoholics, and to practice these principles in all our affairs.

Prayer for Serenity

. . . .

God, grant me the serenity
to accept the things I cannot change,
the courage to change the things I can,
and the wisdom to know the difference.
Amen

—Reinhold Neibuhr

Index

· ·

Index of Twelve Step References

. . . .